Love's Many Mysteries

Edited by Aimée Vanstone

First published in Great Britain in 2009 by:
Forward Press
Remus House
Coltsfoot Drive
Peterborough
PE2 9JX
Telephone: 01733 890066
Website: www.forwardpress.co.uk

Book and cover design by Ali Smith

SB ISBN 978-1-84418-488-0

Foreword

Although we are a nation of poets we are accused of not reading poetry, or buying poetry books. After many years of listening to the incessant gripes of poetry publishers, I can only assume that the books they publish, in general, are books that most people do not want to read.

Poetry should not be obscure, introverted, and as cryptic as a crossword puzzle: it is the poet's duty to reach out and embrace the world.

The world owes the poet nothing and we should not be expected to dig and delve into a rambling discourse searching for some inner meaning.

The reason we write poetry (and almost all of us do) is because we want to communicate: an ideal; an idea; or a specific feeling. Poetry is as essential in communication, as a letter; a radio; a telephone, and the main criterion for selecting the poems in this anthology is very simple: they communicate.

This collection includes a fabulous plethora of voices on the elusive subject of love. Though sometimes contradictory, each poem communicates its own truth as *Love's Many Mysteries* delves into and explores the many aspects of the feeling we call love.

Contents

The Poems

She Was Just Called Love

In a pretty little hamlet
Down a winding leafy lane
In a cottage that was crumbling
Rotting wood and broken panes.

Lived a broken-hearted lady
Battling pain and toil and strife -
To her husband - now departed
She was once a loving wife -

Who was busy in her kitchen
Baking pies and cakes and bread
The smell of cooking filled the house
Her family were well fed.

The fire was burning brightly
There was laughter in the air
The highly polished furniture
Gave a sense of love and care.

She fussed around her family
Her love sincere and kind
However much she did for them
She would never ever mind.

Though worn out - she felt needed
She had a very treasured life
She gladly gave her heart and soul
To be a caring wife.

Then nothing! There was no one!
Alone, forlorn and scared
No one to love and care for
In the lovely home they shared.

In the fireplace a black hole
Where the embers once had glowed
No smell of cooking in the air
A house unloved. It showed.

She was rundown and so poorly
Yet she really didn't care
It was different when she felt love
Now it was feelings of despair.
She dragged herself around the house
Life was just a pointless chore
What didn't seem too urgent
She tended to ignore.

This desperate lonely lady
Who was painfully so sad
Truly thought on her own
She would surely end up mad.

Then suddenly - out of the blue
Her life was to change overnight
For what she then encountered
Was a sad and pitiful sight.

A kitten starving, hungry
Weak, just skin and bone
Frightened and crying
It was lost and all alone.

How could she ignore it?
How could she not care?
How could she not tend to it?
That would be cruel and unfair.

She stroked the poor baby
She lit her a fire
Put down a blanket
She purred with desire.

Now from the kitchen
The smell of rabbit and fish
And a little fresh cream
In her best Sunday dish.

Her eyes were now smiling
A gift from Heaven above
She never had a name
She just called her *Love.*

Jacqueline Rowlands

Congratulations Jacqueline!
The Forward Press editors have chosen your beautiful poem as the deserving winner of the £500 prize.

Ebby

We spent fifteen beautiful years together
Through the changing seasons always thought it was forever.

In the spring we would go on long walks through woodland
Where the spray of warm sun rays fell upon us
Through the leaves on the trees
The carpet of bluebells beneath our feet
Gave our senses a thrill with their sweet aroma
And the sound of the bees.

Always close by each other's side,
When we glanced into one another's eyes
Soft, dark brown eyes where I would almost melt
As it touched my soul, from the glance I had to almost myself prise.

We would spend our summers chasing each other
And playing like children through the golden corn fields
Oh, that was bliss, that was freedom
In the evening just be with each other
In a comfortable silence, our home.

As the years went by, we hardly noticed,
Then one autumn as we walked in our favourite woods
Through the crunchy, golden and bronzed leaves
Where we normally had a game trying to catch the falling leaves
She could not jump to catch the leaves,
It was a shock and hard to believe.

Winter's frost arrived, then snow, our walks were usually fun
Sliding on icy puddles and playing in the snow
But this year she is ill and cannot go out
Whether we will go on our walks again, we do not know.

I wonder if you have guessed?
This is the story of my beloved black Labrador
I miss stroking her beautiful shiny black coat
And looking into her soft, dark brown eyes that say she adores.

She became ill, I had to let her go
I know she did not want to leave my side
I did not want to say goodbye to you either my beloved Ebby
But to hold on to you would have hurt your pride.

The love we have shared in this life and I'm sure in the past
Will live on, at least now you suffer no pain
Your presence is here with me still
And I know we will be together one day again.

Sheila Richford

First Love

At a private nursing home
I worked when I was young
And fell in love, head over heels
With Matron's handsome son.
Louis was an actor
In a London play,
Which I had booked to see him in
And quite enjoyed the day.
Then as I got to know him,
He kissed me once or twice,
Which was my first experience
And I found rather nice!
He said - Who taught you how to kiss
I knew not what to say -
Surprised he'd even noticed me
Up until that day
For I was young and innocent
And only just fifteen,
I knew not then how to respond,
So shy I'd always been!
I'd always led a sheltered life
From the age of two,
Brought up in a foster home
With girls and nothing knew.
When young, I was attractive,
Most handsome too was he,
And on occasions when we met
It was unexpectedly
He said that I was like a boy,
I knew then what he meant,
I'd offered no encouragement,
Which made it evident!
He also said, 'You're much too nice,'
And wished not too offend,
I knew that he respected me,
On that I could depend.
Once he gave me photographs
And said surprisingly,
'I'll have a place soon of my own
And want you there with me.'
That night quite close to me he lay,
His kisses stole my breath away,
Deciding if he were to stay

Then - no offence there'd be.
He whispered, 'Do say something,'
But I said not a word
For I was inexperienced
So nothing then occurred.
He kissed me very tenderly
As through the door he went,
Leaving me excited,
Though he'd made no sex attempt!
Remembering his promise
He'd caused me no offence,
For Louis was a gentleman
Respecting innocence.
He later went to Hollywood
And there he made his name.
Several films he made out there
And famous he became!
I'm left now with his memory
And dreams that won't come true,
T'would have been nice to meet again
And friendship then renew!
Life can be just a bit unreal -
At least now I can say
My first love was quite innocent,
But that was yesterday!
Years later when I married,
A virgin still was I,
I thought that sex was not quite nice,
Remaining all too shy!
I'm glad I met dear Louis
When I was just fifteen,
For as I write my poem -
It reads just like a dream!

First love is an awakening
One feels an inner glow
Exciting! - The experience
As heightened feelings grow!

Sylvia Russell

The Washing Up Bowl Is Floating In The Sink Again, Matilda

The washing up bowl is floating in the sink again, Matilda
The dog's been sick upstairs and the cat has run away
Will you please apply the ointment to my piles again, this evening
Before we go to bed and end another lovely day?

I've put the money in your handbag, can you pay the man on Thursday?
I know you're off to town with Jean and Sally, Glad and Flo
We've got behind again, dear, with the payments for the telly
And we need to keep him happy or else it will have to go.

I'll unblock the outside loo, dear, something nasty down the pan
I'll sort it good and proper, dear, and leave it spick and span
I'll scrape the fungus off the walls, dear, get the mushrooms from the floor
Leave it lovely, smelling nice dear, like it used to be before.

Here's a shilling for the meter, I don't know how long it will last
But we need the gas to see with and a shilling goes so fast
I've put cardboard in your shoes, dear, to keep the wet out for a bit
And we've run out, again, of polish dear, so I've had to use my spit.

I must say that you're looking very pale, dear,
Do you need to see a doctor or the nurse?
Our little home, which long go was cosy, dear,
Now lets in all the draughts, which are a curse.
I'll tuck the scraggy blanket round your knees, dear
Now you keep still and drink a cup of tea
Try to eat this sandwich what I've made, dear,
Can you take a bite or two, dear, just for me?

Open wide, and swalla down this pill, dear,
There now, down it went, dear, what a treat!
I think that you are thinner than you were dear,
Shall I sit and rub your aching feet?
Oh, two little blocks of ice you seem to have, dear
On your two thin freckled legs
You used to say, that they were your best bits
But now they look like two chapel hat pegs.

Well now, it's time to say goodbye, dear
Your bright blue eyes have closed for evermore
A smile is still upon your rosebud lips, dear
Your coffin sits upon the kitchen floor
The men have come in great, big, shiny cars, dear
To fetch you now and take you far away
You'll rest forever underneath the flowers, dear
Until I come and join you, one fine day.

The washing up bowl is floating in the sink, again, Matilda
But you're not here to help me sort it out
Our little house is not the same without you, dear
And I'm lonely now, dear, now you're not about.

I'm sitting on the sofa on my own, dear
Drinking good strong tea from your old mug
But there's not much sugar in the china bowl, dear
And the milk has gone quite sour in the jug.
But on the little table, here beside me
The one we bought together long ago
Is a box of little pills I bought in town, dear
Because, dear, I think it's time for me to go.

There now, they all went down a treat, dear
I'll just sit back and take a breath or two
I'll close my weary eyes for just a moment, dear
And in my old mind's eye, I still see you
You hold out both your arms to me in greeting
And to your warm embrace I step with pride
You look to me, as lovely as you did, dear
On that far gone day, when you, dear, were my bride.

I'm feeling oh so very, very tired, dear
But it's not bad, I know you're by my side
If I reach out my hand, I can almost touch you
And feel your loving hands hold mine with pride
And as I stand and shake off my old jacket
And leave it laying crumpled on the floor
You and I, my darling wife Matilda
Will be together, now and evermore.

Kathryn Fowler-Brookes

Day By Day - Flipside

Day by day I'm falling more out of love with you
And day by day this feeling seems to grow
There isn't any end to my fault-finding
And with you I get more stressed than when baby-minding
Disturbingly, day by day, you're making all my nightmares come true
So come what may, I want you to know
I'm certainly not yours alone, nor in love to stay . . .
And I'll ring your flaming neck if we stay together, one day.

Delphine

Love Is . . .

Part One

Is Love created?
    Or is Love creation?
I would say I love God the creator.
But my human inabilities
    mean I cannot imagine what God is;
        but can marvel,
         be in awe
        and in wonder
          at creation.
In my humanness I like to picture God.
I like to try to explain,
to understand.

I would say I understand God
from the teachings of Jesus;
I understand that God is love.
            Love is harmony
            Love brings peace
        and love makes co-operation.

I see love at the heart of creation.
Maybe Love produced the 'Big Bang'.
            Love
         made the electrons spin,
        this energy co-operated, and
         positive spun with negative
          creating a working atom.
This turned nothingness into power,
                and it *exploded.*

            Love
drew atoms together to make molecules
            Love
brought these together to form crystals;
            Love
put life into the cell.
        All was made in love.

(I should add - I think dark matter is that which did not work together)

So love is creation and love is God,
        and God is love.

As humans we can think about this, we can imagine and we can create.
        We can praise
        and be in wonder.

We can understand love,
and co-operation
and working together,
and we can try and live in love.

Part Two

As well as other great teachers,
Jesus gave us a way to live in love.
Jesus was a genius.
He understood the human condition
and He had a deep understanding of God.
He showed us a path
and told us He would help us.

Jesus is a great leader,
a great friend
and a great teacher.
He is a part of my life
and reminds me not to be offended,
not to hate,
not to be greedy,
and has shown me there is a way to co-operation and harmony
beyond our human understanding.

I keep failing!
However love says,
'Get up and try again!'

B Sommer

Everlasting Love

To a special person on this special day
To wish you special greetings today and the years ahead.

On a day like today, special memories come flooding by
Of happy years spent together as time kept flowing by.

The memories have doubled since our family has grown
Bringing with it special happiness, which made our union, extra strong.

The years have flown so quickly, but the memories have stayed fresh
And hope that now and for always, will always keep it that way.

May this special day repeat itself for years ahead
And leave us with special memories of the day, we were wed.

Mary-Magdalene Kiddie

My Angel

That's my Angel there,
In his long black coat,
With his lush brown hair,
And his face carved to perfection.

His bright blue eyes are elegant so,
Framed by his soft brown curls,
And his cheeks that flow,
So perfectly under my hands.

His hair springs to my touch,
Curling and bouncing in copper locks,
And it smells sweet, oh so very much,
And he laughs at my wondering face.

That's my Angel there,
In his long black coat,
With his lush brown hair,
And his face carved to perfection.

When he plays with my hair,
It makes me soar,
And I no longer give a damn or care,
He is such a joy, such a delight to be with.

He reads with me, he cares for me,
Just as he would a child,
Knowing that we can be free,
That we can be together and have a good time.

That's my Angel there,
In his long black coat,
With his lush brown hair,
And his face carved to perfection.

When he holds me close to him,
He is always warm,
And I can hear the love and laughter from within,
In his spacious, loving and forgiving heart.

He tells me I look wonderful always,
Whether I'm dressed up or down,
And I know he means it, I know when he plays,
And he always takes time to show me off.

That's my Angel there,
In his long black coat,
With his lush brown hair,
And his face carved to perfection.

He'll sing his favourite songs badly,
Knowing I'll laugh and complain,
Which makes him sing evermore loudly,
Until I lovingly silence him with my hand.

And when I'm crying,
When I'm miserable and sad,
He'll pull me close, softly laughing,
And tell me that he loves me and I'll be fine.

That's my Angel there,
In his long black coat,
With his lush brown hair,
And his face carved to perfection.

And today, I told him,
I told him that I love him,
And that I'll never leave his side,
I told him *he* was my Angel.

'No,' he says,
'You are my life, my friend and my love,
You are *my* Angel,
From now until the end of time.'

The sun goes down,
As we kiss and embrace,
And we are Angels there,
From now until the end of time.

Katie Stimson

Dreaming

I'm down the canal fishing,
dreaming of a girl
I should be kissing.

Her name is Jane
from Cooper's Lane,
I fear I may never
see her again.

It's her I keep missing
and for her I keep wishing,
but I guess for now
I'll carry on fishing.

Francis Page

My First Italian Love

I whisper your name
but you're dimmed now, black and white
I try to focus, like a photograph,
Bringing your image aright.
You move, stand before me
brown eyes level, holding clues
to the feeling between us,
we tried so hard not to lose.

Your lips sail like a gondola
I strain to hear you speak.
Your hands animated, seem to capture my gaze
the emotions you're evoking would truly amaze.

You dart, tantalising between boy and man grown
I want to possess you and make you my own.
Whatever I'm feeling, you anticipate all need
where did it come from this insatiable greed?

I've no will left to question what's wrong or what's right
I just need to be with you, both day and night.
I don't feel no, can't say yes,
am I separate from you, can only guess.

I don't feel relaxed, though I'm not tense;
just living each moment in defence.
What expectations have you now?
For myself, I need a vow.

I'm just a child, this has no name
but there's a strategy, it's still a game
shall I win, no I shall lose,
I have no choice, I cannot choose.
This should not be but I sense no shame.

You win me now with haunting sounds
etching your music on my very soul
lilting Latin melodies profound.
I mouth the words, I can't possibly understand,
my senses filled; yet I'm incomplete, never whole.

I never seemed to have a say
like a moth, I stuck it through.
Blinded now, I battle by your side
my only need, to be with you.

You held my hand, we walked along
you picked a rose, and gave your gift to me.

You called out loud, and sang the words
but, I fear I heard a different song.

You may well have walked this road before
the words are clear, and known to you.
You play along, the game of love,
but now I know, it wasn't true.

The sky once blue has just turned grey,
my silent tears begin to fall.
I'll love you 'til my dying day
but, for you, it was not that way at all.

It's over now, you turn and say,
and smile, and hope that we'll be friends.
I clutch my pride, my feelings hide
so I just turn and walk away.

A knife has cut into my soul
no single thing could me console;
'You're very young - you'll soon forget'
is what everyone would say,
but it hasn't happened yet
the thoughts are never far away.

Sheila Evans

Visions Of You

I see your vision clearly as I sit here in the dark
Where you said 'I love you dearly'
As we sat there in the park

Dearest heart for you I pine
I long to feel your lips on mine
To hear you whisper in my ear
Words that no one else should hear

To feel you close beside me
To hear you speak my name
And in your tender eyes I'll see
A spark which I alone can tame

And as your vision disappears from view
Until I hear these words from you
And if they're kept for me alone
I'll be waiting when you come home!

Grace Campbell

Your Wedding

To a special couple on this your day
There are a few words I'd like to say.
To wish both of you all the very best
Of health and happiness - plus all the rest.

Mr and Mrs as you start married life,
Her with a husband and him with a wife.
I hope the love that you share now
Will deepen, strengthen, prosper and grow.

You grew up apart but don't feel down in the mouth
Because he's from the north and she's from the south,
Away from each other you couldn't always hide
So found your own cure for the north/south divide.

At Birmingham Uni you two first met
Pursuing your studies with the mathematics set,
Then various student houses were shared
They weren't all of the best - but no one cared.

Although not always an easy ride
You finished the course, side by side
But that wasn't enough, you both wanted more
And studied again till your heads were sore.

Another four years to the next graduation
Now 'Doctors' this called for much celebration.
Then goodbye to Birmingham you started to sing,
Goodbye to the uni, nightclubs and Bull Ring.

To find a job was now the number one task
And by the Trent seemed a good place to bask.
One company was very keen to employ
And it sounded like a career you both could enjoy.

So moving to Nottingham, No 137
That house was soon your small piece of Heaven.
You painted and decorated and then some more
And both worked very hard, that is for sure.

The garden as well was kept in trim
She helped a bit but mainly by him.
But all work and no play is not very good
So you played and travelled as much as you could.

By now seven years had almost passed
When he popped the big question - at last!
Back to Birmingham again for quite a nice thing
When in the Jewellery Quarter you found *'the ring'*.

With holidays here and trips abroad there
You had to keep working to pay the fare,
And a wedding isn't cheap - as I have found
So when the bills come in, please stick around!

For today the planning and prep is done
And you two finally have become one,
So enjoy what's left of your wedding day
Before we disperse and all go our own way.

May God bless you both in your life's new phase,
Let nothing and no one your happiness erase,
Cherish each other with much love and care
As together you go on the future to share.

I hope you enjoyed these few words in rhyme
I could have done more - if I'd had time
But that's the end of my verse, I can think of no other
So I'll sign off now - with love from your mother.

Esme Murfitt

Pebbles In The Sand

Angrily he kicked the cold wet sand
Desperately trying to understand,
Conversations spinning 'round in his head
As the deserted beach stretched far ahead.

They had been so happy on summer days
Laughing at sunsets when the fiery rays,
Danced on the water . . . flashing gold and red
'I'll love you forever,' is what she had said.

But suddenly she was gone one winter's morn
Driving swiftly away at break of dawn,
Each day he took pebbles to cast in the sea
His mind in a turmoil reliving the memory.

Unexpectedly came a shout from the rocks above,
'Wait for me,' called the voice of his love
He turned to see her clambering down to the shore
She had returned to be by his side once more.

He held her close - she murmured, 'I still love you so'
But his question went unanswered . . . 'Why did you go?'

Jean F Mackenzie

My Man

This gentle man he was to me
My true love for all to see
Always there with a guiding hand
To live our life the way we planned

The love and care for me, was just the best
Until the day he was laid to rest
The sun now is not so bright
For he was my guiding light

To the Yorkshire moors we would often go
Like Heathcliff and Cathy our love did grow
To a special place, walking hand in hand
Drinking in the view, which was so grand

On the Shawl at Leyburn we would stand still
Looking across the valley at Pen Hill
'The beauty of all this,' he said one day to me.
'Is like the love I have for thee.'

I returned to the Shawl one day alone
Before starting my journey back home
I felt the breeze upon my face
As I walked deep in thought, upon our special place

Silently my heart cried out to my love
As I looked across the valley at Pen Hilll
Thinking back, tears came into my eyes
Of my man, then time stood still

It must be the magic of this place
For I truly did see his face
I had drifted into the sands of time
And for that sweet moment, he was mine

Both together, so much in love
I closed my eyes, it was divine
Feeling his arms around me again
For a brief moment in time

To hear his laugh filled me with joy
Deep in my hearrt I felt so glad
I opened my eyes and he was gone
Strangely I did not feel so sad

For the tender times that we did share
To me, is just beyond compare
He was also my best friend
True and loyal to the end

Now, as I turned to go on my way
I will always remember this special day
For I know he will always be with me
Locked in my heart for eternity

He was a special part of my life
I was so proud to have been his wife
Going on at times is hard to bear
Without him in my life to share

I ponder on the love he gave to me
And the sadness will from me flee
I am truly blessed, I know in my heart
To have been so loved by my sweetheart.

Lavinia Bousfield

Years Gone By

28 years have flown so fast
Our kids, memories so precious, will always last
You have such a kind heart and a good sport
Liking a good laugh and a wee drop of the port
Generous and loving, in your own special way
I am so lucky to have you, what more can I say?
It's hard sometimes to put thoughts to the page
The years have been kind to you, I must say

Humorous, fun, secure and true
Always there . . . yes that's you

Laugh lines add character on your expressive face

Destiny led us together back in '71
But 8 years on then my heart was won

From then on life as so full of love
So special you were sent from Heaven above.

Do love you with every beat of my heart
We are soulmates forever and never will part

You're one of a kind, different from others
Generous, charming, but not one that smothers

You'll always be there I know that is true
I'll always be here . . . always for you.

Karen Holm

Crashing Through Time

Crashing through time,
Crashing through time,
Life is sublime,
Crashing through time.
That's fine,
Just fine,
So fine,
Altered images from within,
Let's start at the start and so begin,
I am just human,
Or so they say,
But live for the future,
Not just for today.
Do I exist, or am I a figment of your imagination?
Think for a while,
Just for a while,
Think for a while on what I say,
Shall we live for tomorrow
Or just for today?
Are we a fantasy
Living on Earth?
From the time we begin,
Yes the moment of birth.
Crashing through time,
Crashing through time,
Life is sublime,
Crashing through time,
That's fine,
Just fine,
So fine.
Is your head spinning?
Mine is just now,
But then so is the Earth
So don't take a bow.
No we're not drunk,
Well
I'm not I know.
I'm legless on love,
So let's go man, let's go.

Love is so real guys,
Although I may be fake,
I'm in love with you,

So let's let the Earth shake.
You are the one now,
That I adore,
The wonderful light,
You're just ten out of four.
Crashing through time,
Crashing through time,
Life is sublime,
Crashing through time,
That's fine,
Just fine,
So fine.

Janet Ann Tosini

Twinkle

I saw a twinkle in your eye,
And mirrored the one in mine,
Yet we had this moment met,
Suggesting to me a sign.

In the twinkling of an eye,
Between us had been formed a bond,
We two strangers from out the blue,
Had no choice but to respond.

The devil dancing in your eyes
Was a magnet drawing me to you.
All you did was smile at me,
I was bewitched, life began anew.

The laughter I could see in your eyes,
Accentuated the loveliness in your face,
At this moment something happened,
Something wonderful was taking place.

The light in my eyes,
Then burned brighter,
I had succumbed to your obvious charms,
My immediate response had to be,
A longing to take you in my arms.

The twinkle in your eyes
Will live with me always.

W G Stannard

Lesley

(Dedicated to my wife, my true soulmate, whom I have loved from before the womb and will continue to do so forever after the grave)

You make the diff'rence;
You make things right.
You balance my world
And soften my plight.
You understand
All I've been through,
So when folks talk of special things,
I tell them about you.

You are my strength;
You are my song.
You are the reason
I keep going on.
You are the rhythm
That my heart beats to,
So when I hear a love song,
I sing about you.

You are a gem
Of the purest kind.
You are my treasure trove;
A truly rare find.
Your priceless qualities
Are beyond value,
So when folks talk of riches,
I tell them about you.

Your smile is a candle
Which burns through the night.
You take my darkness
And flood it with light.
Your thoughtful ways
Govern all that you do,
So when the preacher talks of angels,
I tell him about you.

You lift me up
When I am down.
Beautiful things happen
When you are around.
Just the touch of your hand
Makes me feel brand new,
So when folks talk of miracles,
I tell them about you.

And you are my anchor
Against life's savage tide.
You are my refuge
When the storm is nigh.
You are the rock
Which I cling to,
So when I talk to the Saviour,
I tell Him about you.

Michael J Parsons

Never Boil Your Cabbage Twice

'Never boil your cabbage twice.'
The wise lady once said to me

'You get hurt if you go down that road twice,
Mark my words you see.'

His smile melted my heart
His hair was so soft to touch
His gentle voice with dancing words
Meant to me - so, so much.

Oh how my heart missed a beat
But the missing beat was not found

Oh how the butterflies danced inside me
But there were no butterflies around

Oh how he lifted my two feet
But my feet were on the ground

Oh how the music played so beautifully
But there was no note to sound

Her words of wisdom came to life
His promises that flowed had gone
Pantomime, merry-go-round dreams
Were all but a song

Liquid dreams slipped through my fingers
Onto the slippery floor

Never boil your cabbage twice
I now gently close the door.

Kim Elizabeth Reeder

Rosalyn (A Lost Soul)

(Reflections on advice given to a beloved daughter, who later died aged 36 in 1990)

Change your lifestyle they said . . . meet new people, stop smoking.
I'm 32 next birthday and know they are right.
My entire savings are sunk in this property . . . only 22,000
But the garden is a bit of a fright.
I've penetrated the jungle and planted a tiger lily too
And observed a climbing clematis strangle a stick or two.
I've lingered beside a lavender bush, pinching it twixt finger and thumb
Before drawing the pungent perfume deep into my lung
Safe in the knowledge that this time, it surely will do me no harm.
The orchard is gnarled and neglected, but has borne a harvest of fruit,
Windfalls lie sadly scattered like drunks on the tipsy-turf,
Scarred by the unwanted attentions of an army of wiggly worms
Feasting their way to life.
Whilst teams of stripy competitors dressed in yellow and black,
Jostle, pester and parry for possession of the pulpy zest.

The rising damp is cured now after nauseous layers of gunk
Followed by copious coverings of creamy cream-coloured paint.
I started a job with the Council . . . 'couldn't do better' they said,
They didn't know it was in a basement, debased of sun and sky.
I type forms all day . . . type forms all day . . . type all day,
Another kind of factory, but no extra is ever paid for this taedium vitae.
My colleagues are waxwork models, imprisoned by this dungeon door
Too long . . . grown pale and silent . . . like fungi on the forest floor.
Strangest thing is . . . my flat is a basement too but I can see . . .
Trees and green grass . . . birds and blue sky . . .
I can see and savour freedom . . . I cannot let it die.

Change your life they said, meet nicer people
Not the lame duck layabouts you often seem to know.

So I met a guy with a guitar who never has any dough,
But who'd want to know a demented drug addict who wears
Accidentally distressed clothes, he thinks I'm wonderful . . . no, no, no!
Try evening classes they pleaded . . . there's yoga and art,
Even pottery, all part of life's pageant or purpose . . .
An unknown lottery, but I lean more towards self-defence lessons
Than to sit waiting for break-ins or rape, wondering what I may be
Doing by the time I am thirty-eight.
Then if life should happen to deal me a toxic tarot card
There's always my heavenly garden where the darling buds
Will burst into life again . . . next spring . . . and the next . . . and the . . .

Memoriam to a sleeping beauty

The years of heartache, sorrow and pain,
Can never touch or hurt you again.
God in His wisdom seems to know best,
Only He knows why you suffered this test.
Safe in His kingdom, a world without cease,
Loving with love in a haven of peace.
Time cannot age nor the memory dim,
Our beautiful blue-eyed . . . *sweet Rosalyn.*

Betty Deadman

Only A Dream

He lived around the corner,
When we went on our first date,
The pictures maybe, or a dance,
For these I could not wait,
Going out was really fun,
Till he got into my heart,
From that first so gentle kiss,
I did not want to part.
My mind was full of only him,
He left me wanting more,
Passion took the place of love,
'Twas him I did adore.

And then he left.

My heart was drowned in many tears,
As on my soul he marched
And trampled over all my dreams,
My future bleak and parched,
Still through the changing of the times,
The flame remained a spark,
Glowing softly in my mind,
To light a life left dark.
Then, by chance, we met again,
Mem'ries began to fade,
It wasn't him I truly loved,
At last the ghost was laid.

And then I left.

A P Keenleyside

First Night

We shared our eyes
You and I
And I at the river
The stones in the river
Blank-eyed pregnant stones
Stones of silent dreams
River dreams
Of those who dream
Beneath the green reeds
And greener weeds.

I saw myself
Within your eyes
And you in mine
Through night's long journey
Down the river
Over stones
Facing the sky
Rolling and tumbling
Under the sky
The full moon
Shining from our eyes.

And on the ridge
Wise Raven watching
Shape-changing
Watching the rolling
And tumbling
Beneath the sky
Waiting to catch
The moon pearl
From our eyes.

He was wise
But we were wiser
Disguising our moon song
Beneath the flow of water
Was it the water?
Or Raven's laughter
Shape-shifting laugher
Dancing for Orpheus
Dancing through rapids
Of rapidly dancing
Pregnant stones.

Love's Many Mysteries

Don't look back
Orpheus
Never look back
The stones will dance for you
Entranced by you
Swallowed by
The black Raven
Dancing in the shadow
Of our moon pearl eyes.

Tara-Jane Hulligan Zuk

Teenage Love

Psst!
A screwed up piece of paper torn from the back of a history book
The embarrassed boy in the corner giving you an uncomfortable look

An awkward smile then the turn of his head
Next your nosy friends asking what the paper said

My immediate reaction is, 'No, definitely not,'
Your teacher suddenly shouts, 'Alright then kids, that's your lot!'

The pushing, the shoving, the snidey remarks
The known thought of the other girls' broken hearts

A grab of your hand and you're being dragged off to the loo
And you find yourself asking, 'Help, what should I do?'

I then said, 'Pass this on, my answer is yes!'
My heart started beating, I felt like a mess

Last lesson a blur
From the urge I had for the bell to ring for the end of the day
Where I would meet Luke and we could both be on our way

We met as a group, laughing and joking
Hard kids on the corner thought they looked cool smoking
(One of the stupid girls ended up choking!)

Luke offered me a piggyback
Then ran off with me down the old dirt track

We kissed on the corner and neither wanted to part
And knew from that moment that was the start . . .

Luke had well and truly stolen my heart!

Hattie Ingham (15)

True Love

The day he came,
She looked at his face,
And knew he felt the same.
Together at last,
A night of love,
Moss and heather for a bed,
Honeysuckle and wild roses overhead.
Shooting stars lit up the sky,
A tear fell from her eye,
For her man was promised to another.
If only she could stop the sunrise,
And keep this moment forever.
He put a red rose in her hair,
They were meant to be together.
The horizon turned red then grey,
In Romany caravans they travelled,
Past country villages and a ruined castle.
Alongside a wood full of bluebells,
Over a bridge and down a lane,
Stopping for the night by a stream.
In the distance,
The faint sound of tambourines,
Gypsy musicians playing faster,
All were loud and drunk.
A full moon filtered through the trees,
By the bridge he waited for his love.
They embraced each other.
He said, 'Now we will be together forever.'
A woman ran over.
She shouted, 'What are you doing with my man?'
And pushed the young girl aside.
Furiously he answered,
He turned to her and said, 'I don't love you.
We were betrothed when we were young.
I love this girl, it's our families who put you and I together.'
The woman screamed, 'If I can't have you, no one will,'
And stabbed him through the heart.
The woman ran away.
It began to rain.

He whispered his love's name.
The girl held him close,
Cradling him in her arms.

She said, 'Don't leave me now.'
She lowered her face,
Crying, she kissed his lips.
He closed his eyes.
'I will stay by your side until the end of time.'
The knife lay on the grass.
A flash of steel.
Rose petals fell from her hair.
'No one will keep us apart, we will stay together forever.'

Sandra Wood

A Love Betrayed

A heart that's been broken, a heart full of pain
That feels like your life will never be the same
A love that's betrayed, filled with memories lain
That dies to leave more than ashes, a love that's been slain
A trust that was given and then abused
That leaves you feeling battered and very much bruised.

With all strength and energy pushed down to the end
No more to give or even to lend
You look beyond to find a way through
This endless turmoil, to know what to do.

A heart that's been broken will one day, start to mend
In time there will be another, on which you can depend
A love that's been betrayed, can some day be replaced
If you cast away all doubts, of true love that you face
A trust that was given, only to be abused
Can be rebuilt, but it's for you to choose.

I know where you are and I know where you've been
I know all the heartache, I know, I have seen
I know where you are going, though it might take a while
I know you will make it, one day you will smile.

There is a love out there, waiting for you
A love that will always be honest and true
Someone to trust, no matter what life entails
A trust you can rely on, one that never fails
Then you will see 'true love' at its best
One that surpasses all of the rest!

Shirley Sewell

A Tear

I am a tear held back in pride
If I were seen no one would mind

Except the one that holds me here
She wishes I would just disappear

This is her story, I will try to tell
One time it was Heaven, then it was Hell!

She finds her childhood is often on her mind
Thinking of her parents, both loving and kind

They cared for each other with every breath that they took
It was plain to be seen in that special look

He would give her flowers or a surprise little gift
The house was full of laughter - are you getting my drift?

She then fell in love with every beat of her heart
Believing it was forever and never would part

Being married, she thought, it would all stay the same
But life took a turn, it was a different ball game

Yes, there were good times when the children were young
But the sadness inside had already begun.

She was made to feel worthless with no words of praise
Instead, would be moaned at and sworn at for days

All that she wanted was for him to show that he cared
For her to feel her life was being properly shared

She needed him, but he was never there
All she remembers is his empty chair

Now, years have gone by and they have gone their own ways
But now he swears - he will love her to his dying days

The vows they took 'till death do us part'
Are still engraved on each other's heart

They no longer kiss each other goodnight
Having new partners, this wouldn't be right

Now, older and wiser she sits and reflects
It's her shattered dreams she mostly regrets

She knows the recipe learnt from her past
The ingredients of the heart make a relationship last

You need a good measure of love, like and respect
Any mix of two can achieve the same effect

She wonders if there is such a thing as an afterlife
If so . . . would they once again be husband and wife?

At last, I'm free and I'm running down her face
But being quickly brushed away, just in case

The grandchildren might see me there
Now, running her fingers through her hair

She sighs and in a quiet voice
She whispers . . . I guess I made the right choice.

Yvonne Stephens

Love Among The Ruins

Where would we but find love
Among the ruins of our lives
In ageless stratagems laid bare
Where others have trod
To find the happiness
That comes with it
Love where all the saints fear to tread
Where all the world just has not a care
And stirs up from ruined lives
And produces something greater still
Of love that can fly among the ruins
And bring its presence to the fore
Love that can give new purpose in life
That stood many before
And stood in the ruins
When life was not worth living
And stood in its fullness
And its time
Among what would always be
Our better held belief

Of love that will be the companion
And guiding star
Of our boat the river of life
Among the ruins
So it springs
Ruined and damaged
Now healed and rising
On the gallant ship.

Alasdair Sclater

Our Love Stayed Strong

That evening I wandered away from the crowd
And stood in the cool of the day,
To see shades of daylight fast leaving
And the sun with its singular ray
Caught in your hair as I watched you
When you paused in its amber light glow,
And the stillness around overwhelming
And I'm back in those days long ago
When we were just children at play here
And we'd run with the wind in our hair
Every day we were laughing, and every day ours to share.

Then we were children with children's eyes
And would walk hand in hand, off to school
Always the same path together then,
Somebody altered a rule and they took you away
And I sat alone, on the bench by the swing in the park
Watching for you every evening,
Waiting until it got dark
But you didn't come back and I'd cry in the night
For we'd never been really apart
Always we'd been together, forever, right from the start.

Though schooldays are past my love still waits for you
And with eyes closed I picture us there
You laughing at me, me laughing at you
And the wind still blowing our hair.
Time it has passed and no longer a child I come back to this place fully grown,
And though others are here, I've watched every face
But still I feel empty, alone.
Then when all talking is over I turn, and gaze at the sky
From the same place where we'd stood as children
And watched summer clouds drifting by.

Now the day's sun, with its final bright ray, envelopes this lone person there
So quietly she turns as though sensing the past,
Then a warm gentle breeze moves her hair,
Then we each see the face there, before us,
And our hearts pound, as feelings grow strong
Now words don't matter, we've found us again,
Just here is where we belong.

The search now for me is completed and her eyes speak of only the same
And our hands now are tight-locked together
For I know that with me she'll remain

Stolen years and the heartaches between us
Yet so strong in her dreams, did love stay
Being childlike again, and the laughter and being together each day

So, leaving the crowd far behind us, almost floating on grass near our feet
We follow the trail of our childhood, to the gate where each day we'd meet
Then wander away down the tree-covered lane, to the bench by the swing in the park
Where my love waited for you every evening, waiting until it got dark.

Rosie Oakes

Love Story

(In memory of the Royal Artillery 'Ack-Ack' Regiment based at Primrose, Jarrow 1939-1941)

The Stukas dived down, screaming guns ablaze,
and looking for their prey,
it was not going to be their day.

The *Ack-Ack* threw each other three foot shells
and blew them all to bits,
these were the best of British men with
'A' class British wits.

They had all trained in India and were the best we had,
the ladies followed them around, off duty they were glad.

Tall, bronzed and blonde, these gods were gifts from Heaven,
the dance halls did not close till it was past eleven.

Mother loved to dance, she did the Charleston great,
she chose a British *Ack-Ack* man with quite a Scottish trait.

The people all adored them, they had free cigarettes,
the ladies knew some day they'd leave but, they had no regrets.

Mother, she was taken to our Sunderland Empire here,
'It was then all the rage',
Jock loved live entertainment and if you were good
those days you might survive doing a turn upon a Glascow stage.

The Sunderland Empire is still going strong,
Mother's grandchild walked across its stage
for her degree in a sincere throng.

Those stolen moments away from the gunfire,
were worth a thousand nights to those with real heartfelt desire.

Jean Paisley

My First Love

The touch of his lips,
His tender embrace,
The look in his eyes,
When he held me close,
The magic of his voice
As he whispered,
'I love you.'
The thrill that tingled
Down my spine when he sighed,
'I would like to marry you.'
The fascination of his existence
Overwhelmed me with emotion,
The thought of my parents,
Would they approve or scold me?
The pain in my heart with his
Boisterous and wayward ways,
The jealousy I felt in me
When his roving eyes
Saw a pretty face.
The idea of being married
At such an early age,
The foolishness of it all,
Made me think again.
The blow to his pride
Made him go astray,
The tender, loving spark
Just drifted away.
Time waits for no one,
So I've heard say,
He lost no time and
Went on his way,
The new love on his arm.

Soon made him a married man,
With lots of love and a baby
On its way.
As the lovebirds glowed with happiness
The tears filled my eyes,
To think, he could have been mine,
If only I hadn't been so stupid.

He loved me once, in happy times,
But now he's left me
With a broken heart.

The weeks went by,
Without a word,
Then he came around to call,
The cheek of him, I thought.
Made me wonder,
What I ever saw in
That geek at all.

Doreen Brialey

The Rose

(For my friend Brigitte)

It was early this morning when I looked up at the moon
A crescent high up in the sky
The light of it shone down a frosty glow on the ground
And a picture caught my eye
There, at the top of an overgrown bush
Was a Rose glowing bright with the dew
So clean, so yellow, a rare beauty to see
And it made me think of you
How strange that a light shining high from above
Could bring such a warm glow to my heart
But seeing that beautiful Rose on that cold morning
Made me sad that you and I are apart
Could it be a sign sent to me from above?
To show me the wonder of such a bright sight
To make sure that I would think of the beauty in you
In that cold, bright, morning light
I feel lucky that it made me think of such a treasure
Though sadly, we will always be apart
Yet, forever now a rose will give me the warmth that I crave
And bring new thoughts of you into my heart
Each morning now, I will search for you in the moon's light
To bring new pictures of you to my mind
Where your beauty will give me pleasure
Which now will be easy to find
You are like that Rose and your beauty astounds me
And you are the light that I see
And forever now, when I see a Rose
I will know that you will stay part of me.

Don D

Just For One More Night

Maria,
when I am gone
If you need a friend or lover
or a place you can hide
I will always be there,
even though my hands are tied.

I know deep down inside
if you consider what we shared
maybe you'll see you were all I need.

There's never been a better time,
there's never been a better place
for you and I together
here alone
and face to face.

Oh,
I'd do anything for you,
thanks for coming into my life,
    I love you.
I've been spending all my time
never giving much to you,
but you were always
on my mind,
in all the dreams I hold on to.

I tried to tell you
how I feel but the words
just came out wrong.

Wherever you go,
I want you to know
    I love you.
All my life
I've searched
for someone like you.

No matter how hard I try,
no matter what I do,
    I love you.

Before I die
if only
just for one more night,
let me hold you tight.

All my life I've been waiting for someone like you.

Could it be the brightest star
so close yet so far!

don't you know
    I love you?
I'm calling
for you right now.

Norman Huxtable

The Strength Of Love

Mark's quietly sleeping, I'm crying,
I'm holding my husband's hand.
There's so little time. He's dying.

I remember how, strangely we
Became in love, one day on a bus.
Our first encounter, our instant liking.

My bus fare clinked, I looked around,
He sat alone on a sideways seat.
I was impressed when he looked round.

I meant to go on up the aisle,
He daringly forced me to stop.
His long legs prevented my passing.

When he'd completed his manoeuvre
By shifting his big feet away,
These playful tactics had won me over.

Now sitting opposite I explained
I hadn't very far to go.
He nodded, yet without warning disappeared.

Dejected, sadly I got up to go.
I stared at a dent in a green plastic seat,
But turning, discovered he'd waited for me.

Our true happiness of many years
Life together has ended now.
I'm left alone to dry my tears.

While grieving alone by our empty bed,
Mark's smiling ghost momentarily came
To let me know he'd wait for me.

Isobel G King

Loving You

(Jackie, Pamela, John and Kirsty)

As I put this pen to paper, it takes my thoughts back fifty years
On Saturday night I went to the dancing in Balloch
I stood and watched as others danced, I was always a bit shy
Then from across the hall came this chap who asked me to dance
We danced and talked and talked some more
And before we knew it, we had spent all night in each other's company
He asked to walk me home and that was the start of our romance
After two weeks he asked me if I would marry him one day?
And I said yes.
We spent lots of time together having long walks
Into the countryside or parks
He gave me a ring until one day he could afford an engagement ring
The ring I wore around my neck on a chain
With the ring next to my heart
It was our secret.
We planned our lives as man and wife and even thought of children
We thought four would be just right
When I turned seventeen we got engaged
My ring had three hearts
The hearts were one for each other,
The larger one for the family we planned to have
You even changed your job and worked in the same factory
And we spent every lunch hour together.
We both had bikes and you cycled me home each day after work
In the year 1961 I had just turned nineteen and you were twenty-three
We got married and took our vows to be man and wife.

Over the years that were to come we had a special daughter
Then two years later a special son
The years went by and our love grows stronger
This strength and love we passed on to our family
Then nineteen years later what a surprise
Another special daughter did arrive
Sometimes the road of life gets hard,
But our love was stronger and got us through
Our older daughter and son made us parents like we planned
Then our daughter gave us two grandsons
Making us grandparents, it was great
Then our second special daughter who arrived so very late
Gave us a chance of parenthood again, we hope we got it right.
As our family got older, our second daughter gave us another grandson
We had a second chance to share our love with our special family

Only two more years to go and we can celebrate fifty years of marriage
Our love still strong as when we met as we knew it would be.
It was special right from the start
So no matter what our lives bring along
Just stop for a moment and feel
My special love in your heart.

Jean Adam

Waiting

Mist from tunnel now clearing
Train coming into view
I stand on the platform
Waiting for you

Two years have passed
Since I waved you goodbye
To fight for king and country
Wiping tears from my eyes

In your smart army uniform
You made me so proud
Many others were boarding
But you stood out in the crowd

Letters and tokens
You sent from the front line
Proclaiming your love
And confirming you were mine

Would you remember our parting kiss
How have you changed after all this
Time can protect memories of you
Marriage vows taken honest and true

The mist now returning
Steam train pulling away
Crowds all dispersing
No more passengers today

The letter in my hand, crumpled and old,
Confirming the news which had to be told
Over the top you went on that day
Silent and peaceful, on the battlefield you lay.

Anne Hulbert

Love Is A Journey

Love is a journey
It starts with a kiss
The road may be bumpy
Pitfalls to miss.

Jealousies lurking
To mar what is pure
It makes you uncertain
It makes you unsure.

A mother and child
Their bond set in stone
The birth is a milestone
No longer alone.

A clandestine meeting
Masquerading as love
Its lies make it murky
Like cheats 'hand-in-glove'.

A longstanding union
That's weathered the storm
As rare as its precious
No longer the norm.

Today's fleeting moments
Of love cast aside
When problems start mounting
And tempers arise.

Still searching for love
That elusive, prized dream
Where will you find it
To boost self-esteem?

God is love
The believers say
Not everyone's convinced
Of religion's way.

Love is a journey
A daytrip or trek
It can leave you ecstatic
Or an emotional wreck.

Whatever the price paid
We search for it still
Risking rejection
That bitterest pill.

A mixture of feelings
Both noble and tarnished
Hope springs eternal
Never extinguished.

Sonia Richards

Pursuing Love

Was it love
That prompted me
To carve our names
Upon that tree?
I took a chance that
That he would see

Was it love

That persuaded me
To cycle round
The long way home
Hoping he might
See me come?

Was it love

That tempted me
To walk the dog
In the same field
Where I hoped
He would be?

Was it love

That guided me
To visit him
In sympathy
When he was ill
And welcomed me?

It was love
We both could see
How well we grew
Accustomed to
Being together.

Betty Gilman

Until You

I listened to the songs
Heard the whispers
Of how great it is
Seen the dewy-eyed looks
Heard so many say those three words
So simple to say
With so much meaning
That really doesn't seem enough
But never really understood
How it could be
That was

Until you came along
With your smile
You melted my heart
Gave meaning to those songs
I'd listened to so many times

Until you came along
I had this vision of how it would be
Of that perfect moment
When the candle flickers
A spark in an eye
A bolt of lightning
And I would have known
That was

Until you came along
And in that first second
Love struck me
And those words so simple
Became so hard to say
Until it was too late
And I was just a memory to you

Until you came along
I never knew
What love really was
Nor what regret could be
Or how empty a person could feel

If only I had spoken
Not been so shy
Taken that risk
Told you those words
But I didn't

So I'll tell you now
Even though it's too late
And you may never hear me but
I love you.

Oliver L T Waterer

Me And My Gal

I'm an Octogenarian
And simply don't agree
That romance is just for young 'uns'
And not for folk like me.
So if you've a mind to listen
I've a tale to tell,
'Tis about two (still young) lovers
Me, and my 'old gal',
I recall when I first saw her
She were barely seventeen,
Fair took my breath away she did,
Her like I'd never seen.
So I showered her with love letters
And swept her off her feet,
She had many more admirers see,
And I had them to beat.
Then as the years unfolded
Time (it seemed) stepped up the pace,
And transformed 'We' oh so sneakily
Into 'Wrinklies' as they say.
So how do folks now see us
As we toddle down the street?
Just another sweet 'old couple',
Or two more liabilities!
But it doesn't really matter
For we no longer care,
With a lifetime of love between us
And the outlook, pretty fair!
For in our 'enchanted cottage'
Where time quite oft stands still
My gorgeous seventeen-year-old 'gal'
Sets my heart a-beating still!

Austin Baines-Brook

In Defence

You ask me to be sure,
When your hair
Hanging like willows
In the swollen river of my senses
Conceals
That super-sensual point
Where infinity's great wheel
Bears down the button
Of my being.

You ask me to be sure,
When, hearing the ripe
Cornfield rustle of your
Eyelashes,
I watch the lapwing
Wheel into a cartoon
Allegorising
The soul's seven-valleyed
Journey:
When I hear syllables
Below that tune,
Soft and insistent
As the melodic chink
Of colliding shadows,
Which you play upon
My taut tendon's harpsichord.

Being unable to speculate
Dispassionately
Whether your body's whiteness
Mirrors
My unconditional delight in it
Or the immaculacy
Of the lily
Voluptuously
Contemplating itself,
I am sure of one thing only:
That those senses are not
Infallible;

Their authority being rejected
When conversant
With their limitations.

All else flows
Through the insubstantial
Trellis of my hands,
Forming and drifting
Like patterns on the sands.

Jeffrey Amor Pickford

Alone Again

I thought of you this morning,
As dawn crept through the sky,
Too numb to feel,
Too hurt to care,
But not too strong to cry.

I thought of you this afternoon,
You see, I love you still.
Eight endless weeks,
Have come and gone,
No heart, no strength, no will.

I thought of you this evening,
Far on some distant shore,
I heard your voice,
I sensed your touch,
Felt close to you once more.

I thought of our beginnings,
When you were just my friend.
It was our destiny,
To be, to meet,
To love, to end.

I'd hoped to see you just once more,
I long to take your hand,
To hold you,
Tell you gently,
I am trying to understand.

Patience and time will give me strength,
To break these prison bars,
Unlock my heart,
Spread wide my wings
And fly free to the stars.

Norma Fraser Reid

The Alluring Immediate Magic Of Him

A gentle she-thing bedazzled
is incautious, mazed, thunderstruck;
slightest touch of him sending razzled
seismic tremors, I stood still, as if stuck.

Breathing softly, lifting my head,
pulling me tightly against him,
moving me towards the bed,
fitting my mouth over his, lights dim,

tears in my eyes, I held my lips tightly,
I sighed against his mouth, Cupid arrows darting,
my lips went warm and slack, lightly
lips of a sleeping child, mostly parting.

Finding the concavity of the small
of my back, he stroked it, weaving
gently and something new came all
into my lips, into my breathing.

My arms tightened and a new
urgency overwhelming and rare,
I drew in a long breath, soft as dew
like a diver coming up for air.

Whispering sweet words in his ear, a blurring,
he exuded an intangible flavour,
but in spite of the wonder and the alluring
immediate magic of him, oh divine behaviour!

In spite of his wonderful scent,
closeness and dark eyes to drown in,
and the shallow, breathy feelings and pent-up
expectancy, the logical sobering

part of my mind kept moving forever
in decreasing circles; a constant swirling.
Airport departures, time together,
warm soft kisses, but possessing

slightly tart flavour of nostalgia,
so I told myself it was a fine world and wise
and filed away doom-laden thoughts of neuralgia
and we kissed long humid goodbyes.

And I laughed and I cried
not in hysterics but because of the joys of laughing
and the release of crying, we tried
our best and found something

rocking us both to the centre of our souls, oh eternal hope!
Before leaving he slung me a look from
the door that tightened around me like a rope.

Judith McCarthy

To My Valentine

Will you be my Valentine
And love me with good measure
Love me gently, love me bold
Love me at my leisure?

Show me the man that waits within
For Cupid's darted arrow.
Whisper that you love me true
So my full heart can follow.

Pick with care the time, the place.
Make right the situation
For I long to climb the hill
That started with creation.

Try not to lose me on the way,
It makes my journey harder.
Then sadness comes and fills my heart.
Your wrong move kills my ardour.

At times my many moods of love
Change quickly like the weather.
Come we have to catch them fast
Before they're gone forever.

Once gone, I have to start again
To climb the hill of Heaven,
When you feel me melt with joy,
When you hear me sighing.

You will know I'm at the top
Do not give up on trying.
I will love you in return.
I will not give short measure.
So will you be my Valentine
My Valentine forever?

Estelle Goldberg

That Day In 1969

'Twas the year of sixty-nine
That was the happy nineties
She was a bride so fine
Lovely as in her teens

The crowd cheered - what a din
And threw some rice at them
Still stuck there in the tin
Oh boy! She does look nice.

'Who is that man by her side?'
They did murmur loud
With him she'll now abide
This is a 'know all' crowd

Next came the festive board,
'Shut that window' from a guest
Speeches made - guest so bored
Much was said in jest

Now it is honeymoon time
All aboard for 'Lossie'
So on the train they climb
The bride is now the 'Bossie'

Years of nearly forty gone
They passed so really fast
Still our pair just jog along
Youth has long since past

Multiplied they have no doubt
With children young and old
Still they can really shout
Each precious as pure gold

Grandchildren quite a few
All growing well and strong
Good to see a healthy crew
All knowing right from wrong

Time speeds on - our couple crawl
They still say loud and clear
'The Lord is our all in all
Filling us with so much cheer

Thanks be to God above
For that year sixty-nine'
So much overflowing love
With Him they're doing fine
Look back
Look forward
Look up

Erica Menzies

Romance

Dancing days, meeting lads
Always looking for romance.
Then over he came and asked me to dance.

Engagement followed heady with love
No worries to spoil our mood.
With marriage to come
The future, expectations were good.

Years hurried on -
    A daughter a son.
A family complete
    Together such fun.

Next phase of our life
It's happy, exciting
Children studying at uni
The years go like lightning.

They grow up and leave
We're a couple again - a pair
Holding hands when we meet
Romance in the air.

But . . . there's always a 'but'
To spoil that loving glance
When things turn around and
Fate announces the 'last dance'.

Now alone, life's bittersweet
I make a brave stance.
And hold on to memories
And dream of the past . . . romance.

Sheila Westwater

Just A Dream

Last night as I lay sleeping
I had a dream of you
And oh believe me, darling
I hope my dream comes true.

I dreamt we were together
Walking down the aisle
You dressed in pure white satin
And trying your best to smile.

The church bells they were ringing
So soft, but yet so clear
I felt you hug my shoulder
I saw you shed a tear.

I spoke soft words of courage
And told you not to fear
Tho' it took me all my time
From shedding one small tear.

The organ had stopped playing
All went quiet and still
The parson broke the silence
His voice seemed loud and shrill.

I heard him ask the question
I heard you say, 'I will.'
The ring went on your finger
Oh darling, what a thrill.

I kissed you then my darling
Not once my dear, but twice
I wouldn't have missed that darling
Not at any price.

Then we cut the wedding cake
We used a bright new knife
And from that moment darling
You were mine for life.

But then alas, I woke dear
I found it all a dream
I found us not together
Nor to church had been
No, my dearest darling
All this had been a dream.

But with your help my darling
My dream could all come true
So now you know my darling
The rest is up to you.

Gordon West

Quiet Love

The gentle breathing of many years
soothes her sleepless night.
Feather-soft the sound absorbs her,
light as a dandelion clock
the murmur drifts around the room -
music of their quiet love.

He sighs. She turns and wonders
what he dreams this moonless night.
Ambition unfulfilled perhaps -
but no, his peaceful face conveys
contentment in the life they share.
Their tranquil life, their perfect love.

The night seems long, but not unpleasant.
Shining stars cast gentle light
as she remembers many nights
passed, for her, in just this way.
Happy at the sound of breathing
regular as heartbeat patterns.

So comforting each tiny sound,
a gentle cough, intake of breath,
by her side as she lies dreaming.
Light as air they soothe her worries
ruffling her peaceful dozing
as the dawn begins to break.

Rousing as a snowflake's fall
his inner clock stirs him to rise,
knowing she can sense his movements
through a perfect understanding
grown through years of love together.
Smilingly, he brings her tea.

Joan Bell

A Pair Of Brown Liverpool Eyes

Eyes brown, brown eyes,
Such simple words to describe such gems,
Such precious stones.
Millions of beings worldwide have brown eyes,
But not these eyes:
These eyes are unique
They are a pair of brown Liverpool eyes.

Becoming horizontal, they smile,
Then laugh and effervesce,
To scold, they suddenly close their lids,
But then flirt with an optical caress.
They censor by staring without blinking,
Splitting wide open to condone.
Brown Liverpool eyes - eyes I want to own.

Lignite eyes,
Damp woody eyes,
Eyes the colour of Irish peat
And just as volatile.
Eyes you talk directly too,
Eyes which demand immediate replies.
Living eyes. Impatient eyes.

Ever since they first opened,
They have been searching for another pair of eyes,
Eyes of the same quality as their own.
But is there such another pair, in this world?
Cosmic collisions would occur
If such an unusual nuptial,
Were ever to take place.

Umber eyes,
The eyes of a golden tiger.
Two brown pieces of opaque quartz
Smile at me, flirt with me,
Don't censor me,
Be kind to me,
And I shall remember forever these two Brazilian agates.

Eyes brown, brown eyes,
Such simple words to describe such gems
Such precious stone.
Millions of beings worldwide have brown eyes,
But not these eyes:
These eyes are unique.
They are a pair of brown Liverpool eyes.

Ann Fogg

Memories

Once in my life I knew love for a while
With it brought happiness and many a smile
Words were spoken and promises made
Which didn't even last a decade.

I loved him with a love that was more than love
I knew God blessed us from above
His smile for me was very bright
We loved each other with all our might.

No longer do I hear his footsteps on the stair
I look at his chair, he is no longer there
I would love his dear smiling face to see
But alas, he no longer comes to see me.

I think of him often and shed many a tear
His face I cannot see, his voice I cannot hear
We exchanged gifts, mine I still treasure
Look at them often and bring me great pleasure.

He moved away but didn't keep in touch
Four years ago today he moved away
The very next day was my birthday.

I often wonder when he goes to bed
If memories of me ever enter his head
Two years alone I tarried
And after a while I then got married.

I often wonder if we'll meet again
My loving him causes me so much pain
The torment's with me all my life
Dear God, why couldn't I be his wife?

Mavis Shaw

Devotion

(Dedicated to my little Yorkie Bonnie)

I sit here lonely, lonely and afraid
Afraid of what life might hold
Alone with my thoughts
Nothing right, nothing as it seems.
The world beyond my window
A bare and lonely place.
Where you struggle to survive,
Strange faces pass me in the street
But mean nothing to me.
I wonder why I go on,
But then know it's because she is there,
By my side she sits no matter what,
People come, people go,
But she's still there,
She asks nothing from me,
A bit of love, some food, a gentle hand.
A small being, a pint-sized bundle of fun
Cheers me up when sad, makes me laugh instead of cry,
Licks my tears away.
Welcomes me home, always pleased to see me
No matter what mood I may be in.
To her I am her king, the most important person in her life,
When people desert as they will she will stay,
Through sickness, hunger, poverty, she's there,
A true friend I can always rely on, wherever I go she will follow
Through wind and rain, sleet and snow,
Even with no roof but the sky she will remain beside me,
I may be sad or happy, beautiful or ugly to her
It does not matter.
Although I may be unhappy with what I have around me,
She is happy because she has me.
If my bed is the hard floor, so will hers be,
If the sky is my roof it's also hers.
If I have no food or comfort neither will she

But try to take her away from me she will not go
She wants no other master, no other friend,
No other home, her home is beside me wherever I am,
And even in death she will still remain,
For her love is constant,
Am I worthy of such a love as this?
I do not know,
But then I'm only a human being.

Hazel Webb

Agony

I guess . . . I have long been forgotten
Like dust buried in the basement.
But I remember your fragrance
An aroma of freshness and shelter
Swirls in my head and wakens
Every memory cell in my body
Has anyone told you that you are a drug?

Not until now that I know
At the instant we met
I have lost. Lost in your game
You always stand still on the other side
Of the bank. Waiting or maybe not
All along, I am the one who makes the first move.

I am also the one who slips away first
Sorry. Sorry that I could not tolerate
Big mouths, make-ups and slangs
Sorry that I am not used to wearing masks
When I was given a chance to leave
I left with a glimpse of hope, which then
Scattered with a drop of red.

'Long time, no see,' you once said.
Shoulders shrugged with unease
Hands in pockets. Truly, I spot you
In a crowd of clowns every time
Yet my face never lands on your eyes.
Since when did the bridge between us break?

I forgot.

Chiu Tsz Ki

The Déjà Vue Rendezvous

(For Nicola Bowerman)

It is time past
That time future has seeded
The continuous moment
In a never-ending now.
It is a welcome star
Buried deep in erotic caves:
This is the Madonna of the rocks
Come to toll the midnight bells again.

We see through vague longing
Most of our lives, and passively let the world
Wash out our hidden dreams.
But there is an eternal hymn
Under all the surface dross
Singing an anthem
To the undead winds,
Singing like the music of the spheres
To the dark infinite space
Of Truth's heady years -
The romantic ocean
Rising and falling
Usually on deaf ears.

We echo our secret loves
With ambiguous endings,
Small waisted
And curve thigh'd;
Posing with black corseted relieve
And red-stained homiles.

This is the way we attain enlightenment
Through open flesh doors
And pointed hearts.
Life, carved into split second frames
Bursting with remembrance in old age,
While the polished patina
Of our time together
Gathers a brilliant waxy sheen.

It is both nostalgia de la boue
And divine revelation,
The opening of the final chapter
In a dialogue with the universe
Where you and I are one.

Peter Corbett

My Man

Emotions stir, as life's aroused
I wake with ease and gladness.
Who gives me all I have,
when some have none.
What bliss so good a sigh . . .
A hand outstretched, he's there
to share with me all this.
I feel afraid and reach once more for him.
I turn I see his face so dear, he smiles
and then I know that all is well,
and we shall share another day,
with kin we hold so dear.
Who show concern, as time draws nigh,
and lend a hand with love and care.
So blessed are we,
our life, so rich, so filled with love.
We've shared this life, my man and I,
our toil and hardship, made us one.
Our life was hard in years gone by.
but we surged on and closeness grew
with love so strong that nothing
now we cannot face.
I love my man and he loves me.
We see the day when work is done
and we shall know when time has come
to say goodbye.
But do not cry for us,
because we shall begin a wonderful
new life, that's blessed with peace,
and all the time we need
to share our love forever.

Joan Hosker

True Love Is A Wondrous Thing

True love is a wondrous thing
For some it means a wedding ring
Love is showing that you care
Love is always being there.

Love is long-suffering and is kind
It doesn't seek to look behind
It isn't jealous, does not boast
It takes the least and gives the most.

It never thinks to see the bad
Believes all things, both good and glad
It is forbearing, full of hope
While in all things it strives to cope.

Love never fails when based on trust
To say 'I love you' is a must
Love is saying, 'I was wrong'
The sweetest end to any song.

The song of love is very sweet
Making true happiness complete
Better eat herbs where love is present
Than hate - with roasted ox and pheasant.

You are so blessed if you know love
It's like the very stars above
It shines on to infinity
A jewel of divinity.

And in the words of a much loved song
'Love lifts you up where you belong'
Uplifting to hear someone sing.
'Love is a many splendoured thing'.

Love and longing play a part
In comforting the human heart
No one can take that joy away
It just grows stronger day by day.

Love is the food of poets and sages
Handed down throughout the ages
Romeo and Juliet, Abelard and Eloise
And other lovers such as these.

Love is like the April rose
In early springtime, then it grows
A golden crown fit for a king
Yes, true love is a wondrous thing!

Moira Wiggins

Another Time, Another Place

Dirty tramp!
Cold and damp,
Huddled up on the old steps of the pub,
Begging money to buy some grub
. . . and other stuff
Don't you *ever* have enough?
'Keep away!' they say.
Don't look my way,
Go and beg some other street,
You're not the kind we want to meet!
Drunken bum,
Smackhead scum,
Dirty hands, greasy hair,
Clothes worn and threadbare.
Jacket full of paint drips
From when you woke up in one of the skips.
This is what they see, week after week,
They don't see the tear falling down your cheek.
They don't see inside to a broken heart,
To a life rejected and ripped apart.
I turn to leave you there in the rain,
But it's too late now, I will never be the same.
Staring into the saddest eyes I've ever seen,
My soul is torn by what might have been;
I hurry home, haunted by the beauty of a half-starved face:
Another age, another time, another place.
A different plane, a different life,
And you could have been,
(would you have been?)
Should have been
The love of my life.

Beryl Messham

Lost Love

I wish I can bring my days back
I wish I can bring my youth back
My childhood was glorious
My youth turned radiant
From bud I grew into flower
I blossomed in my childhood
I matured in my maidenhood
I built new acquaintances
Youth gave me stigma
I got married at nineteen
To a handsome fellow, a cricketeer
Who met me all of a sudden
Love at first sight - that's true
We had four smart children
And that was our love - true
My own flesh and blood
We raised family so lovingly
We lived our lives wholeheartedly
My hubby cared for me
I had a world beyond my eyes to see
But, I lost my love unexpectedly
I became strong, but suffered silently
I fought with courage with my fate
And stood on my own feet in a bad state
I uplifted my spirit, my heart did bleed
For my beloved, whom I so much missed
I wrote and wrote in my loneliness
And sealed my wounds in darkness
That drained my 'Silent Tears'
I wrote sad poetry in my 'Silent Tears'
That bravely told about my silent years
I progressed, learned and dedicated
Whole book to my loving husband
That was my lifetime's achievement
That was my breakthrough, in my lifetime
My husband has become a fragrance
And I have scattered petals of roses
All over the world to make scent

And sweet aroma is surrounded
All over and across skies and seas
A great man's deed, shining through
Meaning in death also he shone.

Madhu Chapaneri

How Can I Repay You Darling?

How can I repay you darling?
For the love you gave and still give to me?
You are my heart and soul
When we first met, I was troubled and strifed
You helped me, you supported me
And you paved my way
Cured my broken heart, you took me back
In the right direction
I can never repay to you what
You my darling, what you've given to me
This takes a special person
To give a greater love
Who cures and eases a broken heart
I thought was unrepairable but my sweet
You proved me wrong
It would take forever I thought
You're worth to me more than all
The money and gold in the world
When we first met twenty-two years ago
It only seems like yesterday
I also love your sweet nose
Your beautiful green eyes
Also your beautiful sweet pose
To me you're my rose
In a beautiful garden standing out
More than all the rest
You shine more than any star
The best thing that's ever happened to me
I deeply love you, darling
You're my everything, so precious to me
You're my rock forever.

William Deaves

You Know

You know my
Inner Secrets
You know my
Very Soul
You know because
You've been there
You know because
You care!

I know I'm not
Important
I know I'm not to
Blame
I know because we've
Been there
I know because you
Came!

Do you know I want you
Madly?
Do you know I just
Despair?
Do you know because
'You'
Want me badly?
Do you know because you
Care?

I know not what you're
Thinking!
I know not what we
Share!
I know not how to put it
And should
'I really
Care?'

I wish it could be
Different
I wish it was the
Same
I wish I knew the
Outcome
I know we feel the
Pain!

Airam Llewdroc

Beginning And End

I saw my love one sunny afternoon
He looked at me and I swooned
I saw my love one afternoon
He smiled, I smiled and love did bloom.

I met my love one rainy day
I remember, I thought I heard him say
Be mine, little girl
And together we'll share
Countless, endless, perfect rainy days.

I laughed with my love one cold winter's day
Laughed because we didn't know what to say
I laughed at him, he laughed at me
And the cold winter's day was laughed
Along its way.

I cried for my love one dark starry night
Cried because he had this to say
I've loved you, now I must leave you
And be on my way
I know this is a cruel thing to say
You've given me joy and a beautiful baby boy
But all good things have both beginning and end.

I cried for my love one dark gloomy night
Cried for the light of the stars
Which were no longer bright,
I cried a tear or three
But guess what?
Those tears, they were really just for me!

Marilyn Jones

I Found My Love In Autumn

How long before we meet again my dearest love and true
For yesterday's a journey long
When my heart belongs to you
(Kyrie eleison . . .)

I had lived as far as autumn
When you softly touched my hand
But winter's drawing on my love
And to part how could I stand?
(Christe eleison . . .)

Allow me in your winter's chill
Part of your young life's love
And I will pledge to you my heart
Fixed as the stars above
(Kyrie eleison . . .)

Oh! How I searched in hill and vale
From the mountains to the sea
Yet you came too late my dearest love
To belong complete to me
(Agnus Dei . . .)

I found my love in autumn
So content within my arms
How much will I regret my love
When you find young lover's charms
(Qui tollis peccata mundi . . .)

I shall try to let you go my love
With the promises I made
For I know that deep within myself
With guilt the debt's been paid
(Miserere nobis . . .)

I pray that some of my deep love
Will remain within your heart
And I promise to be brave my dear
When you say we have to part
(Miserere nobis . . .)

Oh! why so late my dear one
Why all the wasted years
When in the end I shall be left
With sadness and with tears.
(Dona nobis pacem . . .)

Anthony Cook

The Spade

I saw him cry twice
My father, cry
It was in their home on the coast,
I'd helped them move from London
To spend their evening days in peace.

His arthritis hurt, I knew, but at thirty-odd
I could not really know how it is when the muscles
Shout, 'No more!'

The first time I saw his tears
Was when my sister's husband, a former rugby blue,
Knocked on our door in London,
In forty-five, or six, back from three years
In a Japanese prison camp in Burma.

In his new khaki drill, he stood there
At our door, thinner than you can believe a man can be
And almost blind.
That was the first time I saw my father cry.

Now, ten years or so later, my father stood, bent,
In his unkempt garden, which his body would not
Let him tend, and offered me his spade,
For he would not be able to use it again
Unthinking, I refused, saying he might need it
He cried and my mother, my wonderful loving mother

Took me aside and told me that his health was bad,
But more, that Dad could not give me an inheritance
Of goods or much at all, for they were poorly off,
But what he could give, he wanted me to have
And needed me to take.

I went back, said that yes, on second thoughts, the
Spade would be useful, and somehow, being English,
I could only, belatedly, act, not speak.
I wish I had told him that I loved him.
I wish I had told my mother that I loved her.

If you have children and you're English,
Read their love in what they do
If you're parents, and they're English,
Offer you a spade
Take it.
It is their love.

Geoffrey Speechly

My Faraway Love

As I sat on a rock looking out to the sea
I was thinking of you - I was thinking of me
Of those halcyon days when we walked hand in hand,
Splashing the waves, digging toes in the sand;
When every soft breeze seemed to whisper your name -
Blowing kisses to heaven for the day that you came.

As I sat on a rock looking out to the sea
I was thinking of you - I was thinking of me
Just a girl and a boy -
An explosion of joy
Who had conjured such magic, who had cast such a spell?
Who had flooded our hearts more than mere words can tell?
Our spirits took flight like birds on the wing,
Our lips uncontrolled in the songs they could sing.
It seemed that all heaven and earth were a part
Of the symphony played on the strings of my heart.

I sat on a rock gazing out to the sea
I was thinking of you - I was thinking of me.
Across the horizon, now far out of sight,
Your destiny carried you into the night.
When you'd looked in my eyes, there were laughter and tears;
When I'd looked into yours, I saw unspoken fears.
But a man must take courage - be ready to fight,
To stand up for justice, for freedom, for right.
Who among us can say what the future will be?
Life has its own ebb and flow, just as the sea.

I sat on a rock looking out to the sea
Still thinking of you and still thinking of me.
The daylight is fading, the world has grown still
The shadows creep silently in at their will.
Another day ending - a still, aching heart;
How long - oh, how long - must we yet be apart?
I look up to heaven, to the moon's gentle light
The moonbeams bring comfort - the guardians of night.

Is that a smile that I see on your face?
A promise, perhaps, of some future embrace?
Once more I blow kisses to heaven above
On the wings of the wind, to my faraway love.
I look up to heaven - each breath is a prayer
That you'll be kept always, in God's loving care.

Valerie Smith

the sea

to stand
'neath a grey sky
upon the bones of eden that thrust
from the crashing waves

and feel
in blood dulled
by unseeing crowds and dotted lines
a rush of momentum

to awaken
open your ears
beyond the ticking of the clock
and hear yourself dying

and scream
as one voiceless given
one instant, one breath, one word to utter
in an eternity of silence

to cast aside
numbers and equations
and the inconsequence of meaning
as salt to the wind

and remember

the moment
she looked into your eyes
opened a window and let in the light
of a thousand suns

to find again
the joy you traded
for self and an office and a cheap suit
dreams that didn't fit

and hold once more
the hand that was yours

feel the beating of
the heart that was yours

to be with the soul
that completed yours

and in doing so

to live.

George Zhou

Everlasting Love

Whilst doing the ironing the other day,
I heard a voice in the kitchen say,
'How will I know when I'm in love, Gran?'

'Well . . . you'll tingle all over and
Your heart will be a-flutter,
Your legs will be like jelly
And you'll melt like butter.'

'Yes, but how will I know if it's real, Gran?'

'Well . . . your dreams will be filled
With the wonder of his face
And you'll quiver and shiver
And quicken up your pace.'

'Yes, but how will I know if it's true, Gran?'

'Ah, well that's a hard one to answer,
Only you will know that.
I remember with your grandad
It was the way he wore his hat.
Believe me darling, you will know
When he stands there beside you
And whispers low, 'I love you'.'

I returned to the ironing with a heart full of joy
In the knowledge that I had married a wonderful boy
We worked together through our ups and downs
Reared two lovely children in a house with grounds.

In our thirtieth year we took our vows once more
With our grandchildren following through the church door
All the same feelings ran through my brain
As I stood at the altar and repeated again

Love and cherish, yes I always will
I looked at my hubby and my eyes began to fill
I have been so lucky to have this lovely life
After a golden wedding still as man and wife.

Going for sixty in four years' time
In my ears the bells will chime
And I know exactly what I will do
Look at him and say

'I have always loved you.'

Alma Brace

How To Kill Me . . .

Take all that I have achieved and belittle it
Make it small,
So you feel tall,
Be sure to stamp all over it.

Take all that I have, question it
All that I am proud of, taint it
Split hairs
Destroy it.

Let your jealousy entwine my child and pet
Compete with me, get some of your own
Lead me to believe, that we can achieve
When it gets tough, leave me to go it alone.

Let novelty wear off, eternal to fad
When I speak, drown me out with, 'When I was a lad'
Let your inconsideration deflate me,
At every opportunity,
Make me feel like a 'victim' be 'had'.

When I'm loving and giving, embracing and willing,
Point out that, in fact, it's my duty
Take what I love as most precious in my life,
Insult it with behaviour most derogatory.

Keep your temper bubbling, surface hot,
Sell it to me like you're doing me a favour
Shout and bawl when you want it all
Hate me when I cannot deliver.

Tell me what's here isn't good enough
Treat me like a nobody, a zero
If that's what it takes, to help you feel tough,
Then good for you, oh, what a hero.

When I plead with you, 'Stop this'
And I'm gluing pieces with 'any means',

Be sure to take it
And smash it to smithereens.

And don't forget, that to finish the job,
As I walk my favourite shore,
Extract this broken heart of mine
And smash it on the floor!

Joanne Hutchinson

For That Special Someone

I write this for you
You are my love
You are my life.

You give me love
You give me hope
You give me purpose.

I think about you
When I look at a red rose
And when I look at the stars.

I wake up every day
Thinking about your lovely smile
Wanting to feel your gentle skin.

You are my everything
You make my heart beat
Beat to the rhythm of love.

Your breath refreshes my skin
Your sight makes me go into a trance
Your perfume delights my nose.

You bring light to the darkness
You are a glimpse of summer when it is winter
Your shining smile outshines a shining star.

When I feel down
I think of you
And I get up again.

You give me strength
When I am weak
That is the power that you possess.

The embodiment of true love
That is what you are
To my heart and to my soul.

I thought about you yesterday
I am thinking about you now
I will think about you tomorrow.

I love you
I love you now
And I will love you forever.

Tawfeeq Elahi Samad

Flowers In The Rain

Death of a loved one is traumatic
You are never prepared for this
But, when that precious one is a child
The agonising pain is trebled
And all they can tell you,
'It's not your fault.'

Anger invades your frozen mind
Numbness grips like a vice
Clutching body and heart and soul
Hiding the precious love within
Yet again, they say
'It's not your fault.'

The gaping hole of emptiness
Festers and bleeds soft tears
No others, but you can hear
In the place where love lives forever
Quietly telling you,
'It's not your fault.'

When, slowly the pain gets less
And hot anger subsides
Feeling returns to your mind
As love opens its petals again
And something softly tells you,
'It's not your fault.'

Time heals the outward signs
Secret pain stays locked within
Precious memories lie hidden
In the special place designed
Telling your heart,
'It's not your fault.'

You make offerings of love
In the marked place of choice
Going there time after time
Where the sun lights up a name
Where love still grows and grows
In the special place where, mixed with tears
You planted flowers in the rain,
'Until finally, you know it wasn't your fault.'

Sue Round

My Darling Jane

My darling Jane, come back to me
Your love has fallen like the autumn leaves
Where you have gone, I do not know
So give me a call and relight my heart's fading glow
I cannot believe you have run away
So please come back, if only for a day.
The mistakes we made, we should forgive
So give me a call from wherever you live.
Tell me your worries, tell me your woes
I've tried my best, God only knows
What went wrong? I do not know
Perhaps in time you'll let me know.

I am not perfect, you know it's true
But my love is strong and all for you
Not knowing where you are is driving me insane
So I'll search this land for evermore
Until I find you, my darling Jane
My love for you is like an endless dream
So please don't make me cry or scream
Our baby's crying in his cot
And you know we love you such a lot
Don't leave him growing up throughout the years
Without having your love or seeing your tears
You are in our hearts, you are on my mind
You are so beautiful and so kind
This child of ours needs your love
His eyes are so blue like the sky up above
A father's love is not enough
To bring a child up is really tough
A mother's kindness and caring love
Is what's sent from Heaven above
Just a phone call is all I need
Before I give our baby his feed
So come back to us, we will welcome you
With open arms and love that's true

The phone is ringing once again, 'Hello? Hello?'
'It's me, Jane.'
'Oh Jane, are you coming home?'
'Yes, oh yes, you know I would never leave you both alone!'

David John Hewett

Gone

Here I am again, opening the door of your room!
Sunlight and shadows, the light's playing tricks!
Yesterday's here, you're here!
My heart is full as I step inside.

Happy again, here in your room
I can see you, sitting cross-legged on the bed
I ask you if you're OK, and you throw me a quizzical look
With that half-smile, 'Yes Mum,' with an exaggerated sigh! 'Why not?'
'Just making sure, that's all,' I say.

The ghost of yesterday vanishes and I'm standing in an empty room
If I open the drawers, your belongings seem to mock me!
All that's left of you inside the cupboards
Are plastic reminders, coated in dust
Your smell is getting fainter!

You were a beautiful child, your silver-blonde hair
Shone like pale sunlight,
Always a look, living in a world of colours and patterns
Looks and talent, behind a silent reproof
Eyes of pale aquamarine-blue, you lived in your own world.

I saw your confusion, but also your light
I've often wished I could have shared a moment or two
Of your perception of things
Perhaps one day we'll find a meeting place of communication.

I'd like to reassure you of who you are
Your difference and special uniqueness are a gift.

I'm so proud to have given you life
Time passes and we both grow older, and wiser!
Years ago my heart was so full when I held you
Your beautiful face smiling up at me filled me with joy
Was it only yesterday? I wish it were so!
I would love to put the clock back
Making it matter, always important, your world all!

My love I throw over you like a mantle
Sent on the wings of every bird that lands on your roof
Every day I see your face in my mind
Have courage, live without fear!
Alleric.

Margaret Pedley

Love Is . . .

Love is
Sharing
Caring
God shares His universe
For us to care
How dare we not do so?
Deforestation?
Ruination!
Trees pin earth to itself
Preserve
Conserve their, our worth.

Our love is a sham
Shame.
Fighting
Not uniting
Not protecting
As we should
Why the big fight?
Why not unite?
Terrorism
The latest name of the game.

Women show us how
To cherish
Channel energy
Constructively
Lovingly
And yes, there is pain
In this game, too.
Eased by the desire
To give generously.

All can thrive
Alive
If they choose
As they must

Before it's too late.
What a fate
Could befall us all
If we hate.

BAC

The Arrangement

His fingers caught in the tresses of her hair,
As he whirled her - high in the dance.
His dark, deep-set eyes held possessiveness
The intensity of her eyes flashed defiance.
He would not be denied;
She would not be promised.
As the music lifted, his arm
Tightened around her belted waist,
Slender - against the breadth of him.
The light from the all-consuming fire
Reflected lambent upon her wilful face,
But it did not diffuse the anger there.
Dust swirled in the charged air as the beat
Intensified its pace; the notes hypnotic
The deftness of their feet tracing a path
Of pre-determined destiny.
Palm to palm, the onlookers encircled the pair,
Knowledge and tradition uniting their eyes,
In the taming of the child.
The strings of the fiddle pulsated
In response to the travelling bow
Enrapturing, capturing the girl with its spell.
As the sweat emerged in silver beads,
Upon his brow, he pulled her in
To the aroma of his manly scent.
Intoxicating her senses, quickening the blood
That flowed through the chambers of her heart;
Infusing her cheeks with a blush of softness.
His rough hands - instinctual - felt the burning passion,
That mirrored his body's own needs and desires.
Detecting the change, he halted in his step
And met the full force of a woman's eyes.
Coquettish - she loosened the red cotton twill
He wore knotted about his neck - tantalisingly,
Feeling its coarseness - running through her,
Soft, velvety fingertips. She was his.
The music slowed - became still - as the evening's breath.
In one body, the onlookers retreated to their beds;
Consigning the embers to shift and settle within the dying fire.

Jan Hedger

Wake Of Tears

The ship, it sailed, out of the light,
A creak of rope, the sails, so white.
The wooden wheel, I'm by Your side,
Subconscious smile, an ocean wide.

Kissed Your lips, a course, We steered,
Waters calmed and weather cleared.
A voyage of love, discovery,
Treasure, adventure, destiny.

We sailed the sea of happiness,
Time's movement, was hard to guess.
Guided by the stars above,
Moments precious, shared our love.

Your smile, contained, within My stare,
Reflections, dancing on Your hair.
An island in horizon's door,
Our laughter, on the moonlit shore.

X marks the spot, I took Your hand,
Wrote our names upon the sand.
Treasure maps, by firelight,
My lost treasure, held You tight.

The ship's bell rang, such clarity,
Alarmed, alone, reality.
An empty pillow, cold and still,
Discarded bottle and a pill.

It Navigates by Your love light,
That ship beckons to Me, each night.
Beside her wheel, please wait for Me,
Life's cruel grasp, won't set Me free.

My Wife, My love, My empty heart,
Bleeds each day that we're apart.
A cruel twist of fate and time,
Snatched Your loving hand, from Mine.

Just memories, of days gone by,
A million questions, each one, 'Why?'
Close My eyes, to see Your face,
A wake of tears, the ship, no trace.

Graham Hollingdale

Secret Love

You came into my life
When I was lost and all alone
Lifted up my heart and hopes
With smiles and love unknown

As one day passed and a new day came
Didn't dare to dream or think of your name
Just prayed that tomorrow, you'd be thinking of me
And that maybe someday we could be free

Free to live and love together as one
To spend time openly having fun
Showing the world exactly how we feel
Making our love forever real

Till then the thought of you will never be far away
If only I could find the words to say what I wanted to say
To tell you how I feel deep down inside
The glow of love and pride when you're by my side

You make me feel like a crazy kid
Something no one else ever did
My heart skipping a beat each time we're together
Longing for that moment when it will be forever

Till then I can't bear the thought of you being with another guy
Although I have no right to ask or question why
To ask you to break up an otherwise happy home
To be with me so I'm no longer alone

But until the day our lives truly come together
I'll cherish what we have right now forever and ever
Filling my days with loving thoughts of you
Feeling deeply about you as only I do

So until the next time that we can be together
The sun shining in our hearts no matter what the weather
Keep thinking of me as time passes slowly by
Knowing that I'm counting the days till you'll be mine

Mine to hold and love forever
No more sharing, just you and me together
Making my thoughts known to all who'll listen
Of the feelings I hold inside

Paul A Taylor

The Secret Garden

There are three large oak trees behind the garden wall.
Two ash trees have grown, not so tall.
A solitary apple tree bearing rosy red fruit.
This was once a sapling I treaded in with my boot.

At the far garden wall a trellis tells a story.
Rambling Clematis and sweet Jasmine in all of their glory;
Entwining the fence a maroon passion flower,
A statue and a fountain complete with water power.

Between the walls the lush grass grows.
Feeling soft, looking green between my toes.
Geraniums in pots, coloured orange and pink,
Yellow Hollyhocks and Delphiniums the colour of ink.

Their different perfumes pervade the air.
As for myself I stand and stare.
I think of the past times I shared with another.
My sweetheart long dead, I yearn for my lover.

He planted two roses for me years ago.
The blooms red and peach in abundance do grow.
The memories flow back, I start to cry.
The war took him from me. Why did he die?

A small stone seat stands under an arch.
Honeysuckle adorns it and climbs up the larch.
The bees are humming, the butterflies flutter.
From branch to branch the birds fly and twitter.

Into a small pond the fountain trickles.
I step into the water my toes it tickles.
He and I used to paddle in days gone by,
The memories flood back, I start to cry.

There is a black and white cat stretched out in the sun.
No war in this garden, the war was won.
I see all the colours, all the perfumes I love,
I think of my sweetheart now up above.

I hope that he sees me through his spirit eyes.
I hope too that he is restful beyond the skies.
Our secret garden is precious, sweet memories we did share,
When my love and I for one another would share.

Ellen Spiring

Sir Godfrey's Tale Of Woe

Twas Day of Sighing at Potter Heigham, the very last day of May
The year was 1741 and this is the tale I say
It was sad and bad and also mad, that things turned out that way
For many a tear was wept for the maid, upon her wedding day.

Sir Godfrey Haslitt lived in Bastwick, a fine uprighteous man
He wooed his love from morn till night and paved away his plan
To wed his maiden fine and fair, 'I'll love her all I can.'
Were words he said to everyone, the day she wed her man.
His love, dear Evelyn, Lady Carew, was a picture to behold
She loved her man, but feared her love was not as strong or bold
She told her mother of her tale, a witch they sought, who sold
To her a potion, in return, she had to sell her soul.

Twas Day of Sighing at Potter Heigham, the very last day of May
The year was 1741 and this is the tale I say
It was sad and bad and also mad, that things turned out that way
For many a tear was wept for the maid, upon her wedding day.

The wedding morn was fine and fair, the blossom soft and light
The church bells rang their song of joy, at such a happy sight
Arm in arm, they left the church, her dress of flowing white
He held her close and kissed her cheek, their longing for the night.

Twas Day of Sighing at Potter Heigham, the very last day of May
The year was 1741 and this is the tale I say
It was sad and bad and also mad, that things turned out that way
For many a tear was wept for the maid, upon her wedding day.

Satan came to claim the bride, her soul he came to take
A skeleton drove the coach that night and blood left in its wake
She kicked and screamed, to no avail, she had to pay the stake
Her husband slept through Satan's spell, he'd put in the wedding cake
Surrounded by a mysterious light, the coach was driven at pace
It carried on until Thurne Bridge, where it would end its race
A thousand flaming pieces fell around her tear-stained face
The current pulling her deep below, she's gone without a trace.

Twas Day of Sighing at Potter Heigham, the very last day of May
The year was 1741 and this is the tale I say
It was sad and bad and also mad, that things turned out that way
For many a tear was wept for the maid, upon her wedding day.

Deborah Wells

Young Love

As a whisper on the wind,
As a shaft of summer sunlight, through the trees
As the white foam upon a pebble shore tingles,
When you first walk barefoot on the beach,

Young love.

Just a glance,
Perhaps a smile
Is that smile only for you?
Only for you amongst the crowd
It's really true; your heart does miss a beat,

Young love.

'Shall we take a walk together?'
The sky is blue, the grass is greener
The whole universe is yours
This is made to last forever

Young love.

It is the nearest thing to Heaven
Laughing, dancing, in the circle of his arms
His hand around your waist,
His lips caress your hair,
Together, evermore,

Young love.

Perchance there falls a shadow
Thoughtless words to cause a tear
That same heart is surely broken
In this world so grey and lonely
How can life go on?

Young love.

Another day is dawning
Dry your eyes and face the world
Who is this you see arriving
Bringing roses, ribboned roses, deep red roses
Sweet sorrow in his eyes,

Young love.

June Holmes

Beneath The Shady Trees

We can stroll, hand in hand, gladly together,
With never a thought for inclement weather.
Rejoicing in the splendour of a summer's day -
Though we may never do much else along the way,
We will enjoy these hallowed moments of ease,
Beneath the shady, shady trees.

Ambling idly, below sheltered arbours of green,
Resting here and there - on a gatepost to lean,
Admiring the beauty we see, the splendour around.
Drinking in wonders - the Master's hand to abound,
Accompanied in the heat of day by a gentle breeze.
Every individual leaf would tease!

Here and there a struggle on rutted, muddy ground,
May detract but little from the beauty all around,
Yet we sense arched greenery - towering up above,
Enfolding us in closed leafy embrace in arbours of love,
And still take in the splendour, the sheltering trees -
Wandering together, over the leas.

Setting forth, hand in hand, into shaded glades,
Where verdant wildflowers jostle grassy blades -
And bursts of sunshine can startle and confuse,
But lead our gaze thro' the trees, to wondrous views,
Birds calling - and flitting wheresoe'er they please,
Around and about the shady trees.

And could we ever know what tomorrow may bring?
Today we are content and to these moments cling
To the heady delights of an English woodland scene,
Where restful souls can wallow, blissfully serene,
Taking in the beauty, the freshness, buzzing of the bees,
Amongst the trees - two hearts appease.

We may never, in our lives, pass this way again
And so will drown in restfulness - long to remain
In our minds; longing to roam these woodlands dear,
Forever empowered by their majesty - and a message clear,
Simply taking a day at a time, one moment only to seize -
As we stroll 'neath shady, shady trees.

Julia Eva Yeardye

I Must Be Unlovable I Do Believe

There is love everywhere.

Everyone I meet, see or greet
Is in love with someone.
There are people in the street holding hands.
Kissing, cuddling each other.
Why isn't it happening to me?

I must be unlovable I do believe.
I turn on the TV, there it is again.
Romantic films, adverts, in programmes.
Driving me insane.
Why isn't it happening to me?

I must be unlovable I do believe.
I go in to the newsagents, what do I see?
It is on the front cover of every magazine.
Why isn't it happening to me?
I must be unlovable I do believe.
I walk past a book shop, what do I see?
Bloody romantic novels are staring back at me.
Why isn't it happening to me?
I must be unlovable I do believe.

I look outside from my bedroom window.
There it is again.
Birds, bees, butterflies, all nature is at it.
Everything is at it, except for me.
Why isn't it happening to me?
I must be unlovable I do believe.

I turn on the radio to escape it all.
What do I hear?

Love songs, love songs, love songs.
I can't take anymore.
I must be unlovable I do believe.

My eyes are filling with tears.
My heart and soul are now truly broken.
Why isn't it happening to me?
I must be unlovable I do believe.

Jenifer Ellen Austin

Moment

The moment she smiled, the instant she shone,
Out from the world, and all that it's done,
The promise of hope, the time of new,
My mind, it reaches out for one like you,
No reason, no why and a chance to say goodbye.

The eyes they glint, like they always do,
Drawing me in another time, taking my breath,
The sky, clouded with doubt, grabs at me with glee,
Grimacing at the fact I would want to be free,
To make a choice and take a chance of change.

And yet you stay, still, not a world away,
Apart from them, different to the rest,
You're you, no change, and no one else,
The one of which life has purposely alluded,
The one of which life cannot discard.

The moment she smiled, the instant I saw,
In a world as wide and full as I've seen,
You are nothing special, just normal, just you,
But, against all those who crave individuality,
You are unique, shining in a glow that could light up the sky.

Though I hesitate, fearing the perspective bait,
To draw me down once more into the well of your eyes,
Seeing through all the past and phony lies,
But I can, I must, if the chance be true,
For I may not regret, my place beside you.

Deeper down I must reside,
In a place in which my heart astride,
Where the dwelling of glee is undisturbed,
For I, to remain unperturbed,
And I can show who I ought to be.

For the moment she smiled, the instant it was,
That second of blinding light,
I saw all my troubles fall away, without creed or plight,
I smiled back at those wondrous shining eyes,
And was happy to know that moment was mine.

Nicholas James Haslam

Eternal Soulmate

Your death fails to prevent me from loving you,
It's just caused an uncertain delay,
And the daily pain I am enduring
Refuses to just go away,
For your absence has left me
So lonely and sad,
Now I can only reflect
On the good times we had.
I fail to prevent myself crying
And with each heartbroken tear,
I find myself constantly wishing
That a miracle would bring you back here,
For you were my soulmate,
My lover and friend,
And I'll only find peace
When my time comes to an end.
Each hour is continuous torment
And I dread to wake up each day,
My heart also died with you, baby,
When you were so suddenly taken away.
You still dominate my daily thoughts,
My body, and my soul,
And your departure has left me, my darling,
With a persistently empty dark hole.
I so long for your kiss,
Your embrace or your touch,
For I am nothing without you
And I need you so much.
I just pray that wherever you are now,
That you are completely pain-free,
And I hope that the star
I see twinkling at night
Is you looking down upon me.
There are demons that live in my head now,
Who tease me and won't leave me alone,
And I am left feeling so desperately guilty,
I'm so sorry that you died on your own.

Carole Bates

The Next Step

(Dedicated to James Prosser)

You can dream a dream that is up in your head
Safe in your heart is where that dream's kept
But when is it right to take the next step
When you're afraid of misery or maybe regret.

You think of your life and how it could be
But you're scared and unsure, there is some uncertainty.

You're happy together, so very true
Even through laughter or times that are blue
Your love's so strong, you always get through.

But what happens if you take that next step?
All the dreams that are in your head
You find out that it's all been misled.

The answer is, you will never know
Until the time is right for you to give it a go.

It could be perfect, total bliss
Better than that first touch, or that first kiss
Which you know by now, you're glad you didn't miss.

But how do you know when that time is right?
Even though your loved one is such a delight.

Your love's so strong and deserves the fight
Of compromise and getting things right.

So when you feel in your heart, so very sure
I will hold out my hand and open the door.

Then we will know if our future together we can explore
As we realise our love is so very pure
And we can pursue it every step, even more.

As mother and father and husband and wife
Together forever and doing it right

Loving each other both day and all night
Like the dream, we locked up real tight
For our head and heart to keep
Until the day we make it complete.

Michelle Barnes

Sleeping Alone

If the need is strong enough,
It can create the reality.

At the borders of waking and sleep,
time becomes mutable -
solid, yet flexible.

Waking thoughts create a framework
which dreams can build on.
Shreds of misty fabric
form clumps of matter,
cemented with the glue of time.

In this dreaming web,
something moves,
shifting like the tide.
A glowing light
streaming out to reach you.

As the mist fades,
she steps from it
and smiles.
The perfect lover -
a soulmate.

You wake with a start.
The sound of breathing -
but not your own -
chills your spine.
Rolling slowly over,
you gasp,
stunned, overawed.

Her eyes glowing
like golden suns,
the one from your dreams -
the perfect lover -
lies beside you.
Gently, so softly,
she touches your face.

Gordon Jackson

Salvus Is Safe

I was told that he was dying
Thought so too and took him in
His ears so torn and raggedy
And oh, so very thin.
Found I was stroking a bag o' bones
No flesh on him to find
I loved him er' I saw him
His state I could not mind.
He had intestinal infestations
'Tis why he can't gain weight
So I set myself to deal with them
Cos he'd become my little mate.
Then gave him some affection
Kissed him on his crown
Don't think he'd ever been kissed before
For he ran me quite around
He crept quietly up onto my bed
Relaxed, I watched him sprawl
Had hardly left any room for me
But I didn't mind at all.
Took no notice of what was said to me
'Twas not his time to go
He'll live in my love a long, long time
For time for the two of us will slow
We'll both learn about affection
When it's right and when it's wrong
We'll share our limitations
Whilst our love shall grow so strong.
As I sit and just caress him
Look deep into his fear-filled eyes
'Tis a look I used to wear myself
And know where the heartache lies.
So shall I keep him warm and fed
All his fears I shall allay
The time will come when he will be free
When all his fears shall fade away

Rosie Hues

Thoughts On Love

Love - has many faces or forms
It's the strongest emotion we share
Growing, spreading, throughout life
Freely given, to show that we care.
Love, for family, stems from birth
A bond, stronger than steel.
Love we share, among our friends
As we learn to express how we feel.
Everyone hopes for a soulmate
A love to last all through life
Someone to give our heart to
Unite with - as husband and wife.
We also have love for animals
There is - forbidden love, hidden from view
Unrequited or rejected love
Love - that is stolen from you!
Love is a complex emotion
All powerful or fragile as - threads
Love can hold you safely, against all odds
Or tear your life into shreds!
Love can be gentle or it can be cruel
Ever giving, or too demanding.
It can be a reason for living
Tender or far too commanding!
My first love, gave his life in war
His memory lives on in my heart
I married a love that lasted
Fifty years from its start.
Now alone, to my offspring, I give my love
The circle of life - ever turning
As a child I gave love to my family
Now - my own family receive all my yearning!
Love is unconditional, irrational, sincere
All-consuming, given free from my heart
Unwavering in adversity, though easily hurt
Love is God's gift, that sets mankind apart!

E M Eagle

The 'Duel' In The Crown

Our eyes first met across the room
I felt a passion I could not hide
His eyes sparkled like two diamonds
Lightening up my sky.

With all my heart I did but love
Thanking God in Heaven above
With all my soul I loved thee
But ignored the storm approaching.

We vowed before God at the altar
To love until our lives were through
We smiled, we kissed, oh yes,
If only I had known what you had planned to do.

Always laughing, having a joke
Certainly always with other folks
He was an expert at playing Jack the Lad
They never guessed he was the real cad.

If only I had known what lay in store
When he came home and locked that door
Unknowingly, I had sealed my fate
This was an animal and I was the bait.

Every attack I thought it my last
Believing this brute would finish his task
But I never said, and nobody asked
I endured it all, to the very last.

So before you stand at the altar
And to another promise your all
Make sure you know the inside of his head
It's far too late when they find you dead.

Love is a double-sided coin
Don't succumb when it all goes wrong
Play it safe, don't hang on
There is only death and destruction
On the other side of love's coin.

Alma Mason

Goodbye Mum

(This poem is dedicated to Mrs Laura Chaplin (Mum) who died in January 2009 aged 90. Up to five years ago, she was herself contributing her own poems to Forward Press Ltd)

Mother in her 90th year
Soon not to be with us, I fear
A fall in her home recently
Brought breaks and infection we see
She is such a lovely dear gran
Loved by all her adoring clan.
Always there, in joy or pain
Telling us her stories once again
Of life so long, long ago
Of little money and hardship so
Of a simple, carefree life
When she became Dad's wife
Of love for her beloved
And of life's path discovered
Always a rock on which to lean
Always a cup of tea after a clean
Never too busy to listen
Always advice to glisten
And to brighten up the day
To help us all of our way
Always happy with her lot
Simple blessings, never forgot
Now at the end of her life
Amongst worldly worry and strife
She is at peace, here below
We don't want her to go
But soon to meet again above
With the ones she does love
To stand praising at Jesus' feet
Her heavenly Father to greet
Thank you for all you've done
And for being dearest Gran and Mum.

David Chaplin

Love Is

Love is mankind's greatest myst'ry
Unremitting throughout hist'ry

Love, the riddle of this life
Bringing peace, creating strife

Love is passion, love is calm
Love is fire, love is charm

Love is humour, 'times denying
Often pleasing, sometimes trying

Times so honest, times deceiving
Love is sadness at the leaving

Love is kindness, love is caring
Understanding when despairing

Love is sharing, love is trust
Even anger, when needs must

So enchanting in the youth
Age does not reveal the truth

Here a touch, there a glance
Oft' a meeting just by chance

Love appears in unknown guise
Teasing only certain eyes

Love respects not age at all
Some ne'er recognise the call

Love's a feeling from inside
Often manifest in pride

Or perhaps in sheer devotion
Love is part of our emotion

Life is formed from love's expression
Not by fighting or aggression

Love makes human life fulfilling
Where's the point in all the killing?

K V Clark

Young Love

We carved our initials, upon a tree
It was there for all, the world to see
Pierced by an arrow, through the heart
A love which would not, be torn apart.

No matter what, our parents said
The long road of love, lay straight ahead
We had a love, none could ignore
We had a love, like none seen before.

And how you filled me, with utter bliss
Whenever we shared, a tender kiss
I loved you, and you loved me
It was what was meant to be.

It was the classic tale, of girl next door
You were for me, of that I was sure
I was Adam, while you were Eve
It was for you, I lived to breathe.

It was decreed, by the stars above
That you would be, my one true love
You were everything, I'd ever need
When we were apart, my heart did bleed.

I know the world could see my pride
When you were standing by my side
We strolled upon, the golden sand
Eyes upon each other, while hand in hand.

Our idyllic love, would not be rocked
No matter how much, others mocked
We were two, joined as one
Our love shone, just like the sun.

Now I look back, upon fading years
And your cherubic face again appears
When carving initials upon that tree
We were both the tender age of three.

Brian W Ballard

Sweethearts

In the twilight of the evening
When the stars begin to shine
Tell me you love me
Tell me you are mine

In the dawning of the morning
When the sky is all aglow
Draw me closer to you
Tell me what I want to know

In the beauty of the springtime
When we walk the bluebell woods
Pause awhile and whisper
'Thank you for your love'

When the summer comes and holidays
Find us resting by the sea
Let us happily share the blessing
Of contented harmony

When the autumn portrays its colours
Reminding us how we too shall fade as a leaf
But the love in our hearts is precious
And will surely never, never cease

When winter fires are burning
And the nights are dark and long
Shall we cuddle close together
And sing a sweet love song

And through the blessedness of our union
Please Lord send us 'tiny feet'
And another little sweetheart
To make our lives complete

For you and I are sweethearts
God gave you to me
You are my dearest soulmate
And I will love you devotedly

Doreen Mary Reeves

Love For A Lifetime

I'm sitting alone by the fireside
Thinking of good times gone by,
Wondering why you had to leave me
Glad of memories which still make me cry.

That night we first met, how could I forget?
Saturday night when the cinema drew.
Was it sheer fate that I arrived late
And was shown a seat right next to you?

Sherlock Holmes was solving a crime
With disturbing scenes most of the time
'I'm so sorry,' I said, when I grabbed hold of your palm
'It's OK,' you replied, 'it will help you stay calm.'

I wondered why I'd not seen you before
And thinking I would like to see you some more
When next night, on a bridge watching the fish
You were suddenly there and I got my wish.

We began dating, taking a chance
This was the start of a lasting romance.
Tender love and happiness grew
Talking any troubles away with a kiss or two.

When you asked me to marry you, 'I will,' my heart sang,
I was on cloud nine when the church bells rang.
This magical day, we'd become man and wife,
Vows made to each other, sealed 'our love for life'.

We had been wed almost thirty-four years
When you woke up not feeling too well,
You said at the time you had pain in your chest
And it was really giving you hell!

Later that day, you were whisked away
To a place that's far better, so they say.
So many memories you left with me
My heart still aches when I turn the key.

Lucy Mary Dean

Fincing Love

You were the boy up my road
I liked right from the start.
We became such good friends
Till the day we did part.

I was cnly 11 years old,
Unsure what was inside.
Feelings I didn't understand
And chose instead to hide.

I often thought about you
And how you made me feel.
Wondering if those feelings
Of love I felt were real.

Then 26 years later,
Dear Gary, I found you.
I was so very nervous
And saw that you were too.

You made my heart beat faster,
Those butterflies came too.
I recognised those feelings,
As a child I felt for you.

Leaning across, you kissed me.
Wow! I'd waited for so long.
Instead of now just beating,
My heart it sang a song.

Holding you in my arms
I felt complete and true.
No one else has made me feel
The way I do with you.

I'm so glad to have found you
To have this chance to say,
I love you more than ever,
With every passing day.

Teresa Brimble

Into A Dream

She had been likened to a summer rose
Fresh
And bloomed as fair
But more than that
Moved through his life
Free
Eyes shining in anticipation of
Adventures yet to come
And vibrated with an inner light
Her strength touching him deeply

It was a decade since
She slotted into his life
Hardly disturbing the surface
As though they had ever been
Smiling at each other

Within a week
Shoulder to shoulder
Between Martini and Guinness
There was earnest talk -
She remembers the subjects
He only the blending
And so it remained

Yet sometimes he took her for granted
The unkind word slipped from his lips -
He felt the pain and hurt the more
Later she slipped into a silent world
Which she would leave with reluctance

Then suddenly she was out of his life
Yet not out of his mind
And on warm skylark ringing days
As tall grass bends to the breeze
Her image moves around in his head
Like some fragmented dream.

Godfrey Dodds

The Love Of God

When God was young He had a dream
And thought up such a wondrous scheme
So sitting on His throne above
He set to work creating love
He started with a mother's love
That was the strongest of them all
A lifetime bond which nought could break
Though devils try and empires fall
He then gave love to all the young
That blossomed as sweet songs were sung
And carried on through wedded bliss
With tender and romantic kiss
To last forever through the life
Of every faithful man and wife.

Then came a very special love
For those whose faith in God above
Had stayed with them through many years
Despite the tragedy and tears
And when fond memories they recall
They'll find the greatest thing of all
Was sharing that deep love they had
That saw them through both good and bad
If all the folk in every land
Would only try to understand
It's love that makes the world go round
Then very soon it would be found
That love if shared among us all
would lift us up each time we fall
To bring us everlasting peace
And all the misery would cease
No more war and no more strife
Sweet peacefulness throughout the life
We each were given from above
To share in harmony and love.

Roy Hobbs

The Ways I Love Molly

(Poem about my wife who passed over 24th April 2003)

How many ways do I love thee Molly?
How many impressions enter my mind?
Each thought I have and lovingly see
For they are mine to find.
How great is love bringing two together
That gleam of inspiration in the eyes?
Caring and sharing, making us feel better
True love has a valuable prize.
So loving a special person
Her ways state her character
We are learning lesson by lesson
Our memories we remember.
I love thee Molly in your kindness
That is yours to show
That brought you such success
For these things I know.
I love your eyes, a dazzling blue
That shine as you talk each day
For this is undoubtedly you
In each word that you say.
I love your purity of heart
From the first day we met
In our togetherness, this played a vital part
Which I will never forget.
And when I'm wrong you state the truth
Thus seeing my errors that I have
For now I see the proof
In the words that you gave.
But I love you Molly being you're so true
A love that eternal throughout my life
Each moment these thoughts I review
Molly, my darling wife.

Leon Gould

08.08.08

Do people spend their whole lives trying to find what we have now?
I don't know, but I heard that some people search for their whole lives
And still they never find half of what we have now
And we take it for granted somehow

The big artery pump has got my emotions going up and down
Casting sentimental spells and creating momentary frowns
Sometimes they spill blood in quarrelsome red
But mostly they'll just frolic and float around in my head

This love isn't new but I still haven't discovered all of you and
I'm loving my voyager status, so curious of the unknown
Like an archaeologist to the bone
Like a bee set free and drawn back to the honeycomb
Being with you feels just like coming home

Two brains run together like trains on the tracks
I still find it amazing that after all these years
We never run out of anything to say
Our carriages contain different people, different names,
Different thoughts and different faiths
But we always meet at the same old place
To fill each other up with electricity
For the next lengthy day

Like a limb I'm afraid I'd fall down without you
I'd find myself shuffling along, dragging one heavy leg on the lawn
Paralysed by the notion of being incomplete
I would sooner or later lose the power of both feet
And spend my days feeling phased just awaiting the dawn

I over-analyse and prise like a tired irritation while we've survived gaps as wide as space congregations and although cracks are mentioned; they're not big enough to cause devastation. We're tattooed on each other like a heart indention, one love: one nation. Your body's my station - when I get there I know I'm home.

When I'm with you I know I'm home.

Abi Randall

My Own Obituary

I've been difficult to live with but I hope you can forgive
The uphill road I chose for us. I wanted us to live
In a pleasant part of England with roses round the door.
I didn't know we should have stayed where we had lived before!
I made us move so many times. I really couldn't rest.
I kept you living on your nerves, just wondering what was next!
You sometimes must have hated me but you'd never ever show it
And if I drove you half insane you never let me know it.

When we first met I was so proud, as I'd just bought a car.
I'd sometimes take you out in it but it never went that far.
It liked to break down often and sometimes on a hill it
Would fail to reach the summit cos I'd forgot to fill it!
I then asked you to marry me. The first time you said, 'No.'
I wasn't having that, young man, so I had another go,.
The second time you said you would. It all was very nice.
(I won't say here I had your neck in quite a painful vice!)

And then we had a daughter. She was such a lovely kid
But still I wasn't satisfied no matter what we did.
Our daughter was so beautiful but I never noticed how
The years sped by, she moved away and I'm so lonely now.
Still, I hope I've learned *some* lessons that life's laid out for me.
I've been lucky that you loved me since I was twenty-three.
I'm sixty now and thank my stars for such a gentle man
Who's walked beside me quietly. I am your greatest fan!

Nobody's ever perfect though some may like to think it.
My life was like Titanic's but you helped me not to sink it
And when I'm gone and turned to dust, as all cremations do,
I hope you won't forget me - or throw me down the loo.
My wish is that you'll think of me when sitting in the garden
And somewhere in your gentle heart you'll finally grant me pardon.
I like to hope you'll wander back when evening shadows fall
And in your heart you'll know we had the surest love of all.

Lesley Robinson

Forgiveness

Whatever your crime may be
and whatever the toll.
Whatever dark secrets
lay in your soul.
Just let me speak a while
for I have grown old.
But I see your beauty
shine like gold.

And though you were hungry
these goods they're all sold.
There's no fuel for the fire
And your hands are so cold.
You say you have nothing
and you say you don't care.
But I caught the sunlight
that fell from your hair.

When you walk through the streets at night
with your secrets all sold.
I've seen men from the gutters
blood run cold.
As you fade in the distance
I feel my despair.
It's falling in snowflakes
everywhere.

So whatever the weather
and whatever the goal.
Whatever triumphs and tribulations
lay in your soul.
Whatever you say to me
even if I'm a slave that's been sold.
Of course I will always see your beauty
shine like gold.

Andrew Eddy

Dragonshield

An ancient knight slowly rode his decrepit steed on rutted road,
And as he neared a wooded glen the sound of screams and shouts of men,
Reached this valiant warrior's ears yet in he charged despite his years,
And there he saw a piteous sight, a wounded warrior in unfair fight,
Who set upon by villainous horde now feebly struggled 't raise his sword,
And defend his lady who shrank behind, with flowing tears and terrified mind,
And entreaties to their foe to stay the wicked sword that each one lay,
Upon her love, who could not stop his chivalrous defence until he drop,
From loss of blood or fatal blow, the enemy thus needs't lay him low
To take the prize for which they fought; his lady fair these heathens sought,
The aged knight now intervened, unsheathed his sword and gently leaned,
Forward o'er his mount's broad head, and cried aloud, 'Why fight
The dead, I stand my ground and challenge all and know this day
You'll surely fall, to fiery breath and winged claw, reward for breaking knightly law.'
The attacking troop who'd spun around on hearing the warrior's defiant sound
Laughed aloud to see their foe, the leader then with unslung bow,
Unleashed a shaft with faithful aim, which hit the knight and caused such pain,
He raised his eyes up to the sky, and cried aloud, 'These men must die.'
More merriment followed this firm command but as the knight held high his hand.
The laughter ceased, for at his back, a monstrous sight all cloaked in black,
Froze their minds with dread and fear, for a scaled monster did appear,
It alighted on the grassy floor and hissed and snarled and begat a roar,
That dimmed the loudest thunderclap and as its wings did slowly flap,
The giant's claws dug in the ground and flames and smoke were cast around,
From gaping, fang-filled savage jaw, 'Behold, say I, 'tis Gorgongore.'
The red eyes dimmed and then a flash as scurvy knaves began their dash,
In vain escape of awesome beast but Gorgongore began its feast,
The entire band of twenty men and tethered mounts which numbered ten,
Were despatched in time of arrows flight for none could best this Titan's might,
Then rose the dragon above the ground, his mighty wings ne'er made a sound,
And thus he left the tranquil scene as though the clash had never been
But three there were that knew it had, and two at least were sorely glad,
For aged knight with wondrous shield, who'd saved a love that would not yield.

John Potter

Return My Sparkle

You see the smile
I feel its pain
And the accused stands there
Being guilty of everything but giving me the love I needed
Sentencing me to a life of imprisonment within my own jail ce l
As each day passes
I feel as if I was the guilty one
Giving you what I didn't want to
Letting you break down that barrier, behind which I stood
Little did I know
That you weren't the person that was going to save me from falling
But you were the car whose headlights flashed so brightly in my eyes
Leaving nothing but tears crashing into my soul
Stealing each breath of mine while I lay there
I suddenly became a statistic that day
She who loved, she who lost,
She who felt each part of her heart breaking
As though it was physically possible
The illusion of a happy ending, was all that it remained
An illusion.
This made so many like her live life in its utmost delusion
When you give your heart away once
The owner of the sparkle in your eyes then belongs to someone else
And when they leave, they take that sparkle with them
That is why you only need to look into the eyes of an individual
And you will be able to see just how much they have loved
And more importantly just how much they have lost in life
For that's why we all walk without seeing
Sometimes the truth you see in someone's eyes
Is more than you could have ever expected
So frighteningly honest and bare
And one day, when you're looking at your reflection
You may not even know whose eyes you're looking into.

Palvisha Iqbal

Lasting Love

To write a poem about our love,
Dear one,
Is easier said than done.
To thank you for all the lovely things
You did for me
Would take me to 3003 (at least).
We always put each other first, you see,
All our problems, we would sort out,
To our best ability,
Together.
Some problems would be very serious,
Perhaps ending in a saga,
Of which at the end, lots of laughter.
Big hugs all round, for just us two,
Maybe a kiss or two for upsetting
Each other so.
It's been a year since you've been gone,
Never known a year so long.
Lots of problems came anew,
You not there to help me through.
But you were there somewhere,
I know,
Loving me still, as only you know how.
I miss you so, and when in bed at night
Holding your pillow very tight,
I just want to be with you again,
But cannot be.
That terrible night, you were in such pain,
The ambulance came,
Leaving our world to just me.
Wishing you were here, just the same,
To love me again
And with no more pain.

Mabel Moore

Unconditional

Like that which is the wind,
Felt, breathed in and enjoyed,
Stronger than the first wish of the sun
For want of warmth.

Brighter lit than the moon of path
In a beam to a forest track . . .
More gentle to a ripple on a pond,
More sincere than the bed of warmth
Cradling sleep to his arms

I am the movement Mother Earth once
Told to a stranger long ago.
The picturesque view, the turning of grey
Winds to a summer breeze.

I am to your mother so dear, brothers
And sisters in each give equal to the amount,
Measured to the overflow of a cup for all.

I am of love, unequalled by the darkest depths,
By the very sum of the whole, I encompass all.
Hold one to the other and to the other I embrace
All that is you

I am unquestioned in purity for within me,
Bonds the love of God I am unconditional
Selfless in gain, but to grain make grow for
Of eating makes of life

I am of power so strong, can burn behind the thought,
To the embrace made fine another's life,
Can carry forward the weight in soul

They call of me, love this though is my son
For I am nameless unquestioned, unconditional
To the family, the strength, indeed I am within.

Alan Boyce

Stay With Me

Will you hold my hand, as we walk.
Let me listen, as you talk.
Let me see the love in your eyes, before we sleep.
To awaken with real memories, mine to keep.

Renee Lowe

You Are

You are the wind, misunderstood, powerful,
I need your touch,
I miss your scent,
Crave your kiss,
Lust for your voice,
Your love is serene, surreal and addictive,
You are the flame which lights my soul,
Skin pure as silk,
Hypnotic vision,
Your tender, alluring touch,
Your lips gently stroke my skin,
Our souls, mind and spirit unite,
You are the air, I need you to survive,
Explore new places of pleasure,
Caress my ears with your voice,
Seductive intelligence,
Fill my body with euphoria,
Soothe me, hold me and love me,
You are justice and I surrender,
You satisfy my appetite with your lips,
Your body, beautifully sculptured,
I crave you night and day,
Extraordinary passion,
I dream you, think you and breathe you,
You are a warrior, fierce stamina,
Uncontrollable, intoxicating seduction,
My vision, my speech, is you,
Your kisses push me into insanity,
Pleasurable, affectionate embrace,
My heart, body and mind ache with your love,
You are, we are, forever one.

Alicia Francois-George

Bloodroses

Covered in bloodroses - she wonders not supposes
Can all that be pretty see - into the mind that harbours me
Alone, aloft, beyond the sea - betrayed her sentimentality
Her song, it too transposes - all the lingering past posies
But draped beneath bloodroses - her love knows, not supposes.

Ade Horton

Enchanting Eyes

The deepest blue of the bluest skies
Is reflected in your enchanting eyes,
When I see them blink with surprise,
I know I've won your heart, my prize.
'Tis a folly to be wise,
To look into your enchanted eyes,
They reflect a thousand summers passing by,
Would I lie?
Not I,
And should your blue eyes
Ever cry,
Who made you cry
Deserves to die.
I wipe your eyes
And keep your tears
And put them in a box
With silver locks,
Down through the years,
And use them as my souvenirs,
And as it appears,
When you are feeling hearty,
Those soulful enchanted eyes
Steal every party,
When you walk in the room
And dispel the gloom,
All eyes turn on you,
With your pupils of turquoise-blue,
And when you're dancing,
And I'm romancing,
You come into view
With those enchanting eyes.

Alan Pow

Love Profound

So unexpected, after years
Of living in a single state,
A victim of a loneliness,
Not gaining any lasting joys;
That was the case, until, until,
In that brief interval abroad,
I met my future, on her own.

From our first meeting, feelings chimed:
Polite conversing ruled at once,
But soon gave way to whispered vows.
Emotions like exploding stars,
Expanded then, forever spread.

We seemed to share the same ideas,
A simultaneity of thoughts:
I can't pretend to understand,
I simply knew inside my heart,
That this was valid, safe and sure,
Which gave great comfort to my soul.

The catalyst was my beloved,
With nature soon dovetailing lives.
High waves of rapture swept me on,
To leave me washed upon love's shores.

The emptiness that formed my life,
Was quickly filled and put to rest,
And smothered boredom of past years,
Avoiding thus life's rabbit hole.

More real emotions, less desires,
More final truths, less fragile dreams,
Pure love, incomprehensible.

Raymond W Seaton

What Love Endures

Thoughts of a Love Divine -
Swept over her -
Such a love is this,
Taking her every waking, sleeping moment.

Intense feelings rushed through her body,
Unimaginable joy -
She was lost to him,
Could not even imagine,
A day without him.

Strong arms had protected her
From all harm -
By night he was the lover
Of her wildest dreams,
Taking her to heights
Only they knew possible.

His electrifying touch lit the flame
Of burning desire in her -
Their mystical union blessed from above -
She gave thanks
For this Love Divine.

Lost now -
As darkness clouded their once
Starlit pathway.
That one dreaded word
Struck him -
Silenced them both.

It is cold outside -
Darling
Cover me.

Nina Graham

Constancy

Was it by chance that I met him
Or was it intended to be?
A dance hall full of young people
Determined to have a good time
After years of austerity
In a wartime uncertain world.
Some became teenage sweethearts,
Got married to live together.
We two were among the latter;
We already knew we were soulmates.

We managed to rent our first home,
Saved to equip it bit by bit.
Our leisure pursuits were charge-free:
We conversed on many subjects
And viewed nature in woods and fields.
We planned and nurtured our garden.
A much used car was then purchased
To attend concerts, seek culture,
Take holidays in this country.
Later, we ventured overseas.

My husband's nature was placid,
Pleasant, kind and honourable.
I still feel his arms around me
And closeness we experienced
As I lie alone in my bed.
His sudden death almost killed me,
At first I wished that it had.
More than twenty years have elapsed.
Time and interests have eased my pain,
Yet no other man will suffice.

E Joan Knight

Ode To My Love - Grief

You were my first and only love
That I can truly say
I hope you watch me from above
I miss you more each day.

The only words that I can say
To show how much we cared
We always found along life's way
The love we always shared.

There was a bond so very strong
Right from the very start
For even when our lives went wrong
Never did we part.

For now you are no longer here
My memories - so very dear
Because of all you meant to me
Half of me just ceased to be.

I still recall those precious years
The laughter as our children played
All my hopes and all my fears
My memories will never fade.

But now, as then, I shall prevail
Although it's hard to bear
The loneliness and grief I feel
Now you are no longer here.

But now I have a new abode
I've left behind my cares and woe
I feel I'm in a better mode
Although I loved you so.

Janet Towells

Alone

Only when you are alone, are you truly happy,
When you are one with the wind, the sea,
And the trees, flowing with God's breeze,
Laughing high on the winds of love,
Looking at eternity from above,
Where every moment is silent and free.

Mario Servadei

Come Feel My Heart's Love

So soft and tender are these kisses,
Sweeter than ruby-red wine
Tender is my heart that beats to love
The very rhythm of the divine.

Take my heart, this heart of mine,
For it is open with mercy
A heart born of love and forgiveness
This heart that beats so carefree.

The moon still in the midnight of sky,
As love flows like a gentle stream
Flowing through loving hearts
Upon heavenly angelic wings.

May the night-time consume you,
Each and every star high above
Where the magic would truly begin
With hearts filled with love.

Draw near, draw near, serene love of mine,
Let me feel and embrace you
May I hold you with sweetest desires
For within beats a heart so true.

Close your eyes to the night,
Opening your loving heart for me
A sensual heart that burns with love
And a spirit too that runs so free!

So soft and tender are my kisses,
This love of mine burning forever
The celestial light fires within
As each our hearts beat together.

Simon Foderingham

Love Song

I will write a song and I will sing it to you
I will dream a dream and hope it comes true
I hold your heart in my hand and feel a bright glow
I will dance to slow music with you by my side
I'll return your heart now to you
Will you love me as I love you?

Ann Warner

Sacred Love

Into the life of everyone
There be a sacred love
For everyone whomsoever under the sun
Covering thy soul as a hand in a glove

We be all blessed with such love
A few folk may fail to realise
It is perfect love comes from above
Into our hearts for us to materialise

Sacred love be within thy heart
To inspire and pass to another
A love which will never depart
And can neither be smothered

Such love is wonderful to attain
Fills thy heart with inspiration
Will with thee always remain
Folk following with emotion

It is for us to seek and understand
The perfect love given to us freely
Giving strength as folk walk hand in hand
Everyone greeting each other friendly

It be pure love with feelings divine
For us to pass pleasantly to another
Uplifting folk to enjoy and admire
A sacred love shared together

Love be sacred when found
Comforts thee with feelings divine
Thou feel uplifted and bound
In a heavenly grace sublime

Josephine Foreman

Love Is Blind

Rosy cheeks, sparkling eyes
Thinks that she is worldly wise
Knows it all - and tells you so
You're old-fashioned - don't you know!
When asked if she's in love she says,
'I only know he's good - in bed!'

Jean Gibbs

Awaiting My First Romance

When I was a young man of twenty,
I felt my life was empty;
All because in my teens,
I did not meet the girl of my dreams.

Each day without love, is a day of sorrow,
Why wait until tomorrow?
Each day without love, is a day of sadness,
Why live anymore in this madness?

All that love and kissing,
Is what I am missing;
If I am too shy,
This chance in life will pass me by.

The thing that I yearn,
But still have a lot to learn;
Older people said to me, 'Young man,
One day you will understand.'

That feeling I want to chase,
To have someone to embrace;
I see other couples having a romance,
Why should not I take a chance?

If each night you say your prayers,
God will send you someone who cares;
It is not too fantastic,
To have the desire to be romantic.

There is a feeling for a turn of the tide,
For someone at my side;
Someone to love you is a feeling within,
At your first romance is when your life begins.

Robin Robinson

Searching For You

I searched the moon and the stars but I didn't find you
I searched the sun but you were not there
Even the depths of the sea but still I didn't find you
No place I did not search . . .
But when I searched my heart the answer was there
I found you

Deborah Ayis

What Is Love?

Love can be strong, like a mountain,
Powerful, mighty and high,
Something that can't be diminished,
Something that will never die.

Love can be long, like a river,
Travelling true to its course,
Something that goes on forever,
Never revealing its source.

Love can be bright, like the sunshine,
Shining so happy, all day,
High on a midsummer's morning,
Chasing the dark clouds away.

Love can be fragile and tender,
Like a snowflake that falls from above,
Virginal, pure, unaffected,
Warm, like a hand in a glove.

Love can soar high, like an eagle,
Free without worry or care,
Beautiful, strong and majestic,
High in the clear mountain air.

Love can be hard, like the winter,
Bitter, relentless and cold,
Freezing, like snow on a rooftop,
Something to have, not to hold.

Love can be all that I've mentioned,
All that you've wanted, and wished,
But above all, love is precious,
Something that should not be missed.

F W Cumbes

A Poem Of Love

We sat on the roof the whole night through,
By the light of the silvery moon.
'Oh, how I long to marry you
And may that day come soon.'

We raised our voices to the stars,
We did not care who heard us,
Nor when they shouted loud and clear,
'For God's sake stop that fuss!'

We met at a party, some months ago,
Across the room our eyes had met.
I loved you then, at just one glance,
And always will my pet.

But you were with another beau,
And so were not alone.
Though when the evening ended,
It was I who saw you home.

The course of true love does not run smooth.
I had a rival, from next door.
Who said that you belonged to him,
So I knocked him to the floor!

And now the wedding day is nigh.
I almost shed a tear.
For I am such a lucky guy,
To care for you, my dear.

I'll take you away in a pea-green boat,
And I'll sing to my small guitar,
'What a beautiful pussy you are, you are.
What a beautiful pussy you are'.

Eve M Turner

The Veil

You are a veil, so red and painfully torn
Through battle thorns and emotions wild
Your mind cannot repair you, so deeply worn
You hide yourself away, blemished little child

Through battle thorns and emotions wild
Friend and foe, confused in your threads
You hide yourself away, blemished little child
You cannot hide, even thinking weighs as lead

Friend and foe, confused in your threads
Trust - a long-lost myth, hope amiss
You cannot hide, even thinking weighs as lead
Hopeless you mend your threads and reminisce

Trust - a long-lost myth, hope amiss
Anger rises, as tears solemnly fall
Hopeless you mend our threads and reminisce
Good times fade while threads disenthrall.

Anger rises, as tears solemnly fall
Comforts fly as darkness laughs
Good times fade while threads disenthrall
Wounds expand, you're near in half

Comforts fly as darkness laughs
You question the light that loves you still
Wounds expand, you're near in half
Yet a light is growing and slowly fills

You question the light that loves you still
Your mind cannot repair you, so deeply worn
Yet a light is growing and slowly fills
You are a veil, so red and painfully torn.

Jeremy Paul

Your Sweet Voice

Your sweet voice
Is like music to my ears
Whenever you speak to me
You remove all my fears.

Your tender touch
Is what I desire
You make my feelings
Climb ever higher.

Your beautiful smile
Is what I strive for
When it falters
I do fall.

Your companionship
Is all I need
When I'm with you
I need not feed.

To wake up next to you
Is a dream come true
I would be scared
If it were anyone but you.

Though I have made mistakes
Now they mean nothing
For when I am with you
You mean everything.

And though I may never
Be able to convince you
I want you to know
My life would be nothing without you.

Tony Wenham

Love On Bonny Harris Isle

When the sun, it met the sea
Was the day when you kissed me
Rolling waves and sand collide
Crashing thunder in the tide

Your beauty took away at first
My breath, for you I'm fit to burst
In all the world I've never seen
A bay deserted, so pristine

Rainbow changes green to blue
Swimming deep in love with you
Soft the grains, my skin they rest
Caressing on my aching breast

In pink champagne, a dusky light
Mountains close in for the night
Stars they twinkle in the sky
Gazing in each other's eyes

Spread upon the castle bed
Underneath the sheet of red
Floating warm, a satin throw
Delightful shepherd's crimson glow

Drifting in rose waters clear
A visitor in grey appeared
Quietly bobbing, looking round
Lapping gently homeward-bound

Gold it poured throughout the land
On the night you took my hand
I cannot wait to see your smile
Again on bonny Harris Isle

Rosemary Gladwell

Legend

I switch on my radio and hear your sweet voice
Purity and innocence floats over the airways
Dead to the world but to me you live on
You sang your songs the way you felt
From your heart, your mind and your soul
I switch on my television and I see your face
You smile and I know it is meant for me.

The day you died a part of me died
The day you died part of the world died too
You were a hero in your time
Your music spoke a language of its own
Misunderstood at times by critics who set out to destroy
But you survived them all and proved them wrong.

I switch on my radio and hear your sweet voice
Tears fall from my eyes
I switch on my television and see your face
Smiling eyes but behind the smile
A haunting sadness engulfs and swallows
The world of music and song.

The years have flown by in the blink of an eye
Seasons change
Life goes on
I look out my window at the leaves on the trees
Changing from green to brown and red to gold
I look in the mirror on the wall
I see my reflection looking back at me
From a girl to a woman, how I have changed
The world changes but one thing will never change
My love for you.

Linda McCarthy

See View

Moving always over the sea
which meant there was less
chance of obstacles towering
into the sky. Claire drove a
time machine and was always
keen to hear about changes
like wind turbine windmills.
Steer clear of those when
you enter the twenty-first century.
She must be a queen of
her species from a land where
love has taken root. I met her
one day walking on Brighton
beach, she was counting stones.
She looked cute in her spacesuit,
a Union Jack bikini. Around
her neck a strap and from it
hung a small box. Perhaps a device
to keep in touch with three thousand
years ago. She looked me up and
down and levitated me off the
ground. My heart was hers and
then she uttered these words. 'That
deckchair is four pounds a day
hire and you're sitting on it.' From
that mysterious object around her neck
she wound me a paper ticket. No
doubt with my money she would
buy fuel to return to her world.
I just wanted to go with her.

Vann Scytere

The Ode To Joe And Mabel

The time is the eighteen eighties.
Wedded Joe and Mabel are now aged.
Both are presently in their late sixties.
'The Potteries' not yet elected a city.
The height of the five towns' productivity.
This locality then a smoking nightmare.
Many soot-belching pottery bottle kilns,
Coal pit mounds smouldering volcanoes.
Etruria's massive iron and steel works
Nightly glow like the flames of hellfire,
As men tap furnaces of molten pig iron.
Deep craters of extricated red clay,
That pockmark this ravaged landscape,
Are filled with pernicious orange waters.
The pair recall the area's raw beginning,
When much of this was bleak moorland.
As kids they roamed this place together,
Neither youngster knew anything better.
Steam train journeys out of the question.
In a back to back terrace raised infants.
Most died before the tender age of five.
Their surviving offspring industrial fodder.
Coal mining for Will, their remaining lad.
The two girls became banders and gilders.
Soot, coal, dust or kaolin-clogged lungs
Even the apprenticeship trained, lowly paid.
Attended the Methodist chapel on Sunday.
After forty years married - to be separated.
Destitute - heading for the workhouse
Gender segregated, their cruellest blow.

John Pegg

Romancing The Notion Of Love

It probably began with Adam and Eve
A love or understanding and the urge to leave
Everything else, not as sublime as the feeling
For the focus of your life and your senses reeling . . .
Whether for your partner or your country's shores
The longing ache inside you, that opens your pores
Maybe it's a pet or a familiar place
Or a reliable car or a much-loved face
There's a feeling aroused, that's hard to explain
But when you're apart, there's a deep down pain
Some say it's love and a need to be near
Your centre of attention that you hold to be dear
Maybe it's called romance by those 'in the know'
Others may scoff - hard exteriors to show
Some are unsure about their need and desire
Until reunited, then it's like coals on a fire!
There are many forms of love of things all around
For people and creatures or even plants without sound
So the notion of romance and love are entwined
Not always to end with wedding vows signed
Even in battle men have died for their brother
Is this the same love they had for their mother?
The idea of romance to some may be quaint
With roses and ribbons and new coats of paint
Around little love nests where a couple may dwell
However, to others, it casts a different spell
The romance of travel and the journey's return
To a place much loved and end of heart's yearn
So what of romance and of love and of passion?
Whatever your beliefs - all three are the fashion!

Alan R Coughlin

Heartbeats

When destiny issued this command,
'Take a walk into the American night dear child'
I did not know
What I was about to find
The skies were light
The stars' choir were right
For a pinnacle of newness
Lavished my every heartbeat
The moment was ripe
A face I saw before me
Our eyes twinkled a melody
The rhythm rewinds, rewinds, rewinds,
'I'm Carlos,' his right hand extended
'I'm Carol,' the echo was kind
Hands now cushioned in a flower bed of softness
Oh the pleasure was a majestic rhyme
Love in all its splendour, continued to chime
Meetings from yester time said a quick 'Hi'
For days ago, Steve had wooed me with roses
And charms from his heart
Terrence too just had to appear
For our meeting at the bus stop, was still being played
Now here in this moment of honey and veal
I'm thinking which one would melt me completely
Each one held a semblance an honour so free
All so very handsome with qualities of their own
Carlos' surprise kiss to my cheek brought me back to reality
His scents were euphoric, my heart wowed, my soul did speak
We walked on in a state
Knowing that destiny had sealed our fate.

Carolie Cole Pemberton

Waiting, Keeping Cave

Her solitary walk into her waiting room, which is full of deafening, crying silences
Her imprisoned darkness with eyes constantly staring
Her fragile tears slowly falling, unaware of love's acceptance waiting
She cleans her lenses, and cleans the window again and again
She is at a point in time at which paths intersect and branch out
She is expectant, yet she knows she is waiting in a womb of time
Does she still wait for the past?
Ghostly imagining of steam from yesterday, pluming underneath a glass canopy
With greyhound dogs stretching and yawning, waiting, watching,
being watched, waiting for their master
She waited, amidst high piercing voices as girls vocalize their
excitement in an otherwise silent station
She waited, love waited, silent waiting for her beloved
Waiting in present time
For the next heartbeat, for her next breath, for her next thought
She remembers lakes shimmering and flower scents
Now it is only the rain on the window with dry, dusty imitation flowers with no fragrances
She remembers lying on a rock in the hot sun, becoming part of the landscape
Now it is only the sun shining on the pain
She remains, waiting, but cannot rest
She feels an expectancy of eternity
Behind the veil of butterflies suspended in lace
She watches as tortoiseshell wings flutter for freedom on the woven threads
She frees it
And here she is shadow
Present in reality, but an imaged reflection of herself, which she does not acknowledge
A moon on the wane, washing colour into a tired, slate roof
Bathing it with a silver sheen, transforming it with light so liquid as liken to molten lead
She waits until the shadowy veil of night recedes
And then her heart is touched by the reflected glow of Christ's face

Hilary J Clark

True Love

They fell in love as youngsters do, and wanted only to be wed
They promised to be ever true, as many lovely things they said,
Beneath the stars they sealed the love, that burned within their hearts
And vowed upon the moon above, they would not ever part,
But angry parents are no match, for sweethearts, not of age
Trembling they could only watch, the grown-ups vent their rage,
So they were parted there and then, the young man sent far away
And she barely 6 years plus 10, broke her heart in every way,
But life goes on, the years sped by, and both did older, wiser grow
Then, with upon their lips, a lie they promised others, they'd be true,
She gave birth to two children to the man, whose ring she'd pledged to wear,
And tried so hard to understand, he seemed never once, to care,
When at last her children grown, and she a widow of many years
Her son and daughter both left home, blessed with her love and tender tears,
Oft time she dreamed of her true love, and wondered where ere he went
She gave her life to God above, and lived her days in sweet content Then one bright and sunny day, in a busy city shop
She saw him heading her way, and thought her heart would stop,
Their eyes did meet, their hands entwine, he whispered, ''Tis you my dear,
After all this time I find you,' he hugged and held her near,
His gentle hands so warm and firm, embraced her to his heart,
He kissed her lips, just to confirm, no more they'd be apart,
Yes he had wed a kindly wife, though children had they none,
And had led a sad and lonely life, regretting the things he could have done,
They talked, and laughed and she did cry, letting go to pain and misery,
Blessed with a love she couldn't deny, 'twas there for all eternity,
He took her home, his precious one, and loved her 'til the dawn,
And in his arms, she saw the sun, in all its glory born,
She turned and kissed his smiling face, 'I love you, dear heart,' she cried.
Then safe, at last in his embrace, she closed her eyes, and died.

Barbara Daniels

What If?

If we were to meet again,
suddenly,
I wonder, would I still gasp
as a fresh salmon in a grass basket?
Would I still imagine that I suffered
the effects of bad migraine?
if we were to meet again,
suddenly,
while turning the corner of a busy street
in our small town
would I feel my blood pounding,
hear it rushing to my head as a Niagara
one afternoon in June?
I taste you in retrospect
as I do the wine I had yesterday at dinner
and I must admit,
that though sweet to the tongue then
I had a lot of regrets
when I greeted the sun today -
for my indulgence.
If we were to meet again,
suddenly,
after all these years;
would I be tempted to slap your face,
something owed you since forever,
or will I let laughter escape my body
in a roaring cascade
at myself, mind you,
for thinking that you would have waited
for me to grow up?

Lila Joseph

In Some Far Tomorrow

I will know you in some far tomorrow.
In some future lifetime to come.
It cannot be love at first sight,
For we've met so many times before.
Always there have been difficulties.
From age, religion, race or status.
Some obstacle that always faces us
Defeat, never the twain should meet.
Never to publically plight our troth,
To be the lovers we're meant to be.
History sets traps for the unwary,
If only we'd remembered earlier,
On our past lives' futile encounters.
Pleasures shared in half measures
Treasures only to found in Heaven.
What games do the old gods play?
This time somehow we recalled them,
Though this time our age difference,
Made ours an impossible situation.
Something too unbearable to rectify.
Produced a snare like some poacher,
Yet the scales fell from our eyes.
Surprised not to have recalled sooner.
The pages of previous shared lives.
We avidly read, chapter after chapter.
Shared many tears and much laughter,
From the deep roots of our beginning.
Roots and trunks binding and entwined.
Each time our unity developing stronger.
One day our seeds will make new worlds.

Julie Pegg

Love

What would you have me say?

Would you have me say I see it in your eyes?
Would you have me declare my undying love for you?
Would you have me father your child to prove my loyalty?
No

I say it is
Without it I am nothing, nothing I say.
With it I *am*

With it I cross mountains, I cross time
I *am*

With it I am complete.

It is true power.
That which will level armies, that which
Can turn all enemies into friends.
That which can save you, if only you could see

Where do I find this love?
Look inside.
Put aside your fear.

So what is love?
It is the beginning and the end.
The start and the finish line.
It is all and *one.*
Is it what you call *God?*

In this space I feel no more conflict.
I can reach out across the universe itself should I need to.
But I seek no more, for I am home now.
I have found love.

Simon O'Donnell

'For Christine: My Love!'

(24.12.08)

Oh heart! My tears pour forth, as summer's rain
When I recall just how much I love you.
Through such strong desire, aches my lovelorn brain,
for when we part, painful echoes ensue.
Sweet love, my heart, even more purloined,
by your first fixed gaze, I was 'undone'!
When smiles, azure-eyes, by me are joined,
in awe and wonder, my poor heart was won.
So, what love stirred, like our sun's rising,
illumines by its warm, loving gaze,
to banish night's veil, so unsurprising,
removes fear in these most darkest of days
when alone with thoughts, 'self-centred' sighs.
Oh, my sweet angel, hear my aching cries!

Cleave me, thus I never really live
unless we entwined, in lifelong kiss
embrace future days, in 'symbiotic' strives,
where our two hearts are 'blended' tunes of bliss.
You are not here, caressing tears of joy;
Oh dear, enfolding love, do please give ear,
and my furrowed brow, your touch employ;
Expel, (my 'undone' crying heart) of fear.
Sleep betrays my eyes, my crazed 'estate';
Will you, my love, thru' tears, betroth, bestow
though silent hours cry, 'The hour is late!'
Unknown to mortals, is this 'Divine' glow,
their 'selfish' lusts blind such hearts, 'Philistine!'
Love! Pure, unblemished, so refined!

Cuba N Briton

I Remember

A monument in time
Is like a drop in the ocean
I remember the love we once shared
Inspired by the family
That grew from our love
As the flame of eternity
Burns in our hearts.

Pamela Javes

A Dark Love

An angel I have seen with my eyes
In this world of hate and lies
She walks these roads in the dead of night
'Cause she fears the light.

As she has fallen from grace,
Her wings torn as is her heart,
She cries alone as she walks the dark
Graveyard where she stays.

I do see her every night
Around 12.30 till sunlight
My feelings for her have grown strong
But she has not heard this song.

For I wish I could tell her so
How much I want to heal her so,
But for I'm just a man
How can I love an angel so?

But this I know to be true.
This feeling will never leave me,
So even though it's maybe wrong,
I should tell her this some day.

And she was an angel true,
And she walked in the skies of blue,
Her only crime was being true to her heart,
And for such she was cast out for loving someone.

So tonight under the moonlight
I shall tell her I know it's right,
How much I love her so.

John Black

Closer

When I saw you in this place
And you shone just like a star
I swear I knew your face
Now I don't know who you are

Even when you come in here
I still hear you loud and clear
It's like you're right next to my ear

And I just can't pull myself away
Even though my heart will break
And I just can't bring myself away
And I don't want to escape

When I saw you in this place
Who knew you'd break my heart
But I still see your face
And I don't know where to start

Even though I said be friends
You are still in my heart
And I knew this was the end
Even with this 'fresh start'

Now I see you in this place
And dread the day ahead
And when I watch your face
I wish I was dead

Every day I see you smiling
And laughing without me
Just know inside I'm dying
And in time you'll see.

Natasha Bowerman

Literally

She was not from this world,
Her white skin - too white,
Her blonde hair - too blonde,
Her magnetic eyes - too blue
For comfort, as cerulean as
The generous sky she came from.

She never mixed with the rest of us,
Always kept herself to herself,
Ate her lunch alone, her eyes
Darting this way and that, almost
Too beautiful for this world,
Too perfect for the insanity of
Being human, of talking and sharing,
And arguing, and winning, and
Losing - she was above it all.

A goddess in our midst, giving all
The right answers in class,
Wearing her neatly-ironed clothes,
Smelling of flowers from an ancient
Civilisation that had to be reborn,
But I'm sure she had a soul, different
To ours, but still a soul throbbing
With the knowledge of doom for
This planet which was not her own.

How do I know all this? My spirit guides
Assure me that we used to be
An item a long, long, long time ago,
Before the human race was even born.

Carlos Nogueiras

The Absent Presence

She was completing her floral design
On the stage during her Christmas show
Placing the flowers . . .
Lighting the candle . . .
'Shall I tell you about next door?' she said.
'Wonderful place, nice people.'
Old man, she told us your story.

You and your wife had a beautiful garden, she said,
Your wife died, you continued
To look after it lovingly,
Just remembering, just . . . remembering
Silently grieving, until you
Could look after it no more,
Until you . . . could look after yourself

No more. 'His children,' she said,
'Decided it would be better
For him to go to a nursing home.
They put 'next door' for sale.
A property developer bought it,
They have permission
To demolish the lot. House and garden.'

She was talking to the audience
Whilst she was arranging the flowers.
We were sitting, and watching . . . the changes.
'These cuttings . . . gorgeous, aren't they,' she said.
'These cuttings are from 'next door'.
I was told I could take all I wanted
Before the developer comes in.'

Claire-Lyse Sylvester

I'll Call You Mine

I call you mine
Because we meet as one,
One life, one spirit bound
Through all the years to come.
Not with the chains that drag
The ties we cannot face
But with the bonds we can't escape
That call and plead
Through time and space.
A spirit without a soul
Until we meet, when hand clasps hand
And two hearts have one beat.
Then the divided parts
Become a whole,
A perfect being
A creature with one soul
Which glows and loves.
Whose limbs we see
Dancing down the years -
Who's free.
Until such meeting
Must we limp forlorn
Severed from that other half
Crying in the darkness
Lost and torn.
Only together is our world made whole
Walking as one through time
Thus - if God wills -
I'll call you mine.

Margaret Blake

Expression

Watching
Watching you
Searching, for what I do not know
Hesitating, to tell you of what I know
Of what I feel within me
How just your touch
Though it may be only as you pass
Leaves an empty ache within
An ache that only grows, as the days go on.
Wanting
Wanting you
Both physically and mentally
Watching you and your ever-changing moods
As within yourself you struggle with your emotions
You strive to find your inner strength
Through both your ups and your downs
Struggling within this web of humanity
Within time and pain and laughter
Sometimes you win; you lose.
You're just you, you're incomprehensible
A human form.
Afraid
Afraid of what I feel and of what has been felt before
But this is life
We have to learn to live with our emotions
To control them; we live to learn.
Loving
Loving you
As only you will know.

Tracey Skivington

Forever

Moonlight walks starlight wishes
Dreaming dreams of Mr and Mrs.

A whisper of softness
Catches the tender nervous voice.

Exchange of rings
Sacred vows of promise.

On a solemn oath of loyalty and trust
Two hearts so in love, beat as one.

Mother and father to children of joy
A house together for a family born.

To seal a bond joined in sickness and in health
Sharing both good times and the bad.

No matter what challenges fate has in store, from this day on,
Supporting each other is no problem for this Man and Wife.

Groom and bride stand side by side
A wedding day celebration, let the party begin.

A handsome prince with a rose of valentine
David and Cheryl surrounded by friends to wish them well.

A couple of reserved seats on the honeymoon train
A 'Do Not Disturb' sign keeps the ticket collector at bay.

Forever is the destination that lies ahead
For future planning there can be no arrival time set.

I wish you all the best Son and my new Daughter-in-law
On this Valentine Day, 14th February 2008.
Lots of love Dad

Nigel Astell

So Would You

I have never been a married man,
But I find love when and where I can;
And when I love a girl there's nothing I wouldn't buy her,
If I desire her, I get the fever and couldn't deceive or leave her.

I fall in love with just a talk and a sweet smile,
It only takes me a very short while;
But I don't like to rush; I like to take my time,
Until I know she is really mine.

My first love I have loved all my life,
When we first met I wanted to make her my wife;
We used to laugh and have some fun,
But then I found I was the lonely one.

She was not what you would call sincere, given an inch,
She's been married four times since;
I still love her but not so dear,
And wish her the best throughout the year.

Tracy is now the love of my life,
I have known her for eighteen years;
I love to see her face when we kiss or embrace,
And I couldn't bear to see her in tears.

When we're together we have a wonderful life,
I try really hard to make her my wife;
We never have unhappy tears,
And have never been closer over the years.

I love her more than anyone I ever knew,
And if you knew her, so would you.

John Walker

Lines For Valentine's Day

I love you as the swallow loves the sky,
I love you as the salmon loves the stream,
I love you as the blackbird loves the dawn,
I love you as a dreamer loves her dream.

I love you as the forest loves the spring,
I love you as the desert loves the rain.
I love you as the darkness loves the stars,
I've loved but once: I shall not love again.

E Margaret Kidd

The Gift Of Love

The love of a father,
to discipline his child.
The love of a mother,
so gentle and mild.
The love of a sister,
to help and to cherish.
The love of a brother,
so tough and yet boyish.
The love of a grandma,
so old and yet wise.
The love of a grandpa
with tired-looking eyes.
The love of an aunt,
kind and so thoughtful.
The love of an uncle,
strong and so helpful.
The love of a godparent,
to pray and encourage us.
The love of a friend,
of whom we can trust.
The love of a child,
looking for guidance.
The love of a woman,
to find an acquaintance.
But the greatest of all love,
which will never sever,
is the love of God in dear Jesus,
which is now and forever.

Teresa Street

To Mother

Cherished possession, a mother's love,
Borne in the heart, unshaken
By the bitterest strive, it shall prove
A guiding light, never darkened.

Dulled though it be by constant touch,
Awakening comes, with separation
To stay, just as such;
A bond of deep appreciation.

George Beckford

Dedicated To Miss X

Peter, sometimes I wonder
Whilst at night I lie in bed
What is the girl of your dreams like?
I mean, the one whom you hope to wed.
Is she a woman whose kisses
Lift you to heavenly heights?
Is she exotic and charming
A vision of dreams and delights?
Her beauty, does it entrance you?
How neat is her figure, how trim?
Would Hedy Lemarr be envious
Of one so graceful and slim?
In your heart will she always linger
And reign like a Queen on a throne?
When she speaks is her voice soft, yet husky
As she whispers, 'My darling, my own'?
Has she tresses that shimmer like moonbeams
As they fall on her shoulders so white?
If so, are they wavy and golden
Or jet-black like a raven's in flight?
Do her eyes gleam like stars in the twilight?
Are her lips like rubies so red
Or when on you she flashes a smile
Do you think of pearls instead?
If Peter, you find this description applies
To a certain young lady named 'X'
Then take her dear Sir, to the altar
And marry the gem of our sex.

Esther Hawkins

Widowhood

Before me many a table has been spread -
I cannot eat, for appetite has fled,
However wholesome and refined the fare,
It would be tasteless, after your spices rare.

And I've been offered many a brimming glass -
I turn my head and let temptation pass,
No stranger's cup could quench this thirst of mine,
My craving is for your rich vintage wine.

Eileen Whatmough

Love In My Life

Love always helps the world go round
As it affects every person's life
And is the most important feeling
For parents, kids, husband or wife
Work at times can be hard and troublesome
And may make you sometimes feel alone
But what will help you through the day
Are the folk you've got at home
Initially it was my wife just being there
When my job was s*** and hard to take
That made a bad day seem much better
Saying, 'It's only work for heaven's sake!'
Now work is good, no problems there
And we've been married now for years
Now maybe taking each other for granted
Could be our greatest fear
When both of our kids came along
First our daughter, then her bruv
We were both absolutely ecstatic
And then knew the meaning of 'real love'
They both still mean the world to us
And regardless of what they may do
Our love for them grows year by year
And just keeps on shining through
I really love our beautiful kids
And also love my darling spouse
And if by chance they all feel the same
We must have a very loving house!

Christopher Leith

Before I Sleep

I wish for me a peaceful night
My soul to rise into fanciful flight
And when it returns on gossamer wing
Let me wake and enjoy what life's journey may bring.

If that moment arrives, should my soul not return
But take off into some endless flight,
Let the loved one I leave, recall when they grieve
My last words, 'I love you - goodnight.'

Derek William Gresty

First Meeting

We met as many friends would meet,
As passers-by along the street,
But little did we know
That our friendship was to grow
Into a long and happy love affair
As we passed by on the street out there.

I'd seen him before at the local dance
And often hoped I'd have the chance
To dance with him one night,
Just to feel his arms hold me tight.

After the dance, it was quite late
He walked me home to my garden gate.
He kissed me fondly on the cheek
And asked if we again could meet.

It was as if we walked on air.
Happiness was ours beyond compare,
Our love grew more and more each day.
We knew that it was here to stay.

At the village church we made our vows.
In a cottage made our home.
For forty years we shared our love
But now I'm on my own.

He was my love, my life, and my all
And the memory will always be
Of the lad that passed me in the street
And said hello to me.

Margaret Sparrow

Sophie Louise, My Granddaughter Aged Eight

Witty and pretty, mischievous too,
When she does a dance, we never feel blue.
She has strange little habits like folding her arms,
Just like Les Dawson, but with more than his charms (bless him).
We thank Heaven above for Sophie Louise,
We love to be with you - it's really a wheeze!
God bless you my grandchild, long may you reign,
I'd love to be nursing you all over again.

June Picken

I Had Everything To Give

Love, desire and attraction
You took me in your arms, bright eyes.
Behind the lust, and abundance of lies.
I had everything to give,
Together we did live.

Love with joyous beliefs
Along the riverbank, lusty days,
But I am amazed how beauty lies
And I behold a grief.

Feelings, love is like a baby in the womb
That love lost, buried in a tomb.
Hence, we grew old,
And our bodies naked, grow cold.

Summer lingers on, bright eyes gone.
Abundance of lies are within and left.
Feelings I buried and felt bereft
But life continues, and the river flows on.

Love, desire and attraction
A lust for truth and honesty bright eyes . . .
To relieve the pain of and passion, with no lies
A devotion to live.
Everything I had to give.

A consequence reflecting my joyous beliefs
We reflected, on our life, full of lusty days,
Passion heightened and forgiveness of lies.
How I long for bright eyes.

Ann Hubbard

Doris

Fifty-seven years I've shared your life,
Fifty-five years you've been my wife
In life on Earth you did your best
Now God's decided you need a rest.
So until we meet again up there,
For you I'll say a little prayer
'Au revoir' dear love of mine
I'll love you till the end of time.

Alan Parkinson

I Remember When

I remember when we first met in the park
We sat upon the seesaw it really was a lark
We strolled the paths together by the flowerbeds,
Two old dears on a bench, chatting and nodding heads.
        Oh I remember when

I remember when sailing on the lake, you showered
Me with water. I cried, 'Oh stop for goodness sake.'
You furled the sail and we got out, I stubbed my toe
I gave a shout.
        Oh yes I remember when

I remember when you first kissed me on my cheek
I'm sure I blushed a rosy red, I could hardly speak
Your arm went round my shoulders, my head was on your chest,
I thought, *oh dear me whatever will be next!*
        Oh yes I remember when

We stood beside the garden gate, the moon was high
It's getting late, you looked at me, a look of love
My heart fluttered like a dove
        Oh yes I remember when

Though many years have now passed, a teardrop
Glistens in my eye, dear Jed, although no longer here.
Yes I remember you liked a beer.
Dear man, I miss you very much, I miss your kiss,
Your gentle touch
I have your sons and grandchildren too 'tis all
I need for me, from you.

Doreen Christopher

Atypical

Asexuals challenge the words of a song -
'Everybody loves somebody, sometime'
And prove those lyrics oh, so wrong!
For ne'er there will be a wedding-bell chime.
Non-tactile means forget a group hug -
No instinct - maternal - to give a child bliss.
No 'our tune' at the heart strings to tug -
Thus forever and ever 'love' is given a miss.

Anonymous
pp B E A M

Story Of My Life

It's just a passion paradise failed
All I want right now is the power to forgive
But I can't look at your face without feeling pain
You were the one I couldn't un-crave
I rejected the idea you may have found love
I believed your emotions for me ran deep
I was crazy and stupid and immature to think for so long you could believe in me

It's just a lost opportunity
All I got was an unfinished dream
It's crazy you're the one I never wanted to run from
Never banked on becoming some kind of enemy
I hope you know I could have loved you
If you had given me half the chance
I was patiently waiting, I guess a fool, to think I could pick up a feeling passed

It's just a damned crying shame
Why did you throw it all away
I can't stand to look back and face it all again
So I'll move on, time to turn the page
You just gave generous false hope then expected me to give it all up
After all there is no happy ending
No ending at all to our story

I can always think of could've been
I can always dream of what if
But for the sake of my sanity
I'll put it down to the story of my life
I guess it was just bad timing.

P Dixon

True Love

My late husband, John, was my only true love,
So I'm sure he still loves me, from his heavenly home, above
I gave my heart to him, when I was seventeen years old,
And his love for me then, was worth more than pure gold.
He suffered war wounds, and heart attacks,
But he never complained
So my love for him, has always remained,
Now eighteen years have gone by, since he sadly passed away,
But my love for him, grows stronger, thinking of him, every day.

Jean Hendrie

True Love

I remember when I saw you first, as I
Walked home in the rain,
I looked and smiled, and then passed by,
And went on down the lane,
But all that night, you filled my thoughts,
And I hoped and prayed you'd be
Tomorrow too, in the place we met, and
Looking out for me.

So when I saw you there again, I knew it must be fate,
As by my side, like a lifelong friend,
You came with me to my gate.
Then as I turned to smile at you, so lonely
Was your glance,
How could I hope but ask you in!
I simply took a chance.

But I never will regret it dear, as you've
Been so good and true,
My life is so much richer now, I have
Your love - and you.
Now, as we sit together here, so cosy by the fire,
We're happy and contented pair, and have
All that we desire.

So if you and I had never met, these lines
Would not be written
Then for this too, I thank you dear -
My own sweet darling kitten.

Josephine Quinton

Untitled

I fell in love and I became
the sparkle of the sunshine on a dewdrop in the mist,
the thrill in the whisperings of the trees,
the tingle in the trill of the blackbird's crystal song:
I became the ultimate me.
Now my being brims high with the meaning of life
that runs, giggling, into my soul
and I know that forever that blackbird will sing
and the thrill of that tingle will never grow old.

Eileen Caiger Gray

Lost Love

Love was once
the warmth
of my life.
Now I feel
cold, lifeless
alone.
In life
with low
energy,
strife.
Tears flow
I cannot
control.
I long to
feel complete,
plus whole
with a warm
sunshine
array,
to warm
my way.
Oh why
was my
love lost,
in a
mist
array?

Denise McDonald

A Soldier And His Girl, 1960

Her well-rounded curves
Soft, dark hair and brown eyes,
With features beautiful
I truly love each memory.

His smooth, silky, fair hair
Blue eyes filled with passion,
Twixt desire and delight
I treasure every moment . . .
Together true love was found.

Elizabeth Murray Shipley

A Poem For Brian And Geri

In the beginning,
Geri used to fear Brian.
But he adored her.
He worshipped God, too
Brian always cherished Him.
Now, she is joyful!
Geri thought she died.
Brian resurrected her,
And he cherished her.
When the day begins,
Geri comes and speaks with him.
His words bring her light.
When the day is done,
Geri comes and speaks with him.
He soothes her to sleep.
He enlivens her!
Brian fills Geri with zest!
Brian delights her!
Below lights from stars,
These two both feel marvellous!
The lights are glowing!
Moonlight sends a breeze!
These two are both passionate!
This world is for them!
They are enchanted!
The night sky is wonderful!
Their world is perfect!

Laraine Smith

Permanence Lost

You kissed a rose, its petals bright
And scarlet in the gentle light
And scent caressed your nose and you
Sighed gently for the cool of dew.

But days have slid and slipped away
And though beside your rose you stay
Its petals darken, wither, fall,
Do you, my lover, still recall,
Why once you kissed your rose at all?

Harriet Nuttall

Distant Love

I feel so very deeply
For the man who's in my life
I felt such joy and gladness
When I became his wife.
I felt my life had started
When I looked into his eyes
He was so very gentle -
So adorable and wise.
But years roll by as they always will
I still love him oh so much!
But long for him to hold me -
I long to feel his touch.
Each time I see him look at me
I often wonder why
Instead of feeling happy
I somehow seem to cry.
The love he used to show me
Has dwindled with the years
My feelings of such happiness
Have each dissolved in tears.
But still this man will always be
The only one I'll love
Until my life is over and I'm taken up above.
So whilst we are together
I'll cherish every day
And thank our heavenly Father
For the day he came my way.

Wendy Souter

Cruel To Be Kind

I try to forget you, but you are always on my mind,
At the time, I thought I was being cruel to be kind.
It seems that for once in my life I was wrong,
That maybe I should
Have bitten my tongue.

I watch you from across the street, hoping you will notice,
But you don't and I lose focus.
Why did I let you go, why didn't I see
That you were in fact the most important thing to me?

Jennifer Starkie

Aladdin Boy

Oh, Aladdin boy, where are you now?
I remember when we met in the park
All those years ago!
You rescued me from a life of woe.
Oh how I miss those walks with you in the wilderness,
Holding hands and skipping happily.
I'd jump up and down and you'd
Call me your happy bunny.
I'd dance round the room for you.
It would be Kate Bush, Water Music and Madonna.
You would watch happily and make me
Feel the star I wanted to be
Even though it tired you endlessly.
Those long, hot summer days in your garden of paradise!
Bushy trees encased all around
A stone, ornate bird-feeder.
We'd while away the hours talking and laughing,
The prettiest rainbow of flowers splattered everywhere.
Kisses and cuddles all day long with a tender one.
You had your hobbies, I had mine.
We would look up at the stars on bitter-cold nights
And talk about Jupiter and Mars,
Along with Venus, the mother of all stars.
Oh where art thou now, the golden boy of dreams?
Lost in another sphere!
It's been many long years,
But I hold onto your memories and my tears.

Stella Robinson

A Mother's Love

Jesus is sitting there in Heaven,
Jesus calls Peter,
'Peter, go and see where
all the people are coming from.'
Peter goes and comes back,
He calls Jesus,
'Jesus, it's your mother again.
Every time my back is turned
She lets everyone in.'

Alice Collins

What Loving You Means To Me

(For Alex)

If I could build a rainbow
I'd colour it bright with a warming glow
If you felt depressed and needed love
I'd lift it down from up above.

I'll give you a hug if you are sad
I'll calm you down if you are mad
If you ever need a sensitive ear
Within your heart, you know I'm here.

We got together I know it was fate
It was meant to be, you're my soulmate
You gave me your jacket when I was cold
I knew right then you had a heart of gold.

You're there with a hankie if you hear me sneeze
You'll bring my inhaler when I start to wheeze
If I need anything at all, on you I can depend
A husband, a father and my best friend.

I love you lots, you mean so much
With the kindest smile and a tender touch
You are there for me no matter what
I'm so very thankful of what we've got.

If I died and went somewhere far
I'd write your name on every star
Then everyone could look up and see
What loving you means to me.

Kelly Kinross

A Special Time

Candles light a darkly lit room.
In a vase flowers loom.
Music plays a classical or romantic note.
Voices enter and sit gladly.
A waiter hands a menu,
For the two renew.
A special time as they recall
The meal that started it all,
As the waiter has the call.

TS

Dignity

Life can be long, love only brief,
Words of a woman, lost in grief.

Lonely days, long lonely nights
Sat all alone by candlelight.

Family and friends with no time to spare,
Cast you aside and leave you there.

Lessons to be learned from love
I'd say, as you never believe
Love will go away.

But to another's arms my love did fly,
No final words, not even goodbye.

He promised to love me to my life's end
Then wanting me only as a part-time friend.

So please someone love me
And really care.
Make up for the man who
Left me standing there.

Hope he never knows just
How it feels, to lose to love,
When the scars won't heal.

So I hold my head up
As revenge not to seek.
For this man I loved deeply
But no longer could keep.

Fay Morgan

Forever Love

Rest your head upon my shoulder
You're tired my love as the wind blows colder
Sleep gently, let the silver stars in the skies be your eyes
Let the tears of happiness be the rain
As you're in my eyes again
Let your smiles be the morning sunshine
Let the time disappear
We're in love forever.

Isabel Taylor

Deliverance

You gave me carbon crystals,
10 on the scale of hardness,
cut from dull stone found
in some foreign gravel bed;
but you did not offer them
with your eyes,
your hard eyes,
so take them back,
I will not call them
diamonds.

You enticed me with
corundum from Burma,
lucent, red,
and metal silicates
green as grass, hacked
from transatlantic rock;
but they came without your hand,
your heart,
so do not expect me to see
rubies, emeralds.

See me now
bespangled with this
jazzy glass,
green, red, crystal.
Why not a little vulgarity?
A little bad taste?

Christopher Highton

Secret Love

My heart has a wall built around it,
Keeping my secret love locked inside,
But secret love will break my heart,
If I conceal it any longer.
I want to release this secret love,
And free it upon the wings of a white dove,
I want Cupid to come with his arrow and bow,
The seeds of love I want him to sow.

Tina Rooney

Secrets

You can always tell.
The way she walks.
The way her hand hesitates,
restraint proving need
as much as any brief
incidental touch.
Her eyes rarely stray.
See how she waits.

His shoulders, tensed,
reveal more
of feeling than hours
of talking
sense or sex.
No chance of him
concealing nerves
beneath transparent
practised nonchalance.
When she smiles,
he barely hides relief.

For a spell, watch,
then look away.
None of this is new,
for they
are not alone.
Our secrets, too,
are not our own.

Phil Rampton

Jacqueline 1949-2008

I will not mourn, well not for long,
I will not cry, for you've not gone.
You are my darkness and my light,
You are my daytime and my night.
You make me happy and never sad,
You are the best friend I've ever had.
I will not mourn, well not for long,
I will not cry, for you've not gone.

David Morgan

My Love

I have come back
You hurt my love,
My love, here I am.

I loved you and I love you so,
You left me, you had to I know,
My love never left you, only bruised.

I have crossed seven seas
And flown through seven skies,
Just to see you, to be with you.

You can't see me but I can,
You can't hear me but I can,
You can't talk to me but I can

Your sigh, it is over me, I know
I will swallow your sighs,
All your sorrows too, my love.

That unique gesture of hand
To the time gone by,
And that silent smile is just the same

Now, I will not let you leave, my love
I will be with you and watch you
Until the judgement day.

When you will see me also
Hear me and talk, also endless love talk
Of the days we once had.

Dr Ahmed Jamil

I Want To Be That Close To You

I remember the racing heart,
the dropping sensation in the stomach,
the mind's fixation on the beloved.

I don't want misunderstandings -
I want to be sure of you -
to love and be loved.

I want to be the sleeve of your shirt,
the strap of your sandal;
to enter you through an intake of your breath.

Di Perry

My Coat Of Many Colours

On a wintry God-forsaken day
of scowling, scurrying clouds,
I huddle, umbrella-sheltered
burdened by a deep despair.

Stinging rain falls in a deluge,
thunder applauds, ironically;
streaks of jagged lightning
sear the sulphurous sky.

Suddenly, urgently, your voice
echoes on the howling wind

'I am your coat of many colours.'

The memory of your sun-bright smile
shakes off the shackles of gloom,
your spirit dances on the edge of
a dissolving cloud. The candle
of your life burns ever brighter
as the sun breaks free, bathing me
in its blessed warmth.

Above my head appears the shimmering
halo of a double rainbow:

A shining promise of the other side of life,
when we two happy prisoners of the wind
will dance across the silence of eternity.

(For Ralph - forever)

Grace Galton

My Garden Rose

There is, for me, but one that glows,
As does the lovely garden rose,
Which, a beacon of light in leafy bowers,
Outshines the loveliest of lovely flowers.
And does, with tenderness, disarm
Dreary shadows with restful charm,
As do you, my love with tender guile,
Enlighten sylvan corners with your smile.

Geraldus John

Love's Lottery

Love manifests in mind, body and soul
Affectionate thoughts, gestures of care
And produces tenderness.
In Love's beauty, she beholds
As she plays the lottery of life.

Love overlooks via rank, culture and kind
Unconditional, blind to race
And does not discriminate.
Via Love's glory, she respects
As she plays the lottery of life.

Love generates to pride, pardon and joy
Brilliant achievements, sheer forgiveness
And brings exhilaration.
To Love's delight, she aspires
As she plays the lottery of life.

Love overcomes with faith, courage and hope
Distressing trials, problems of fear
And never fails when needed.
With Love's power, she believes
As she plays the lottery of life.

Love promises in life, patience and death
Vibrant emotion, apt endurance
And feelings that last forever.
In Love's wonder, she marvels
As she plays the lottery of life.

Eunice Ogunkoya

The Flower Of My Heart

I could see a thousand men in a day, but never like you.
Because you are the flower of my heart.
When I am with you, I feel I have the power to stop
The waves from splashing on the shore.
You have touched my core!
Every day my passionate love for you is more!
It can be snowing outside, but you always keep me warm.
The flower of my heart!

Edie May Tustin

Remember Me?

Remember me?
From way back when,
the flighty, flirting days of yore;
days of light, you to adore,
playing with fire beyond our ken.

Remember me?
When the longing grew,
when passion and tenderness filled the air,
when I held you close and you stroked my hair,
feelings but held by a favoured few.

Remember me?
As a friend in time
sharing so little yet sharing so much
enjoying our interests, inflamed by a touch
just happy together - your place or mine?

Remember me?
As we were in our prime,
enjoying the now, many years still to come,
still optimistic, when all's said and done
for one day it all will be fine!

Remember me?
Now that we are old,
still the warmth of our memories light us inside,
just a few more steps and we'll catch the tide
swept back together, our story told.

Brenda Heath

A Letter To My Wife

My darling, thank you for sixty-six years of love,
For caring, friendship and advising, day by day,
Thank you for the concern you showed when I was ill
And in hospital, you came through snow and ice, till
I was better: I still remember '64.

For me the experience was wonderful,
After thirty-one years of intense pain, I knew
How wonderful it was to be at peace, and full
Of gratefulness to God, the surgeon and to you;
You had your times of trial too my dear how true.

I was so sorry to see you in any pain,
My heart was in turmoil when you were ill, my dear,
But I was glad to be able to attend your needs,
We prayed to Jesus that He might help us through,
And were we not closer to each other because

Jesus was always part of our lives, yours and mine,
How well we worked together in so many ways,
We both knew sorrow and pain and joy, all our days;
But I'm sure our Saviour and His love made us one:
And how wonderful was our temporary parting.

Now we look forward to our next meeting, quite soon,
When I have finished the work God would have me do,
Then my dear, I shall come to my Lord and to you,
So shall our love continue, blessed by God forever:
Lord Jesus, thank you for life, and for Violet.

W Herbert G Palfrey

Chanson Bagnoles

There was something in you that called out to me and
I heard that voice,
like a siren song,
pulling me out of shape,
invading my mind
opening my body and desires to desecration.

A weaving melody of love
refashioning the shape
of paths to come.
I no longer heard clearly the beats of the drum
that is mine.

The tenor of my life changed in a cymbal crash
of shattering, tinkling, beautiful, delicate shards
of crystal pain.

But, should you have gone,
left me now,
the refrain of that music
will have lingered on
my life immutably interwoven
with your soul's song.

And, now and then
when my heart is teased by
light glancing from a silver thread of memory
I will smile
and eternally thank my God.

Padi Vincent

A La Recherche Du Temps Perdu

(A Remembrance Of Things Past)

Pert Miss of the Bible class,
Penny how I loved her,
Soulful eyes at morning Mass,
Sensuality and myrrh.
Could it be so very wrong
Kissing during evensong?

Wild child of the travelling fair,
Jenny how I loved her.
Eyes berry-black and sable hair,
Cherry cheeks, soft as fur.
Everlasting bliss was ours,
Down among the dodgem cars.

Blue Jean girl from Liverpool,
Wendy how I loved her.
Tattooed, studded, no one's fool,
Hair dyed red as ember,
Our love just the briefest whirl,
Now she loves a *girl* called Pearl!

Marriage came and marriage went
Still we had some happy years.
I just think of good times spent
Silly just to dwell on tears.
Life goes on - it twists and bends.
Now I have the love of friends.

David Lorkin

The Proposal

I love your eyes
Your perfect smile
Your wit, your charm, your humour
I love the way you held me close
When I thought it was over
Your touch, your smell
I love as well
I hope that you can see
That what it is I'm trying to say . . .
Is will you marry me?

Barbara Kinsey

Loving Inspiration

I, attending the Business Professional Women's
International Candle Lighting Ceremony
Africa, Asia, Europe, Latin America, North America, UK Regions
After supper our guest speaker, Keith England,
'Walking the Great Wall of China'
He lost his young wife to pancreatic cancer,
Raised £200,000 for the Macmillan Nurses charity.

He flew from Paris to Beijing, entering the Forbidden City
The apex roofing is fluted outward for good luck
Final courtyard is Tiananmen Square
He camped outside the Zhongyan Hotel
The restored wall snow apex one side Mongolia - the other, China.

Steepness contours of hill 30-40 feet centuries of stones,
wilderness incredible
Temperature varied 30° to freezing - wildlife non-existent,
A few goats walking the deep steps
He walked seven hours daily, the experience awesome.

Beijing Summer Palace - the land hand-dug, with magnolia tree,
Che-Hang House;
The warriors, monuments, terracotta army,
horses to be in the afterlife
Keith experienced togetherness with other people in his party
May we strive to touch and know the great human heart
common to us all
Let us not forget to be kind.

Patricia Turpin

Everlasting Love

He was the man of my dreams
The apple of my eye
The centre of my world
A wonderful guy.
I was fourteen, too young you may say
But I loved him until his dying day.
I was twenty when our marriage took place
And for forty-eight years I saw his sweet face.
I have no regrets - I love him still
And of one thing I'm sure - I always will.

Joyce Evans

The Light Of My Life

I often sit and wonder
If you knew how much I loved you
I don't remember telling you
But I hope that you knew
We all take for granted the love that we share
And just assume
The ones we love will always be there
I wish that I told you
How much you meant to me
All the things that made you special
And so important to me
I loved to spend time with you
A moment here and there
Times that I will remember
The special times we shared
You had a special magic
That was yours and yours alone
A light that shone
You lit up my life anytime you were around
I miss you and your laugher
Your very special smile
The gift you had of being you
That made my life worthwhile
I miss you so much now you are gone
I love you more and more
Your memory will stay with me for now and evermore.

Janet Thomas

Red Roses

Red roses on a hall stand by the door
I hear your footsteps as in days of yore
Petals fall when the winds come like a sigh
Reminds me of the days gone by
I'll meet you again, I don't know where or when
The rose bowl is empty now, I'll pick and refill again
And when I am old, and my hair is turning grey
I'll still hear your voice and laughter in the boys and girls at play
Petals blowing in the wind.
Red Roses

George Camp

Sit

I sit by the door as a good animal should
I await my master's entrance
What has it brought for me today
Perhaps a tasty treat or the scraps from a tray?
If I am good, perhaps I will be spared
The normal grunt or the flailing hand?
I don't ask for much, but just some love
And once in a while, more than a little shove
I do my best to keep out of the way
I hide my face during the long day
The dark nights are worst though
Who knows what is to come?
Perhaps I will be taken out
Or he will not need to shout . . . at me?
Oh, I do hope he has had a good day without pain
And I will be spared a bad night again.
I long to snuggle close by the fire
To share a smile before we retire
Once more to the bedroom where it can be cold
I can lay beside him and my body he'll hold.
But these days a stick to fetch is all I can muster
While around his 'sometime' friends they do cluster.
I know getting old is what happens for sure
And none of us know what is waiting anymore.
But I cannot help feeling as he pushes me away
Why, oh why, did he marry me that day?

Arthur Reeder

A Lost Fragment

I cannot sleep for fear of waking
Nor stem the flow of tears
Through a haze of mist
That vacant and distant look appears
Muscles tighten yet twitch from aching
From the infusion of emptiness
With shivers like of a chill
The heart the chief primate
To a mind that can only relate
To the soul who has lots its mate

J E Gobbin

Did You Really Love Me?

Did you say you loved me?
All those years ago
When we were just silly teenagers
Always on the go.

And I'm sure you said you'd love me
So many years ago
When you gave me that ring
With the bright diamond's glow.

I believed you, when you said you loved me
On that sunny day in May
When together, we were married
It was such a happy day.

I always knew you loved me
On that glorious joyful day
When our beloved son was born
And you named him 'Ray'.

With sadness, you still said you loved me
When your 'call-up' papers came
And you went away to war
Was it the Middle East or Spain?

I'd hoped we would still be lovers
When we were old and grey
We will be together soon my love
And I can say, 'I truly love you,' on that day.

Shirley Patricia Cowan

The Flower

A radiant flower that needs to bloom
Life is cyclical from the womb to the tomb
Receptive to love from above and around
Lay the seeds to nurture the ground
The sound to hear is a blossom awakening
The scent is so captivating
Olfactory note ancient in mind
The noose on the stem can now unwind
Finally set free please can we gather
To look upon this glorious flower.

Louis Cecile

Lost Heart

You've left me for good
All alone and distraught
Has our love disintegrated?
I perish the thought

A Marine boy in youth
Sampling hardships of war
Only he will remember
The heartache he saw

Our bonds were knotted
So no one could untie
Where did we go wrong?
Why did we have to say goodbye?

Siestas at the seaside
Midnight swims on the beach
Summers cruising in the car
All so far out of reach

Tears, smiles and giggles
With fun photographs
Late night loving calls
With plenty of laughs

Memories that will last
Of a husband just twenty-five
A son to be proud of
And a besotted father when alive

Heather Dickey

Our Second Joy

A second grandchild, once again we are blessed
This time a grandson, another little pest
Now at two years, he's a dear little humbug
Especially when he says, 'A hug please, a hug'
And as with our Ellie, when Samuel comes to stay
Our eyes are wide open, when he's out to play
So daring he is, and with a mind of his own
Mischievously grinning, he's his father's clone
But when the day is over and he is fast asleep
The love we feel for him lies within our hearts, so deep

Val McDermid

Have I Told You I Love You Today?

Have I told you I love you today?
My husband used to say
Before we were even married, he said
I shall tell you every day.

Throughout the years he always did
In sunshine or in rain
We built our lives together
With many joys and a little pain.

The children came, we loved them
And then we let them go
We did our very best for them
Without a lot to show.

The grandchildren came, one, two, three
Each one very different
We brought them into this life of love
And watched them grow, still different.

My husband died very suddenly
A bitter blow to us all
But he walks beside us every day
Still gives us a call.

Have I told you I love you today?
The message it comes loud and clear
I still walk beside you along life's road
Remember, I am still here.

Edna Rudge

I Walked Past Your House

I walked past your house on Saturday afternoon
It was a lovely day in the middle of June
I looked in the window you were sitting there
With your dark brown eyes and cascading hair
I thought to myself, *you look so fine*
One of these days I'm gonna make you mine!
With jet-black hair and complexion so fair
I want you to know I really care
I watch from the street, you I want to meet
I'd love to talk to you, if only you knew.

Frank Tonner

Farewell My Love

Now we must part as time decrees
Feel not my pain of loss dear wife
Our time together was a summer's breeze
Blowing through sense, giving constancy life

Such times I've known since contact made
When young wide eyes poured into mine
Your prisoner taken, had no ransom paid
For that thief called love, I walked the line

Was ever a prize so easily won?
Captured enslaved with only a glance
Tectonic plates rumbled just for fun
When fate offered up fulfilment's chance

No deity or spirit that holds the key
Of Heaven wherein souls finally rest
Will feel they're cheated of entrance fee
As you my love bring only the best

At times if clouds darkened life's pages
You never once left me to face them alone
I drew on your strength, my rock of ages
Was there ever queen, loved more by her drone

These lines are conduit into my heart
Carrying all I hold dear and treasure
Before onward journey to dust, as we part
One kiss on those eyes, closed now forever

Charles Keeble

The Affair

The agony of waiting
Footsteps that are not yours
The fierce anticipating
Through the endless lonely hours
Seconds ticking, minutes dragging
Coffee flowing, patience flagging
Then the meeting wild and thrilling
All my longings now fulfilling
Such a love to only borrow
What the future, what tomorrow?

Sybil Marie Curzon

My Light Has Gone Out

Why did you leave me after sixty-four years?
You left behind loneliness and tears
We have never been very long apart
Your going has left me with a broken heart

The Lord has taken you for a long rest
To a new life where you are now blessed
Thank you for the many years of your deep love
Until I am called to join you in Heaven above

You are so very sadly missed
No more hello or goodnight kiss
We have walked life's path together
Rain or shine whatever the weather

A long and wonderful life we have had
Through ups and downs, through good and bad
When you were my young and beautiful bride
I stood at your side just beaming with pride

Your presence made this world a far better place
You lived a life full of charm and grace
That wonderful smile, that warmed the coldest day
For them to light up my life, now I can but pray

Sixty-four years we were side by side
From the day you said 'I do' as my bride
Mending a broken heart is not easy to do
You go to your rest taking my love with you

Leonard Butler

Love

Shaping, showing, changing love
Keeping, coming, tasting love
Taking, rushing, making love
Moving, hoping, wishing love
Waiting, softening, touching love
Timing, shaping, feeling love
Freeing, moaning, wailing love
Wanting, talking, missing love
Meeting, falling, kissing love
Fearing, failing, choking love.

Lisa Harper-Gough

Aspects Of Love

Without love I would not be here
Thus my words to you are sincere.
Love's indefinable feeling
Has power to send one reeling.

Little girls' love may be equine
For a boy, football is divine.
In each case the passion is strong
It's natural, there's nothing wrong.

Teenage love is far more complex
May involve the opposite sex.
The joys, the hopes are so intense
Sometimes defying common sense.

Adult love embraces it all,
Young gent attends the local ball
And spots a girl he'd eyed before,
Shyly invites her to the floor.

Hours later, ball is over,
He becomes the gallant rover,
Escorts her home, up to the door
Gives her a kiss, please just one more.

After this it becomes the norm
Many courtesies to perform.
He will do anything for her,
One day, 'I love you,' she will purr.

Brian Eley

A Vision Of Venus

She stood revealed,
An undoubted goddess,
Her virgin form unblemished; chaste,
Immune to cruel humanity.
Her face pale and clear,
Like the first days of spring
That cling to winter's chill.
For a while, the darkness shone,
And my whole world shrank
Into the beauty of her eyes.

Mark L Moulds

One Head, One Heart

You said hello, I walked straight past,
You said to blank you wouldn't last,
It wasn't fair on all our friends,
To be civil we should pretend.

I'm always stubborn so I said no,
This was the only way to let go,
Although it didn't feel my heart was having much success
At wanting you any less.

The tension between us was on a high,
Still so in love with you I won't deny,
This was too hard to be around you regularly,
In three weeks I was breaking already.

Then I said sorry, so did you,
We both wanted to work things through,
You told me you loved me and always had,
All through the summer when I was mad.

You held me in your arms just like I'd missed,
It wasn't long before we kissed,
You sent emotions racing through my being,
We together were God's miracle for seeing.

Yet this pain still threatens to return,
To trust again with my heart will I ever relearn?
One head, one heart, the fight within,
So with our love stronger renewed let us begin.

Jennifer Smith

My Family

Your love and support surrounds me
It never lets me down
I know no matter what, you'll always be around
I thank you most sincerely for all that you have done
And praise you so completely because you're the only one
I never had to question your intentions and I hope I never do
Because I know who you are
You're the one I rely on
You're my family
There is nothing more important than you are to me.

Janice Bailey

My Gentle Giant

I want to write a little poem
About my darling John
He stands apart from other men
Who have come and gone

He's good at cleaning windows
Cookers, sinks and doors
And if you ask him nicely
He'll even clean your floors

Cuddles in the morning
Cuddles in the night
John Spiers likes his cuddles
And holds me oh so tight!

He says he's always loved me
From the moment that we met
A nicer chap I haven't known
Nor loved as much, as yet

John asked me to marry
To become his bonnie bride
I said, 'Yes,' and promised
That I'd stay by his side

Soon will come the happy day
When we will pledge our troth
We trust that God will guide our steps
And richly bless us both.

Rita Spiers

Tender Love

Love me tender, love me true
This is all I ask of you
When I hold you in my arms
You just fill me with your charms
First a kiss, then a cuddle
Puts my poor mind in a muddle.
I just want to hold you tight
And keep loving you with all my might.
So love me tender, love me true
This is all I ask of you.

Pat Adams

Rainy Days

When it rains I think of you
And all the pain I put you through

I'm sorry that I made you cry
And I left, without saying goodbye

I went with another 'cause you weren't there
But he treated me badly, he just didn't care

I was blind and could not see
How much you really needed me.

Now I sit upon my windowpane
And watch the clouds build up again

The rain falls down just like my tears
The rooms are cold without you here

My heart is racked in so much pain
I'd give anything to have you back again

Even the weeping willow cries for me
She can see I'm in such misery

I know I was wrong, can you forgive me
You are the only man for me.

Never again will I hurt you so
I'd rather die than let you go.

Please come back and free me from this pain
So it won't hurt anymore to look at the rain.

Jean Lilian Bramhill

For My Wife

Tonight, you are the queen of candlelight,
Daughter of Neptune,
Flung from the silver-streaked lining of a wave
To the welcoming palm of the Earth.

You are the body of the impalpable flame of desire.

The seedling swell to please you,
The seas swoop and bow to praise you,
All life strains from its tenements,
To be placed, if only for a second,
Beneath your gaze.

Sean Bennett

Recollections . . .

When 'ere I first sighted her
I noticed her large blue eyes
Amidst a dear small face
And a smile that enlightened dark skies.

Admiring her when glimpsed now and then,
My feelings held back at distance,
Inherent shyness made for awkwardness,
Until, at last, it deemed time to advance;
Seize the moment
Leave nothing to chance,
Walking her homewards one evening
Led to a lifetime's romance.

We experienced life's highs and lows,
Sometimes, temporarily, we fought,
All this throughout those times
Parting company was brief in thought.

During our long life together
Life's been good . . . and not so good.
But life was sorted and there it lay,
We moved on . . . as we should.

My emotions are as loving now as the beginning,
'Won't last,' said the condemnables with sneers.
We have proved them wrong . . .
This year, 2006, we've been wed 56 years . . .

J Fred Jackson

Yesterday

Oh how I wish I could bring back yesterday
Yesterday of years gone by when you two were still here
So happy, so true, the two of you, we didn't need to cry.

But those days are gone now, you have both been taken away
To that lovely Heaven in the sky, I wish I could bring back yesterday
Yesterday of years gone by.

When we were so happy with you both here, we didn't need to cry
But now you are both gone, Mum and Dad
The tears still flow on and on
Today, tomorrow, yesterday, always, now you have both gone.

Trudie Sullivan

Here You Bring Me A Bouquet

Here you bring me a bouquet
With drip drops twinkling
On the velvet texture
During the dullest moment
Of my soul over the toils of life
Bitterness entwined
Within such a hue of dawn
Folded by numerous havocs
That beget our weary bodies
With crimson wrinkles
To hovel in an air of indifferences
While the anguish of loss
Patters and swirls
Before it falls
To the ground

For a feeling cuddly
Like the touch
Of roses manifold
I have foreseen the craft
Of a fine flowerman
At the sight of such
Flawless passion
Lively presented
In a rapturous mood
Of love.

David Lin

The First Flower After The Flood

You're the first flower after the flood,
Taste my lips and be my blood,
I see you and I can't stop blushing,
Is it love or am I crushing?
Every time I hear your name,
I cry and cry and cry in pain.
When but when will you be mine,
And then the whole world will be fine.
I've spent all of my love on you alone,
Take control, and rule my throne.

Jodie Hassell (13)

I Love You

A dozen red roses could not say it.
The petals would not be as delicate and beautiful.
The colour would not be as bright.
The thorns would not pierce deep enough.
The fragrance would not be as poignant,
evocative of joys and contentment a rose could never know.
The stem would not be as strong and long lasting.
The bouquet would not demonstrate the beauty I see in you.
The arrangement would pale into insignificance
compared to all you are.

The only thing you have in common with the rose
is that God made you both
But
Only you were named the Crown of His Creation
Only you are called to be with Him in the secret place
Only you will receive a new name
Only you are inscribed on the palm of His hand
Only you tug at His heartstrings when you are hurt and in pain.

So I can say, 'I love you'
and the words will pale like the fading rose
yet my love will remain.

No matter what we face, or where we go
my call will always be for you to remember
I love you.

Susan Smith

Canine Love

He was my first love,
A curly black and brown
Bundle of fur.
Bright eyes,
Wobbly legs,
His sheer joy of living,
His warm and cuddly body.
A long swipe of his tongue
For a kiss.
My confidant and friend,
My canine love - Bobby.

J Erskine

What's Happened To My Wife?

What is this I see? I suddenly jump for glee
Wow wee! The vision before me has got to be every man's cup of tea
Then suddenly this girl looks up and our eyes meet
She holds my gaze as she walks toward me crossing the street
Yep! The rest is history, we married and settled down
And in no time at all I started feeling like a clown.
'What's this?' I say. 'Dirty dishes? No dinner today?
This is not what I expected I just can't stay.'
'This is not what I'm used to, this is not what it's about
I'm sorry dear lady, but I want out!'
Her eyes mist over as she looks back at me.
'Oh really honey, what do you see?
Cos when I look in the mirror I see an old lady looking back at me.'
'What are you talking about woman? For God's sake get a grip
I don't know what you're on, but it's been a long trip.'
'Darling, dearest, honey pie,' she says
'I have had two babies, my breasts are no longer mine
My waist is not what it used to be and just look at my behine
Nothing about me feels the same, I just want to hide
The fact that I've kept going, dear, is the children and my pride
There has got to be more to life than just the way I cook
And surely honey dear, you married me for more than my look?'
Suddenly I see me again, that young man in my head
And I remember clearly that I didn't marry this dear lady
Just to get her into bed.

Joy Elaine Mendez

For Jean, My Wife

From the first kiss in the morning
To the last kiss at night,
I love you,
For every step I take without you dear,
I feel my heart would break.
I need every precious minute
To prove my love for you
And with each passing year,
The flame of love grows higher,
And when we pass into each our Heaven,
My love will stay with you.

George Till

To Tie The Knot Or Not

The proverb says a rolling stone never gathers moss
So when is the time to rectify and so redeem this loss
To cast the anchor overboard and make a firm foundation
To put aside your wandering ways and home in on your station
And then to say you are here to stay, you'll go no more a-roving
No more doing as you please or risk some disapproving.
You'll miss those hectic days unleashed, not having need to answer
To anyone except yourself, to your tune you the dancer
So think again, my travelled friend, is this the price to pay?
To clip your wings and other things on this deciding day.
Do you want to gather moss unlike a rolling stone
And settle down with loads of dross and say all this I own
Then bovine beast-like tethered up, chewing on your cud
Until your friends of long ago say, 'Who's that stick in the mud?'
Yes! Think again, my doubting friend, before you cast the die
That patterns all your future days, before you learn to sigh
Of how life was and still could be, if just a little wiser
You have a taste of 'settled down' just an appetiser
Enough to learn what life is like tied by an apron string
And to know with just a quick slipknot you can prolong your fling
This undeciding unnerves me, I feel the leash is tightening
My freedom feels in jeopardy, it's just a little frightening
To tie the knot or not, takes some contemplating
So to ease the strain, I'm off again
Round the wide, wide world - deliberating.

V Clarke-Irons

Untitled

A stolen glance across a room
Our eyes met, were held
For a fleeting moment, linked endurably.
I wanted to stay forever gazing at my love.
He rose and came to steal a kiss
Not with lips, but a caressing glance.
Soon our hands were joined, fingers intertwined,
Like our hearts beating together.
I am at great peace in his nearness
Safe and satisfied to know he loves me,
And that all around know it too.

Patricia Laing

Music

Music is the food of love
Played by one and all
So mine I play for you my love
While waiting for your call
I've always loved pianos
Though never learned to play
I just pop on the records
They have so much to say
Since you have left me darling
I've learnt to love to the sax
It seems to bring you nearer
To the day when we are back
Together again once more
Sometimes I play the music soft
Other times very loud
When pressing down on me
I have an awful big black cloud
Then when the cloud is lifted
It is in my head I see
That you are not so very far
And ready to collect me
So my music plays a big, big part
In expressing the feelings that I show
And it's only you my darling
That sets my heart aglow.

Daphne Fryer

Horizons

I dream a dream of you and me
On an ocean, out to sea.
Day by day we play our parts,
No one ever knowing
What's really in our hearts.
The wind is strong, the sails open wide,
Will we ever reach the other side
Where the box can be opened
And we can run free,
In that field on the cliff edge
Looking out to sea?

Julie-Elizabeth Haslam

Love Of My Daughter

Who's the one who understands?
When I'm worried takes my hand
Tells me, Mum, you're looking grand
My daughter.

Who is it that seems to know
When I'm blue and feeling low?
Then says, Mum, I love you so
My daughter.

Who can chatter on no end
Sometimes drives me round the bend?
But will always be my best friend
My daughter.

Who can all the world beguile
With the sweetness of her smile?
Who makes everything worthwhile?
My daughter.

I have sons who love me too
But who can read me like a book?
She just takes one look
My daughter.

Who says with genuine pride
Mum, I will always be by your side
My daughter.

Margaret Kent

Battling For Your Love

Broken by the waves of despair
Overwhelmed, shattered and done
Long lives the inkling
Of that sense of sinking
Deeper into decay

Noteworthy contact
Of your presence and touch
Affection, fondness and lust
Long lives the pining
And lonesome yearning
Battling for your love.

Daniel James Suttill

Roses For Barbara

I gave Barbara roses
That summer's day
With grace, she accepted
Lovingly to say,
She placed those roses
In sweet array
Those roses I gave Barbara
That summer's day.

With memories so dear
Ne'er to fade
'Neath shady bower
As 'oft we would lay,
Radiantly they bloom
Fain do I say
Those roses I gave Barbara
That summer's day.

Where life has its calling
From whence you may stray
From dawn to their evenings
Come sunshine or rain,
'Tis with love, joy and happiness
I lovingly gave
Those roses for Barbara
That summer's day.

Terrence St John

Love

Love is walking down life's roads which wind along the way
Love is a hug from a true, faithful, loving friend
Love is the patience of a soul, which is wide and thoughtful
Love is the touch of a hand of a friend, who is sad.
Love is a thoughtful gift to show you care.
Love is silently to kneel in a prayer which is unselfish.
Love is sometimes having to be strong and true.
Love is correcting and teaching with our Love above
Love is the gift from our Father in Heaven, which nobody needs words for.
Love is always around us if we just bother to seek and see.

Jennifer Lowe

The Test Of Love

Dare I say I love you, would you prove me true?
I have always held respect and adored just you.
It was yours to test and wonder how greatly I admired,
Your manly grace and masculine charm, would surely not disgrace.
Even at an early age I knew you were meant for me,
Although you sought other pleasures, truthfully we agreed.
Remaining constant companions, 'twas without a doubt,
Secretly I wove my web love helped this situation out.

Unsuspecting is your attitude, this make me at a loss,
I thought you would be romantically happy, but you appear so cross.
Having taken far too much for granted he relates,
He is off to woo another and have me, poor soul replaced.
Well to think I wasted all that time thinking he would be mine,
He says he appreciates my company as a friend, only perhaps divine
I being disappointed, as I had all planned for we two to survive
In our own love land.

Gradually I have edged away and left him to his own devices,
He knows that this has affected me but does nothing about it,
Soon he will be forgotten as the many years slip by,
I think I have wept buckets as I am now high and dry.
Finding another true and tender fellow I have placed him on my list,
He came first class, so intellectual far above the rest.
We married and settled down and raised a family
I dote on my loving husband, he is so extraordinary.

Ronald Hiscoke

Fulfilling Ways

Love is tender, love is kind,
Love is a deep, deep expression of the human soul.
Will care for one that has a need,
Will not need to boast or brag,
Love is long suffering,
Love is gentle like a mother with her child,
Holds the power to keep anger out of sight,
Love will embrace all that is good, all that's kind.
When put to the test, will never fail.
Our world would be a better place to both live and dwell
If we all could learn to love on Planet Earth. Amen.

Rowland Scannell

Goodbye Romeo

It was the kiss that never was,
naïvety because,
seventeen, he wasn't to know
a 'goodbye Romeo';
all alone they found themselves,
hanging on that pause -
things the memory shelves?
yet still today explores . . .

Would he have changed anything
if he'd have lit her cigarette,
ignored her wedding ring,
and have those lips met?
She stood there, sensuality,
he was blind,
unaware of his sexuality,
migrant of mind.

They were the lovers that never were,
and ghosts may confer,
over what was provoked,
long since choked,
but she never made the move,
and he was green,
maybe there was nothing to prove,
as love never had been . . .

Andrew Gruberski

Bill

Twelve months have gone since you passed away.
Bill, life is not the same, I miss you dear.
My love goes out to you each day.
There are times I feel you very near.
Memories of the things we did
Come flooding back again.
I see your smile and feel the pain
The tender love you always gave
That still comes back to me beyond the grave.
One day we will meet again once more
And be together as before.

R P Candlish

Bram

Darling this and darling that
How cheap endearments call.
But will she be your darling
When backs are to the wall?
Bikini babes and busty blondes
Give lustful thoughts to men
But will they still be loving
When we lose our basic yen?

Just one test beats all the rest,
Does she love you as she loves life?
Through joy and woe, now this
I know is the credo of my wife.
She answers to a nickname,
I simply call her 'Bram'
But I rarely need to call her
Cos she's close by where I am.

I still gaze at beauties,
A saint is what I'm not,
But I say a prayer to Heaven
In thanks for what I've got,
And when we come to leave this Earth
To find St Peter's grace,
I've asked the Lord so many times
To book a double place.

Denis M Pentlow

The View Of Love

I compare thee to a masterpiece
Pure light and spirit a magnificent view
Your happy smile and kindness fills me with joy
'Such a smile'
And -
I cannot live a life of loneliness, no - never
To feel discontented, unfulfilled, sleep or worry
I dream of you!
I have known a kind friend, a warmer word
And your beautiful eyes touch my soul.

I look for you, a friend that fills me with excitement -
A shy person, yet elegant and you have a voice
Of the morning dove - even an angel singing!
I would ask you for one kiss
I would ask you for one hug
If you were to ask me, I would give you a kiss
A stolen moment.

I compare thee to a masterpiece, snow falling,
Thunder thrashing - love's lasting dream
My wish would be that you would feel the same
I compare thee to a masterpiece,
Would you compare me to the brightest sunbeam?
Igniting, smouldering, stirring passion, 'waiting'.
All I ask for is thee.

Carole Morris

To My Latest Love

'I love you,'
It's just that simple,
I love your beautiful smile
And the way your eyes twinkle,
I love seeing you happy,
It makes me happy too,
But whenever you're down,
I'll be there for you.

Girl, I'll love you always,
Now and forever,
No matter the time, place,
Season or weather,
Good times and bad,
Sunshine and rain,
I'll share it all with you,
From laughter to pain.

I want to be near you,
As much as I can,
In your arms, by your side,
Or holding your hand,
It makes me so happy,
To think of *(insert latest love interest here)* and Matt,
Cos I really do love you,
It's as simple as that!

Matthew R Worthington

Memories Are All I Have

The cruel way you treated me
I cannot understand;
Your love for me was precious
As we walked hand in hand.
My love for you, forever
I'll hold within my heart
And wish you could return it,
And of my life be a part.

Our lives should be together
Not many miles apart,
And I'll never, never know
How you could break my heart.
Our lives were fused together
For thirty years and more,
Giving you my life, my love
As I never gave before.

And as we've been together
We've loved and laughed and cried
We worked things out together -
Our feelings did not hide.
Now I'm just left with memories,
The joyful and the sad,
But most of all I'll treasure
The happy times we had.

Anne Gray

In Perpetuam Rei Memoriam

Time cannot steal my memories,
my treasures of the past,
the way we ran and laughed and sang,
the dances that we danced,
the gentle, caring feel of you
is locked within my arms,
my tears taste of sunny days,
your fire still keeps me warm

and how can I forget the hands
that so well matched my own
as fingers met and intertwined
to tell me I was home?
When every glistening sunset
reminds me you were mine,
you'll always be beside me
till time has outlived time.

Years will not dim the flame of you
alive within my heart,
I'll keep it burning always
though we were torn apart.
Memories are like the stars
they never cease to shine
and such a little thing as death
cannot extinguish mine.

Valerie Sutton

Ballyconneely Beach

I am the shore forever lapping up your waves
taking for granted that you are always there
assuming my right to be forever kissed.
Why should your jewel exist
to moisten my Sahara
through the turquoise of your lip?
You glisten with rays the greyness of my coast
Oh to drink in this sunlit scene, but, what is more, to sip

Still you come, constantly, wave on continuous wave,
with gestures of endearment drawn bottomless from love
I wait, dumb, to be cosseted,
dry, lifeless until your calm embrace
comes and keeps giving, interface
with my long, thin, yellow line,
whose mouth is always open
to taste your special wine

My grains are baptized in the ocean of your care
bathed when they are hardened by the coarsening of soles.
Yours is the shooshing calm of an eternal flow
which gently waters seaweed, stones
in insistent, soothing hum
that outlasts enduring pain
My desert through your soft caress
has become fertile again

David Speed

Remembered Love

Embedded deep within the contours of my head
Are dreams and memories of what might have been
The scent, the feel of saturated skin
Full of love drawn from the heart within.
Bodies lain close upon warm sand at night
Fulfillment underneath the velvet night-time sky
Replete, content beside you there to lie
Storing up memories for a life apart
Embedded deep within the contours of my heart.

Where are you now? Where did you go? When you left me
Did you remember? Do you relive old memories?
Or did you squander all those nights of bliss?
Surrendering them as lightly as you did a kiss.
Will ever time converge, your time and mine
A sound, a scent, will they rejoin you to me?
On leaving this world will we ever meet again
And will the memories we shared be carried on?
As now they are, forever in my brain.

Life passes on, the years forever go
Tears, joy and love, life's constant ebb and flow.
Yet I have been content with my life's allocated love
He and I have a long lifetime shared
But even so within the contours of my brain
A sudden image springs; from long ago, of one for whom I cared . . .

Pamela A Campbell

Love Is The Wonder Of You

(Our favourite song)

Four little letters that mean so much
Holding hands, a tender kiss, a gentle touch,
You were so young when we had to part
I thought I would die too, of a broken heart.

Though I can no longer see you
I know you are by my side,
To listen, guide and comfort me
Just as when I was your bride.

The children have long since grown
And have families of their own,
I tell them all about you
How good and kind you were, handsome too.

Our children, grandchildren and great grandchildren
Have brought me so much joy
My heart swells with pride for each girl and boy,
Their love knows no bounds
(Though sometimes they can be little hounds!)

So many years have passed since you had to go,
But I've learnt to live with my hopes and fears
And you will always be my dearest of dears,
My Gentle Giant our love will go on forever.
For nothing can break the bond we have, ever.

Joy Hanlon

Just For The Love Of Duncan

How many ways do I love thee?
More than I can ever say
The moment I saw you was my moment
Across a crowded room, your clear blue eyes
Looked up at me and loved me that first second,
My whole being in that moment came alive.

That moment at the alter was my moment.
My heartbeat drowned the organ, would I cry?
I am yours and you are mine now
Yes beloved,
For better or for worse now till we die.

Lying in your arms must be my moment.
Harmony together, you and I.
Could there ever be again that perfect moment?
Joyous love and starlight shining from your eyes.

The first of our four daughters was my moment.
New pain transfused to joy and raucous cries.
They're wrapped within my arms, my lovely babies
Looking at me with their father's eyes.

Every morning I see you is our moment,
Each day, new joy beginning, new surprise.
I love you now, and always will remember
The first time that I looked into your eyes.

Kristin MacEwan

My Love

I love, I love you, every day of the year,
I love you, I love you, tho' you're not here.
Our time was so brief, like a will o' the wisp,
But my heart skips a beat
Remembering your kiss.

When I hear our tune, I dance all alone.
Pretending you're holding me, as once you had done.
Memories are sweet, and never will fade,
Tho' times they can hurt, when our tune is played.

I love you, I love you, and always will,
Nothing can change that, I love you still.

E M Pace

Brief Encounter

One day a stranger,
one day a friend,
words exchanged,
kindness to lend.

Love blossomed, it grew,
we talked, we loved
and then we knew
this passage through life
is Heaven for few.

What a wonderful man,
and I, who am I?
I do not know myself,
I wonder why?

A faraway female lost with his love;
I have prayed to God in Heaven above
that he shall find a peace within
to live his life . . .
no need to sin!

Such a brief encounter came our way,
'Was it to be O Lord?' I pray
I look around and quietly say,
'He must go this way, I must go mine.'
A brief encounter . . . but so divine!

Margaret R Bevan

Last Love

Who knows where the seeds of the rye grass fly?
Another season's summer will smile upon their falling.
And so, for a hundred summers more,
The ever-widening traces of this morning's random seeding
Will rise and fade in distant future fields.

What, then, will be remembered of our love?
Who could recall the things we dreamed of?
Those thousand moments from which we built our secret world?
We smiled to know that only we had found some lasting bond
In love which swiftly-hurrying Age could not embitter.

Yet only a poet's futile earnestness can claim
In foolish arrogance that any love can be eternal.
Death will never be defied.
The smothering hand of time will soon extinguish
All we call so dear.

But, like these errant seedlings trembling on the searching wind,
Our kind and true regard may, through example,
Journey through fields of time
To reappear in lives a hundred summers on.

When, in some far-off sunlit afternoon
A girl's eyes smile, as yours do now at me,
We must have no regrets that she will never know
That once, a love like this I had for you.

David Ryan

Battered

After many years
And many months
And many hours,
I was in a fix
I could not fix
With a bunch of flowers.
I missed the kiss.
I kissed the mist.
I kicked the powers.
I drank the moat.
I grabbed my throat.
I fled the towers.

You say enough
And think too much
Till nothing matters.
There's nothing left.
It will not touch,
It's left in tatters.
There is no flame,
There is no blame.
The ash has scattered.
There was a trust.
It just went bust.
It was too battered.

Ian Davey

Love Is . . .

Love is a kiss
Love is a wish
Love is bliss.

Hearts beat quick
Stomachs feel sick

You may walk on air
Or sit in despair

Love is hard work
You must not shirk

Love is delicious
Love is capricious

If it's offered beware
With your heart take care

Love is a cheat
Love is a treat

Love is confusion
Love is profusion

If you are tempted to fall
It might be wise to recall

Love is illusion
With no certain conclusion.

Ron Vickerson

Wait For Me

Once was my heart on fire, but now it's chilled,
Once did my pulse grow fast, 'tis sluggish now and stilled.
The sight of you once filled my soul with joy
But now you've gone my love, my golden boy.
My days are long and weary, I'm getting old, that's true
And how I long for death to be once more with you.
The flowers bloom each spring, the sun each day doth rise,
But I remember when my sun shone from our eyes,
What raptures did we share when you and I were young,
What joyous mingling of limb and tongue.
And soon my love we shall together be,
Oh, wait for me, please wait for me.

Dorothy Beaumont

Our World

Walk you by the harbour light
We talk all through the night
Feelings are concealed
Every breath I take with you
We're gonna see it through
All to be revealed.

There's a mist from the sea
Alone just you and me
So deep inside
Angry by frustration
So full of emotion
Time to confide.

Can't explain the way we feel
Waited for the scars to heal
Memories are revived
Look up at the stars above
No one can deny our love
We have survived.

Our world, time to analyse,
Our world, time to realise,
Our world, is it right or wrong?
Our world, is it weak or strong?
Our world.

Paul Hobbs

Mistress

She is a girl who meets my needs
A thrill of erotica on the side, when I need it
She is the Devil in disguise, a temptation I can't resist

My heart is pounding
Money spent, well worth it
Feelings are growing strong

Yet I have a family
A wife and children
A ring on my left hand

She is my mistress
Who I offer the world to.

Darren Lee

Millie

Love of my life is my dog Millie
Does that sound silly?
Come sun, rain or hail
Every morning she greets me
with a wagging tail.

On our walks by the sea
She is great company for me,
People stop to chat
And give her a friendly pat,
With me pass the time of day
Without her they would have
just gone on their way.

When I am in my chair
On my knee she sits.
Fills the empty room with her snores
Does it matter she covers me with hairs?
Then she gently taps me with her paws
'Is it teatime yet?'

For you see I am on my own
With joy she fills my home
She is such a faithful friend
And that is how my poem about Millie
will end.

E Long

For Colin

'Listen my love,' his mother wrote,
'You're going to be upset,
He died at 3 o'clock today.'
'You'll forget,' they said, 'forget.'
'I can't say anymore, my love
I can't believe it yet.
His last words were of you my love
Perhaps you will forget.'
It's sixty-nine years since he died
And eighty since we met
How many more years must I wait
To finally forget?

Rae Alderson

So I Can Love Again

I know you're out there somewhere
The past I can't forget,
Hanging like a cobweb
With threads of regret.
I wish I could reach them
Break but every one,
Watch them fall and disappear
Along with a heart that's gone,
Out of my life forever
Yet remains tightly bound,
Deep within the depths of me
Where it can never be found,
By anyone who may search my heart
And the secrets that lie there,
This hidden place inside of me
Filled with sorrow and despair.
Within yesterday's shadows
That haunt my sleepless nights,
I think of you often
As my memories take flight.
So breaks the dawn of another day,
And with it brings more pain.
Will God not take the past away?
So I can love again.

Lisa Jane Mills

For My Husband

It is funny how time can mend a heart
That is torn and broken in two
The heartache and sadness will soon be gone
And that is because of you.
You picked me up when I was down
And the sun came shining through
You made me smile instead of frown
And I give my thanks to you.
To find someone that I can trust
And we'll grow old together
I know that you will never leave
And you'll love me forever.

Maureen Baxter

Love

A touch that tingles,
Words to hurt,
Moments of passion,
A manner, curt.
A crescent moon
In a starlit sky,
A song to make
Two lovers sigh.
Loneliness
Beyond compare.
Happiness, then
Deep despair.
Floods of tears,
Broken hearts
Because two souls
Are rent apart.
If this be love,
Why do we glow
When Cupid aims
His fatal bow
For 'tis like torture
War and strife,
Not the mainstay
Of each life.

Florence Barnard

A Love Returned

With a love of old I am now entwined
One who was never far from my conscious mind
With serene beauty and mindful dress
I treasure her loving and thoughtful caress
Having pondered deeply should I lose this love
The answer came from up above
Should I propose on our away day
The dice now cast called for a holiday
So with thoughts conveyed and in gleeful acceptance
I await in patient expectation of the consequence
A love I lost twelve years past
Has now come back and hopefully my recompense.

William Ryan

To The Unknown Self

So much talked about, you should be well-known,
Though we're often deceived by a passion to own.
You dissemble to flatter and strike up a chord
Then gamble freely what your heart will afford.
Whatever the cause, the ideal, the sport
You encourage, embolden, inspire and support.
No servant to reason, though you'll take its advice,
You'll dare anything at a throw of the dice.
For your tender feelings the poor sick-at-heart
Would enslave themselves in a world set apart;
But the strong, the noble and generous of mind
Know how fickle you are when you're kind.
In the shapeless void of everyday care
You create with art where I wonder and stare;
But best of all, when I tire of this life,
You bring me to Earth and free me from strife.
Then shall I win your genius in time
And what achieve by reason and rhyme?
Yet how can I doubt your desire for the good
When the spirit called Love is infused in the blood?
So wreath me in smiles and dark conscience banish
And let the pale ghosts of fantasy vanish.
Give me your truth whence reality springs
And I will fly through hardships on wings!

Brian Green

Repeat Performance

It was your warm brown eyes that did it -
Across the room they trapped me - but I hid it!
You asked me for a dance and I agreed -
Those eyes, that smile, made me weak-kneed.
Just think - that moment, half a century ago, was all it took
One smile, one dance and I was on your hook.
Now all I've left is your firm, promised word
That, at the time I hardly even heard
You said, if you died first, you'd wait
For me at good St Peter's Gate.
Such a long wait, love, that I know you'll say . . .
'Late for your funeral - just like our wedding day!'

Joan Evans

In The Summer Sunlight

In the summer sunlight
Come to me, stay with me
Here I sit so longingly
Underneath the willow tree
Where the sun-kissed waters glide
Let us stroll side by side
Tears and fears we'll override
Because we're so in love
Upon a leafy bough
Whilst we're embracing
We shall hear the sweet thrush singing
Giving out his lovely melody
As I hold our sweetness
Close to me
I'll run my fingers through
Your silken tresses
Thrill to all your warm caresses
Soft we will pray
That God will bless us
When I make you mine
When the evening shadows steal
We won't need to conceal
Just exactly how we feel
Because we're so in love.

Terence Leslie Iceton

Love

Can anyone tell me
Does true love exist?
I feel rather strange
So, if it persists
I'll go round to the doctor's
To see what he says
A second opinion
I think - always pays!
Then I'll wait a while
For his diagnosis
Meanwhile, I'll work on
My own prognosis!

Erica Simons-Croft

What Is Love?

A welcome warm cuppa
On that cold frosty morn
That tiny unclenched fist
Of your new first born
The chin on his chest
Says he's ready to talk
Wet nose on your hand
Means it's time for a walk
Return of the hero
From his war-stricken hell
The welcome home party
Family and friends wish him well
Linking arms with the frail one
You help cross the road
Not one minute forgetting
The day we all will grow old
That broken heart
For a loved one passed on
Teardrops remind you
Tell you they've gone
Comfort and contentment
Are all of the above
So in my opinion
That's what's called love.

Dawn Williams-Sanderson

Unconditional Love

Unconditional love does not see the nose out of joint,
Or the sagging chin
Or the ever increasing foibles of the maturing process.
It sees simply the bright shining aura that is life -
The burning soul that makes everybody, important or unimportant,
A star.
That it is sometimes unrequited does not seem to matter,
It is less complicated that way.
When one enters the realms of performance-based affection,
Then it becomes complicated.
On the other hand, one sees the potential for great happiness
And exciting rushing fulfilment.

Jethro Dykes

The Parting

I knew this moment had to arrive,
I knew this day must dawn,
And I had to be strong to survive
The trauma of this morn.
In my mind I've gone over it all;
You stood in stark relief
Against the light and I looked appalled,
Brimming with disbelief.
My eyes pricked and smarted, and blinking
The telltale tears away,
I stood my ground firm without shrinking,
But fool heart did betray.
It pounded hard in my chest and throat,
I thought that you must hear,
Sweet peace and tranquillity I sought,
But all is lost I fear.
The tears well and cascade down my cheek
Like a huge dam unstopp'd.
I had not wanted to appear weak,
But my façade I'd dropp'd.
I had intended to be so brave,
To smile with empathy,
But needs I find me a small dark cave
To hide from sympathy.

Gwendoline Douglas

Time Gone By

Oh where are you now and how have you been
Oh why are you always still in my dreams
It seems like a lifetime since I saw you last
But I am always thinking about my past
All I ever wanted was to share your life
All I ever dreamed of was to be your wife
But that will never happen now for you never knew
Just how much you meant to me and you still do
I have never wanted anybody else
That is why now I'm all by myself
I was in my teens when I first saw you
Now I have my bus pass, I guess you do too

Eileen Kyte

Everlasting Gift

What a bonus it has paid
That first warmth of love,
For fifty years it cocooned us,
Made reunions after partings
Like our very first meeting.
The family that we raised
Simply enlarged love's range
First our young embraced
Our love and care for parents,
Then it was their turn
To bring new faces to the fold.
How lucky we were in their choices
They too added to their number,
No less than seven joined our ranks.
What a joy to see them grow,
Offering our love to embrace
The times of celebration,
And share their times of sadness:
When half my love seemed lost
At the time of your leaving,
I found it still with me -
For you live on in all we've built,
Evident in looks, in character,
And in God's gift of family love.

Di Bagshawe

The Button

Adventure's calling out my name, it's holding out a hand
Now you see my darling, why the button must be found
I wish that I could find it, I wish it wasn't there
I've been looking for a long time, I know it's here somewhere
I'll turn it off, take it out and throw it in the air
I'll stand and watch as it explodes without a single care
The button's red and really worn, the writing's almost gone
'Self Destruct' is what it used to say, press as often as you want
You'll guess that I have used it, maybe once or twice
When someone gets too close to me or takes me by surprise
But now it's time to close it down, throw caution to the wind
To open up this heart of mine and let adventure in

Lesley Anderson

Memories

(Written for our Golden Wedding March 26th 2005. My dear husband, deceased August 28th 2007)

We had the passion and the joy and the tears,
Now, together still, we face the twilight years
Your memory is dim, your hearing's hard
You say, 'I love you,' still.

I say, 'Remember when . . . ?'
You say, 'When was that?'
But you remembered when we wed,
With all the world before us
And the incredible joy of sharing births.

It was so long ago, yet yesterday,
When we walked on mountains
Or ran laughing in the rain.

Of course, we had our pain
And argued greatly, now and then
But we both kept our marriage vows.

Old age does weary us indeed
I can hardly walk at times
And suffer pain and sheer frustration.

Then you say, 'Shall I make the tea?'
And smile and all is well.

Betty Shipway

Sorry

If only we could talk and talk,
then I wouldn't seem such a dork.
I engaged my mouth before my brain,
and left our bond with quite a strain.
Those words were spoken without a care
- I didn't know that you were there,
you came from behind, I did not know,
but I shouldn't have uttered what made you sore.
It's too late now, the words are out,
if I understand you, there is no doubt
that if I say sorry, a thousand times,
will you forgive me for my crimes?

Warren Fraser

To Margaret On The 'A' Side

The boughs of the larch trees dance in the breeze
Tall flowers sway to its rhythm
Is it the same breeze that once caressed us years ago?

It could have travelled around the world
So many times since those days
When it used to lift your curls, but now you're gone.

Sometimes I think I'll phone
Then realise you'll not be there
You have a life now, all your own
While we still live on the 'Flip Side'.

The loss I feel now is so hard to bear
It seems to get more every day
Would you mind if I met someone I could love to help to take
This pain away?

The gift would be if she could love me too
And unlock the tenderness and love I feel
For so many things in life, it's people, music, nature
And the stars.

You've told me in a dream how close you are
I know, for I feel the same in places we have been
I loved you so, and however much I try,
It's hard to keep this paper dry.

Cyril Payne

Remember Me With Love

One day when it is time to say goodbye
I will look up and reach towards the sky.
For my spirit soon will be free
To fly away like a bird that is me.

With the sea beneath and the sky so blue
Do not be unhappy with what you have to do,
Just lift me up and say goodbye
I will not leave you, I have not died.

You will always see me if you gaze out to sea,
Away in the distance, that is where I will be,
You can talk to me and tell me what you want me to hear,
You may not see me, but I will listen, I am quite near.

I may not stand at your side
But I will help you, comfort you and be your guide.
I am happy, you must be too,
Just do your best in all you do.

I loved you all so very much,
I hope your hearts I may have touched.
I love the cliffs, the sea, the sand,
As I leave you now for another land.

Goodbye to everyone I have ever known,
I thank you all for the love you have shown.

Chris Gardner

Sally

I have a friend, we've shared our lives
for many happy years,
Rarely has there been cross words,
never any tears.
We enjoy each other's company,
more than words can tell,
Our love is just like man and wife,
or that of boy for girl.

She stays at home while I'm at work,
and never does complain,
If I come in a little late;
because I've missed my train.
We go to bed together, when all is
safely locked,
But not before we've had a walk,
then watched the old square box.

Sally is no lady, as you have surely guessed,
She's just a little mongrel bitch,
one of the very best.
We're getting on in years now,
me and my old Sal',
But never have I had before,
a finer little pal.

Peter Mahoney

Tsundere Translation

You speak a secret language
only I can translate.

I'm cold
(let me sleep in your bed)
Get off me!
(never let go)
I hate it when you do that
(how do you *know* to do that?)
Stop saying embarrassing things!
(I want to hear more)
I don't care if you leave.
(why am I crying?)
I don't care if you die
(my whole body feels cold)
You're not important.
(you're everything)
I hate you
(I love you)
. . . Why are you still here?

Others don't realise
who you really are.
That's okay.
I want to be the only one.

Kathleen Ingleby

The Love Of My Life

(To my wife, Mary, happy 30th wedding anniversary 21/7/09)

Love is not a four-letter word
It's a magical feeling, something is stirred
From inside your body, if you're young or old
It's the same for us all, no need to be told
You get all the butterflies deep in your belly
When you meet 'the one', your legs turn to jelly
Is there such a thing as love at first sight?
There was for me, she shone like a light
It might be different for you, who knows
But you'll get the same feeling, from your head to your toes
No, love is not just a four-letter word
It's an emotional feeling that has to be shared
With the one you love, from start to finish
So don't let your love ever start to diminish
Love with your heart and soul all the time
If you don't do this, you're committing a crime
You love your kids, your parents too
But not in the same way that 'I love you'
I may not say it, it may not show
So I've written it down for the world to know
The last 30 years with Mary, my wife
Soulmate, best friend and 'the love of my life'.

Neil Duffy

Love Is . . .

Love is powerful
Love is strong
Love is blinding
Love can be wrong

Love is surprising
Love is open
Love is destroying
Love can be broken

What is love?
Why do we seek?
How do we find it?
How do we keep it?

Katherine Bowers

My Everything

You hold me, I melt in your embrace
The smile that lights up your gorgeous face
Could I ever do without your kiss?
Not me, I live for your caress
Without you I'd struggle through each day
Just your presence takes my fears away

Never stray from me, I want you near
You're forever there to dry my tear
How could I cope without your counselling?
Could a bird survive without flying
Or a rose without loving care?
My all with you I want to share

You're my strength, my rock, my everything
I hunger for the love you always bring
Beside me stay, don't leave me lost
I couldn't survive this world at any cost

You touch my hand and I tremble so
I dread the moment when you have to go
You speak my name, no sound's as good
You lift me up like no one else could
My heart is yours, hold me eternally
No one knows the joy you bring to me

Barbara Lambie

To John

The world became a different place, the day that I met you
I began to see lots of things through eyes and concepts new
A rose upon a thorny bush, looked a deeper, richer hue
Oh yes, the world was different, the day that I met you.

I found that friendship flourished when you became my friend
Because I opened up my eyes and let my mind unbend
I found happiness is when you give more than when you lend
Friends were all around me when you became my friend!

The happiest day of all was when I became your wife
I knew it would not be easy, the path we trod through life
But I felt certain we would overcome the struggle toil and strife
I know I can do anything because I am your wife!

Olga Moorhouse

This Morning

There's icing sugar
On the grass.
The air is a cushion
Of cotton wool.
It feels like we
Are the only people
In the world.

You say something silly
And my laugh makes
Puff the Magic Dragon shapes
In the misty air.

Our gloved hands
Hold each other
And our feet stride
In time -
Crunch, crunch, crunch -
On the crackling grass.

We can't see
Where we're going,
But we don't care.
We're together,
That's all that matters.

Alex Dixon

Untitled

There's a hole deep inside me getting bigger every day
I feel the emptiness even more now that you've gone away
Losing my breath whenever I think of you
I miss you more each day, that I'm feeling blue

Knowing my heart has disappeared off to be with you
I love you so much, and I know you know it's true
Wanting to see your smile again, feel you close to me
I know you're happy with him, so I'll have to let you be

Your happiness is important, I know it's not with me
I know I need to let you go, but my heart won't let it be
Maybe you just don't really see, how much
I really need you here, right next to me.

Chloe Catlin

Our Son's Wedding Day

It happened oh so quickly, it was over and yet just begun
No longer sweet imaginings, it's the wedding to make you one
The months of careful planning slipped into place today
As every step is taken with no doubts about which way
So strong and very handsome with his brother by his side
We watched him as he waited for the first glimpse of his bride
His heart filled with pride when he saw her a vision in purest white
Her smile lit the church like sunshine and we knew this marriage was right
Their love shone this day with such beauty
We all watched them and shared in their joy
They say marriage was made in Heaven, it was for this girl and boy
Too soon the vows and the photos,
The feast, then the speeches all read
Too soon the day was ending and the families' goodbyes were all said
But the magic of every moment will be with us for evermore
As we remember each word and movement
Of these two people whom we adore
I remembered our day my darling, how we made our promise of love
And the wonderful years that followed and the happiness we still have
I prayed for our children's future and trust that they will be
As deeply in love and contented with each other as you and me
Time's passing has made me realise what a wonderful husband you are
Our marriage was made in Heaven and I thank you for being my star.

Milly Holme

Counsel Of An Old Man

Don't speak of love and spoil the day,
Don't strive to over-egg the pud.
The day goes well enough, I say
And we can thrive on leaner food.

This world rotates on thinner fuel
Than kisses hot and wordless sighs.
The lover is the gormless fool
Who's pitied by old men more wise.

So keep your peace, enjoy each hour,
For wisdom shapes these words of mine.
Dull the flesh in a long, cold shower
Dispel all thoughts of Valentine!

David J Ayres

The Dream

The dream into which I had venturec,
At first, uncertain of its theme,
Was a search for a missing person
Who was still here to be seen.
My quest took place on mean streets;
With a glimpse of paradise.
I remember calling out, 'Where are you?'
As I entered the underworld; then
Hovered in empyrean to get an overview.
I saw her leave the rail terminus in
Fawn skirt and striped top;
She looked so young and elegant
With her striking long dark crop,
The way she looked, when we
First met, over forty years ago.
She must have heard me call her name
But she did not pause or stop;
I started running after her, but
Although my legs were moving
They could not get me there!
The dream echoed with my calling:
Begging her to stay, then waking up
To realise she had never been away.

John L Wigley

Cupid's Little Arrows

Having travelled the harsh valleys of sadness
Divorce, lost children, lost house, all seems madness
Then to meet a soul who's suffered similar circumstances
Hardly the usual, sensual start of romances.

But an understanding of practical appreciation and trust
Which has more depth than some showy bubble and bust
The love felt for each other so very sincere
This July we've been married for twenty-four year.

Our love has blossomed with the test of time
It has fire and intensity, rock-like, sublime
Fortune has smiled on us beyond our dreams
Maybe Cupid's little arrows have been up to their schemes.

Len Peach

First Day Of Spring

21st of March, first day of spring,
You will never know what happiness it brings.
So in love but of different faiths,
Both sets of parents said, 'This will never happen. It's a disgrace.'

They eloped, got married in a registry office,
No fuss, no family, just two witnesses
Off the street, June and Margery.

They had their wedding lunch,
Spaghetti Bolognese,
And listened and danced the night away
To the lovely Tubby Hayes.

They collected their suitcases in the dead of night
And left their notes to say they had taken flight.
'Not to worry, we are going to be alright'.

Didn't go down well, of course,
The parents were screaming and shouting
Until they were hoarse.

Forty years on and it's the 21st of March,
The first day of spring,
And I am all so sure
We did the right thing.

Sylvia Papier

The Love Of My Life

(George)

I finally found my true love
But it took many years to find
For this lovely man I married
Is so very, very kind
I showered him with non-stop affection
And you should have seen his ultimate reaction
Loving him so much makes me feel I'm walking on air
And nothing in this whole wide world could ever compare
For our love is something very special
And something we can both share
Forever and ever, just him and me
Forever, as one, that's how it should be.

Sara Jane Berry

Water Baby

Swimming in the rain on a wintry Sunday
Getting all the jitters at the back of the spine
Bathing with you naked in the shadow of darkness
Momentary quiet in the shimmering brine
Nothing but our footprints on the boards of the jetty
Clothes are in a pile on the dock of the bay
Our car on the beach lying still as a statue
Leave the land behind us and step in the fray

I'm not a swimmer
You're not an athlete
Being good lovers is what we do best
A kiss underwater
Then rise to the surface
Hugging you tightly I'm close to your breast

Put all your clothes on and tie up your sandals
Not before drying out and dusting your feet
Pass me the car keys and put on your seat belt
Drive off the coastline and back on the street
Break into the moonlight with the roar of the engine
Just enough time to look back onto the sea
I could spend a lifetime in the drop of the ocean
But wouldn't venture near it if you weren't here with me.

Martyn Leroy

The English Rose

She's imagination on the first glance
Get a chance to hold her hand
If you're lucky ask her for a dance

Her name is spelt across my heart
Etched within my soul
I've known it from the start

Each time she speaks her melody lights up the room
Looking up at the stars
Every night I want to grab and give her that moon

She wears beauty and intelligence like peaches and cream
If she were here now
It would be a dream.

Jonathan Simms

Gift Of Fate

(Dedicated to Robin Haines, my husband and best friend)

You shook my offered hand that day,
so formal, so sincere
and that was many months ago:
I'm glad that you're still here.

We've taken weekends for ourselves
and been away to play,
we've worked together, slept together,
grown closer every day.

Our love has deepened, time has flown
and now I realise
that fate brought us together and
has sealed our future lives.

I never thought I'd find the man
who'd make me feel at ease
by taking time to listen;
you really want to please.

Robin, I'm lucky as I share
my life with you today.
I hope I make you happy
so forever you will stay.

Tracey Haines

Love

Love is a heart that
Falls so deeply into
Sparks of wonder
At your first
Sight of seeing your
True love.

As the clouds
Above look down
Where the sun is shining
You have to
Trust your heart
And wish for
A silver lining.

Ashleigh West (8)

Kulsum

(Love you, your husband Farooq)

When you came into my life,
To be my one and only wife.
It changed my world and the way I would feel,
My empty heart you did seal.

You are the only one I have ever loved and do adore,
You keep me coming back for more.
Your love, your smile and the way you look,
It honours me, that you are Mrs Farooq.

If you were to be lost, what would I do?
Unthinkable, unbearable, I wouldn't have a clue.
How to live or how to smile,
My life would be meaningless, not worthwhile.

My heart is yours and has always been,
The world is my witness, for this is what they have seen.
I have tried to do my very best,
It is nearly time for me to rest.

My love for you shines in the sun,
Together we have had some fun.
I have to say this before it is too late,
We were meant to be together, for that was fate.

Mohammed Farooq

A Love I Do Not Know

A collection of tears
Fell into my cup
It began to overflow

My heart smashed
To a million pieces
All for a love I do not know

My blood runs dry
Like the sands of time
A flame so cold to touch

Will I ever find
The thing called love
That's talked so much about?

Margaret McGinty

The Purple Room

The phone rang to invite me over
to come and knock on the purple door
the house where love hangs from the ceiling
a special place to find the power of give and receive . . .

The warmth of your tender body
swallowed me like a man-eating plant,
the air was clean with your perfumed body
as the smile on your face danced with mine.

Fingertip searches for a sensitive spot
while lips kiss with tongues on fire;
sheets of purple become a body suit
drape us both into one single figurine.

The earth starts turning the other way
as the passion gods enter our minds
innocence gleaming around the room
as inner voices whisper our love.

Uncontrolled, the emotions we share
no clear path to the end of our feelings
feeding the flames of our souls
as fire burns when we ride the waves
of ecstasy in our veins of pure lust.

Werner Wehmeyer

Broken

Why did you tell me you would stay?
You knew one day you'd go away
Why did you say we'd never part?
You knew one day you'd break my heart
You said our love would never die
You said you'd never make me cry
You lied, but that I could forgive
Without your love, how could I live?
But losing you made me strong
And now I sing a different song
Much time has passed, but this I know
Wherever we are, and whatever we do
We are bound by our memories, me and you.

P Cannon

I Am A One Thousand Piece Jigsaw With A Missing Bit

I am a one thousand piece jigsaw with a missing bit
And you're the piece I think will fit

All my edges neat and smart
But there's one piece missing in my heart

Without your piece I feel so ugly
I think that it would snap in snugly

But seriously, what are the chances?
I bet it's someone else you fancies

Your laugh lights up my bits of card
Without your love, I'm lifeless lard

Be my missing jigsaw piece
And I swear I'll never get obese

Join me in my jigsaw game
Am I even in the frame?

Please don't leave me incomplete
If you don't want me, be discreet

It's a thousand to one that you'll be mine
I'll stay nine hundred and ninety-nine.

Rob Barratt

Our Love

Knows no parameters
No territory where it may not tread
A jewel roughly hewn from youth's illusions,
Crude in its innocence
Raw in its naïvety
We seized it with both hands
And shaped it together,
Tempered its form with humour and sensitivity
Guarded its vulnerability.
Now, honed by treasured memories
Shared sorrows and pleasures
The patina of the years reflects
Its many-faceted perfection.

Vera Morrill

A Special Kiss

We decide to meet
I see you
My heart skips a beat
There are children playing around
We don't hear their sound

In front of them we shouldn't really kiss
But each other we really did miss
'I do want to stay with you, now and forever'
'We'll get engaged again, I'll leave you never'

You open your hand and show me you have the ring
This day, this moment on we hope many happinesses it will bring
No forethought on to linger
You slip the ring on my finger

Our feelings are so intense
A seething passion to commence
'I love you'
The engagement of our eyes
'My love, my darling'
The wedding of our lips
'Forever my love'
We honeymoon within our kiss.

Maureen Taylor

My Love

Nothing here on Earth can ever eclipse
The way you kiss me with your lips.

No man-made strength, can keep me from your arms.
I'm so vulnerable to your sensuous charms.

No other smile I've seen, is like yours, so warm.
When I'm far from you, my heart is torn.

Though time passes faster each and every day.
Let's grow old and together always stay.

When our lives expire
And our time on Earth has gone.

Our souls shall entwine together
And we will be as one.

David Paul Heath

My Yearning Heart

You are always with me
And yet, you are not
I loved you so much
But I was soon forgot.

My heart I gave only to you
There was someone else
You said you loved true
Why did I fall?
You were all I could see
I never realised you hated me.

Just to see you around
Made my yearning heart pound
When your eyes met mine
I did nothing but pine
No more do I stand a chance
Now you have a new romance.

My love for you is so strong
To you I wanted to belong
Together for always, just you and me
That's what I hoped for
It just wasn't to be.

Violetta Jean Ferguson

Wasted Journey

It took hours to pick up the crumbs
From wasted conversation, struggling through orchards
Of common failings and antiquated squabbles
Like a pilgrim to an ancient cave.

Inevitable evenings with muffled stand-lights
Highlight the frailties of our kaleidoscopic relationship
The witness moon smiles with mirrored lights
Mask of a perfect hypocrite waiting to smelter in an hearth
To a reshaped reality.

How we carry the moments of desire
On diverse footings through a sea of factual clumps,
Remain unattached; looking for a string of pearls
From a car boot sale of assorted images from life.

Soumyen Maitra

Face Of The Girl

(For Madeleine, 'Min')

It may be a tree;
a bright printed curtain.
It may be a heap
of crisp autumn leaves.
Sometimes a carpet
of regular pattern;
sometimes the swell
of a summer sea.

It may be the voices
of late night conversing;
a background of music;
a wild jamboree.
But sometimes a silence,
a pink crumpled tissue,
a few poignant moments
with afternoon tea.

Whatever, wherever,
I can but perceive
the face of the girl
that is mine. Is for me.

Reg Billett

Broken Heart

You told me you loved me,
You told me you cared.
I couldn't believe what I had heard.

You broke my heart,
I don't know why,
But all you did was lie.

My heart left shattered and not to mend
Will stay that way
Until the very end.

Please go, the damage is done,
To the heart that was one.
So much for the male ego,
Loved by everyone.

Tina Ann Bonner

Sweetly Smiling

You always were attractive,
Even before age had petrified
Into ammonite fossils
The labyrinthine city
That stands shimmering
In the heat haze
Upon timeless hills.

I love the way you lie,
In the languor of a noonday dream
Of long forgotten summers,
With breasts rounded and firm
Bare for the sun to caress.
Silver-green lacework of olive trees
Is folded round your loins
And against your fertile flanks
The Tiber is spent;
Spent and dried up
After an orgy of turbulent insemination
With melted snow from Sabine hills.

But your lap is heavy
And full of growing.

Phyl Jones

Winter Love

Cold. White. Snow.

Taking my footsteps where I want to go
Crisp and deep the snow covers my dainty feet
Chiffon and lace down to my waist
My white dress ripples to and fro getting wet as I go

I hear the bells ringing and the choir singing
My heart skips a beat; soon I will be standing by his feet
My lifelong dream come true
And now there is just us two.

Who could have foreseen at just eighteen
With love on our side, life can be a roller coaster ride
But I will always say, it's true love in every way
Till the end of my day.

Pat Kerr

When Those Leaves

Now days they come
and days they go
I'll love you
through them all
I'm wishing I was
there with you
when those leaves
they start to fall

I never said I love you
because I always
thought you knew
there was no one else
there was only you

Now days they come
and days they go
I'll love you
through them all
I'm wishing I was
there with you
when those leaves
they start to fall

K Lake

Reciting A Love Sonnet

The dictionary of love I gave unto her, whilst she stepped down,
From her blue and gold carriage, with adventure in my heart,
Madame was veiled, immaculately dressed in lace and satins,
Before the adventure I had a strange dream, permeating the ether,
Her presence appeared like a winter-white spirit,
Love comes in many disguises, especially when I think of you,
Dearest creature the passion you cannot deny is so beautiful,
Whilst reciting a love sonnet, underneath tempest stars,
Compassionate, full of sweet memories of yesteryear,
Methinks her ladyship governs with acute senses of the heart,
With pleasures so fond, bright and wonderful, duly I praise,
The beautiful art of continued love, being kissed beside April blossoms,
The immaculate birth of sun-drenched flowers amongst the bowers,
Oh Lydia of Rome, sovereign of the Earth, immortal creature.

James Stephen Cameron

Bittersweet Valentine

I remember when I first waited
For my very first valentine
But when a letter dropped on the mat
I knew it wasn't mine

As I grew older, I expected one
From the boys that I would date
But this never materialised
No matter how long I would wait

Then things got a bit more serious
And I thought I was in love at long last
But although he seemed to be in love with me
He never acknowledged this day till it passed

In due course, I met the man I would marry
And was sure that I'd get a card each year
But despite the times I dropped hints
A card would never appear

Now Alzheimer's has dulled his mind
And on the day, I naturally expected the same
But he painstakingly made me a card
Even though he's forgotten my name!

Louise Maria

My Lovely Man

Your lovely face, your smile, if only I
Could anchor them within my consciousness;
Your laughing eyes that tease but yet express
Devotion time will e'er intensify;
Your voice whose strength and potency belie
A tenderness that only you possess;
My soul would languish should they evanesce,
These priceless gifts you left must never die.

But when decrepitude's grip dominates,
And should insensibility hold sway,
All fear of my forgetfulness abates
As memories return to yesterday,
For I'm assured death's greeting compensates,
My lovely man is my last breath away.

Hilary J Cairns

Deep Inside My Heart

You said 'I do', I said it too
Uttered truthfully with all our hearts.
Two souls, so committed to each other
Not even death would keep us apart.

I have always believed in magic
I see it deep in your eyes every day,
How could I have been so lucky
To have you enter my life that day?

There was something different about you
A difference I could not explain.
My whole body tingled with pleasure
But in my heart it was like beautiful pain!

Falling in love with you was like crazy
It was a matter of life or death to me.
Far away into an uncharted future
I could see us together for eternity.

There truly is 'love at first sight'
I know, because it happened to me.
The happiest moment in all my life
Was the day you and I became 'we'.

Christopher Thomas

Lipstick On The Glass

A sad song plays on the jukebox
mirroring my mood, mirroring my mood
and there's lipstick on the glass
but the beer is cold and strong
slipping down easily tonight.
I never realised this time would come
And yet I am not in pieces . . . just numb.

The song has finished, I visit the bar
for another pint and not my last
and there's lipstick on the glass
as I stare at a lone drinker
with eyes as sad as a chained bear
and now the ghostly past begins to hurt,
In my hands was a jewel . . . replaced by dirt.

Guy Fletcher

True Love

Loving you was so easy
But losing you was so very hard
We had a love, never to be replaced
Yet time soon came to be apart.

Oh how I miss my true love
We made such great plans together
To build a home after army life
To live and love forever.

Alas it wasn't meant to be
My love was taken from me
Never to hold me again in his arms
Nor to kiss away the hurt when I weep

My darling has now gone to a better place
In my dear Lord's loving care
Yet our love will last forever
Until the day I meet him there.

Now at the age of eighty-three I need no other love
But my memories will live on forever
For the greatest love I have ever known
When we two were as one together.

Vera Ewers

Love

Love is a dream,
What will happen,
Where will I go
Marriage, and life,
I would become,
The perfect wife.

It was perfect,
Working on the life
I wanted,
Until it ended,
In death, I
Caught my breath,
Alone I go my
Own way.

Barbara Brown

My First Wife, Janet

Three score years have passed me by
Since that day you caught my eye
Across the office our eyes met
I knew at once you'd be my pet.

As our love blossomed more and more
We courted for those years times four
And then you said you'd be my wife
To love and cherish all my life.

Eight happy years we spent together
Through sunshine and inclement weather
But alas no child was born
And I realised you were forlorn.

One winter's day you left the nest
I know you'd given me your best
The saddest day in all my years
My happiness reduced to tears.

Now in the twilight of my life
I still remember you as my wife
Despite the sadness and the tears
Time has passed, three score years.

G Hall

Shadows Of Love

The shadows of your love
Are following me wherever I go
The forces are so strong
Pulling me to you
I can't say no
Beckoning me to surrender
To your arms and to your lips
Yes, your love's so tender
I just know that this is it

The shadows of your love
Can follow me at any time
Cos I know that when they reach me
I'll be yours
And you'll be mine.

Teresa Billington

Unconditional Love

Love usually has conditions
In one way or another
But no conditions do exist
Between a child and their mother

From long before the time they're born
They form a natural bond
The love the mother gives to them
And the way the child responds

Just watch when they're together
And imagine them apart
No other love's quite like it
It can melt the hardest heart

The love towards a father
Is never quite the same
That's the way it seems to be
Nobody is to blame

But love between a mother and child
Is impossible to explain
It's just a simple fact of life
And should always be the same.

Neil Warren

Hand In Hand

We walk hand in hand,
And with you I feel no fear
We kiss, I taste your breath,
Our hearts beat as one
The love we share, so dear
Holding you gives me peace
Watching you sleep puts my demons at ease,
Feeling your heart beat next to mine,
Gives me life
You are the reason I'm here
And for all my happiness I thank you
And hearing those four little words
Makes my life seem worthwhile . . .
I love you too.

Dale Alun Duggan

To Karen

Other women just stop and stare,
'Who's that woman over there?
The one with the perfect smile and hair?
This whole world is so unfair!'

'I watch all the fashion shows and read all the beauty books
How come one woman ends up with all the looks?
She doesn't even look as though she has to try
It's natural to her, makes me want to cry!'

You walk with such a graceful poise
The male of the species, both men and boys
Can't help but look, though they may try not to
But it's useless in the end, they have to, they've got to!

You possess the most amazing eyes
They sparkle like stars in the dark night skies
And when they catch the flickering candlelight
They come dancing alive and my heart takes flight.

You're fun, fantastic, my soulmate, best friend
I never want my life with you to end
You're the most beautiful, gorgeous woman alive
But most perfect of all, you're my wonderful wife.

Peter Howie

First Love

When I first saw you, my heart missed a beat.
Experiencing the first painful stirrings of love.
At first so awkward, in telling you how I felt.
We were both shy and nervous and innocent.
Slowly a golden summer beckoned and our love grew.
We walked hand in hand, along golden beaches of sand.
Or sat on the bench in the park talking.
Sometimes our lips would gently and innocently kiss.
It felt so good, to hold you close in my arms.
But the summer faded away into autumn.
I waited by the park bench, but you never came.
As a cold wind rustled through fading leaves.
There have been other loves, but none like yours.
Now in staid middle age, I can't forget you.

Keith Davies

From My Bedroom Window

Last summer, when the sun was shining,
From this same window where I stand,
The hills beyond seemed close enough
For me to reach and touch your hand.

The scene, with those suburban hills,
Had come to be my chief delight.
I looked across each day, on waking,
I watched the lights come up each night.

And if those nights were long and lonely,
And dull the days, I did not care,
For our love filled the gulf between us,
I looked across, and you were there.

But now the summertime is ended,
In shrouds of mist the valley lies,
I cannot see you any longer,
For that same mist that fills my eyes.

So empty seems the valley now,
And empty, love, my life is too,
With endless, empty years ahead,
I look across, but where are you?

Molly Mettam

The Dark Side Of Love

Since time began
A force for good has been
Love for mankind
All civilisation
Has been built on this
But there is a dark side too
Love is a destructive force
When joined with power or greed
Bringing misery to many
Often innocent victims
Perhaps it is time we turned
Once more to faith
Before it is too late
And our world crumbles.

Barbara Williams

The Tribute

Just how do you thank your partner
For her care and her love of you,
And those years of support and comfort
From a wife who is constant and true?

She never grumbled when life grew tedious,
Or protested when times were tough,
Just as long as we were together,
To her seemed to be quite enough.

Whenever we were briefly parted,
I hurried to be by her side,
I just couldn't be without her,
It wouldn't have worked if I tried.

To see her each day is a blessing,
She's my sunrise of every new day,
My heart is filled with her presence
And I've loved her each step of the way.

Dame Fortune gave me a fine lady,
I've been honoured to be by her side,
And I vowed to make her life happy,
With the love in her eyes as my guide.

G Thomas

A Shakespearean Love Sonnet

If music is the food of love, what melody shall I play thee
to plight my troth in ardent amour
that seeks to woo thee, fairest maid
in tenderest lays - for 'tis no chore?
Shall I play thee on St David's harp
or ripple the chords on spinet mild?
My love, my dearest, which shall't thou choose
for I swear by faith my love for thee doth drive me wild?
So shall I play along, fairest maid
till in excess of it all I neither sicken nor die
for I can never get enough sight of thee
and would from this day forever with thee lie
in warmest love, surrounded by sweet melody
within my heart - where'er I am, there shalt thou be.

Ann Voaden

Sunbeams

The sun's orange rays shone in the bluest of skies
I remember those days wandering hand in hand
'Was it just yesterday we watched the sun setting?'
God looked down at us and gave us His blessing.

Two very young people and so much in love
Nothing deterred us; then our health was so good
Together each day we would wander the land
In a faraway country, like it was planned.

One day we returned to the land of our birth
Arrangements were made to continue our mirth
Then married in autumn to strengthen our bond
We felt like we'd found a magical wand.

Life very wonderful, with children we're blessed
Age has not changed us, well not for the worst
Of course we had troubles, God helped us through
The good years and bad, we had more than a few.

Now he's gone before me, one has to go first
Memories we made still with me on Earth
Together we'll meet in the future somehow
A Darby and Joan; who stood by each vow.

Joan Prentice

Clouded Senses

If love be blind then praises sing and shield my eyes
Let love be deaf and dumb as well as blind
For I'll not look upon our lovers' casket gnarled with whispered lies.
Nor hear again such bittersweet mutterings to pollute my mind.
Let love not be sweet but sour to taste so I dare not sample it twice.
Do not let memory loose to toy and tantalise me with an echo of love,
To discard the cud and place on a pedestal only the sugar and spice.
Let love fly from my heart; a lone vulture ne'er a gentle dove.
Let not my hands betray my thoughts through letters of affection
Lest the ink turn to poison or the pen should prove a sword
To spurn my heart with an unendurable rejection
From the Romeo I once so adored.
Let not my voice break faith and sully my determined will
To be silent and not confess I love you still.

Andrea Mitchell

Strengthening Love

Love is pain, it is harsh . . . that's not right
It's the warmth that dries your tears in the night
The strength that gives you the will to go on
The lullaby, your comforting song.

The whisper in your ear, telling you not to be afraid
Not to let the faith and hope in you fade
The rainbow brightening up the rain
The reward after you've come through the pain.

When it feels like all hope has gone
I still feel God's love so strong
When no one else can truly understand
I know God's love can and I know it will never underhand.

Love is the rain washing mistakes, doubts and sorrows away
It's the sunshine revealing hope the next day
The wind that sweeps away those painful memories
And it's the calmness when it leaves.

Love can still see you at your best
When you've stood in the storm and all the rest
It still stays even when your hair is a mess
To help you carry on to succeed and progress.

Catherine Gardner

Endless Love

Golden moments remembered, newly-wed,
Clothed in confetti, holding hands, we fled,
Honeymooned in Cornwall, a magical land,
Barefoot on soft, brown sugar, sand.
I cried over his socks as I put them away
Only three pairs, I'd buy him lots next day.
Reality had struck 'n my tears were for Mum,
So far away, she had been my best chum.
Babes came along, two girls, then a boy
Time passed quickly, there was sadness and joy,
50 years wed! 50 years! It's a while
A wondering look as we hold hands and smile,
Our grandchildren come in we gaze at all four,
Golden moments again when they step through that door!

Joyce H Honeyman

To Dennis

So deep, the darkness of the night
But there, a lone star twinkles bright
And then, a flit of moonlight touched a tree
Whose bare 'arms' reflect the ache in me.

Where are you now, my dearest dear?
Now, I can never hold you near
My empty arms reach out in vain
For, you will never come again.

So many years have rolled away
Since on our lovely wedding day
We promised, both to love and cherish
And love held fast, it did not perish.

Through times of joy and times of sorrow
We never worried about tomorrow
Was there enough to pay the rent
Or wondered where our wages went?

And now, I'm old and live alone
But, never truly, on my own
For, tho death keeps us two apart
Your memory lives, deep in my heart.

Lucy Williams

To Emma

I miss the natural beauty of your face
The beauty that with nature's best compares
More frequent sights more hours of your grace
Is my request that with me you will share
For like an air whose melody prevails
Your pictured image lingers in my mind
Constantly haunting yet beauty's details
Gradually fade as light at daytime's hind
But when within the countryside I walk
Your loveliness and beauty are recalled
From flowers' faces frequently you talk
I see your beauty and I am enthralled
For nature gave us flowers to enjoy
You're my flower my beauty and my joy

Leslie Salmen

Not What I Wanted

The tears and anguish
The sorrow and pain
Our lives have parted
It will never be the same

I try to comfort you
My words you do not hear
My heart still remains true
To you my love is sincere

I wish to be close to you
And try to explain
I did not wish to leave you
It's driving me insane

To brush away the tears
Your heart I long to mend
And let you know I'm near
This is not how I wanted it to end

So it's upon this summer's day
As you walk from my grave
It's my heart you take away
But my soul just has to stay.

Bruce Ripley

The Ghosts

I picture you as you turn and see me,
In that instant I run and am encircled by your warmth.
Then from inside you
I look out at the world through your eyes.

There is a road sixty years long
Which we have travelled with other marriage partners.
How many hopes have been trampled for us to arrive here
In this ragged mist, and yet it is only my spirit that flies to you
My soulmate.

In the mingling of future lives will our wistful yearning
Be woven into children as yet unborn
For our love to be realised
And will we, the ghosts, then be free?

Barbara Phillips

Love Or Not Love

Love they say is a very splendid thing
Usually ending in marriage and symbolic ring
But how can we be sure that love is true
Does it warm the cockles of your heart like a good brew

When you choose a partner is it for life
Or are you choosing what seems an acceptable wife
Do they really enjoy the same things as you
Or are they just kidding by saying they do

How do you feel about sharing your life
Compromising and accept the daily strife
Will true love really overcome the negatives
Or do you still heal an aching heart with sedatives

Many things are done in the name of love
Celebrations signified with a rose, a heart or white dove
But how do you know that true love has come
Does your heart beat fast and loud as a drum

So many times we imagine love is real
When yet again we realise it's not the right deal
Is it because people change as they get older
Causing any love to disappear and the heart grow colder

George Alexander

How It Was

And when I think of
Where it was
And how it was
And when.

And then I think of
Who we were,
And what we did
And then.
We loved and loved and loved.

I know
It never could be
Possible,
To love like that again.

Robert King

The Gift Of Love

I heard the whisper of a murmuring breeze,
I floated on this wave, with tender ease,
I felt transported to another world,
Where life seemed a dream, of ecstasy unfurled.

From time to time, I seemed to need console,
Emotions seemed to disturb my soul,
Morning awakening, answering its regular call,
Its beauty passed me by, I simply felt disenthralled.

My stature seemed to alter its shape,
However now quite relaxed, I knew my fate,
Although rather heavy, knowing it's only for a short time,
The gift following, would be all that was necessary for some time.

My gift arrived as a well-earned reward,
I had produced a baby boy, whose arrival was adored,
A child to love and share through his life,
For me the ultimate glory, significance, of real life.

Knowing for a little while family duties would slowly increase,
For now everything around us held a perfect peace.
Because miracle of miracles, my arms held our baby son,
Our journey as a family had truly begun.

Lorna Tippett

A Love That's Forever Near

When dawn's first gleam of golden glow
Burgeons in the eastern sky
And its luminous lights the darkness
Of the night doth put to flight.

When sleep her cradling arms do me unfold
'Tis then across the yawning gulf of time
Flooding the corridors of my mind
Come those marvellous memories of all those years
Of your wonderful love and care.

That brings the tears I cannot stem
And I weep that you are now and forever gone
And yet in my lonely heart
You are forever dear and forever near.

Victor William Lown

Love

As I survey my Christmas cards
I feel a sense of being loved
Each written message (not emailed)
Yearns for yearly keep in touch.

I also cherish sibling love
Their interest - my little world
Much talking point - extremely proud
An artist brother - Poet too.

My mother - who is eighty-six
Appreciative - devoted fan
Grateful for my recent help
(Still her first born Maltese son).

I also have a special girl
(No sweetheart - just delightful friend)
Sharing all our joys - our woes
Over coffee - sticky buns.

People like me - which is nice
Companion - held in high esteem
My acts of kindness, warmth and wit
Rewarded by endearment now.

Steve Glason

Kiss, Kiss, Kiss

Kiss, kiss, what is a kiss?
A kiss is something that lovers don't miss.
Kiss, kiss, kiss, can you take anymore?
Does she kiss you in the morning as you walk out the door?
Have you missed a kiss as you're reading this?
Kiss, kiss, kiss, it's too good to miss.
The most memorable kiss I can recall
Is the one told to do as I stood in the hall.
Weddings and birthdays and funerals and births,
There are different kisses all over the Earth.
Kisses for nations together unite,
Kisses in the bedrooms as you all say goodnight.
Kiss, kiss, night, night.

David McNiece

Three Valentines

St Valentine, the patron saint of lovers young and old
Was martyred while so very young - or so we have been told.
Since then he's been remembered on this very special day
With flowers, cards and little gifts wrapped up so very gay.

Great Grandmama had saved her cards, beribboned, edged with lace
A faded photo in a box - a young moustachioed face
Mementos of a bygone age, a heart that never healed
A silent grave, the resting place in a far-off foreign field.

My grandmother had also kept her little souvenirs
The Valentines my grandad sent, 'With love from Armentiers'.
Inside a card, a poppy pressed, and marks where tears were spilled.
A telegram - three little words - 'Missing - presumed killed'.

Another box - more Valentines, my mother has preserved
And medals that my father earned from the Airforce which he served.
A snapshot of a smiling boy, the Spitfire which he flew
Shot down across the Channel, he was just 'One of the few'.

These Valentines are all we've left of the lives that have been lost.
Sweet memories, the price that's paid - we dare not count the cost.
How many more such Valentines we'll cherish 'ere wars cease.
The saint was slain for love they say - our loved ones died for *peace*.

Celia Westbrook

My Secret Smile

The day begins and the sun comes up.
Thoughts of you fill my head,
And a secret smile cannot be hidden.
Will you be there today?
My friends all know how I feel
Yet you are in the dark.
Your voice, a smile, the light in your eyes
Separates time and space.
I am caught in a moment where all that exists is us.
Do you feel the same?
My heart hangs on your every word.
Yet you have no idea what you do.
So you remain my secret smile and live inside my dreams.

Anne-Marie Pratt

Heartbreak

The empty space,
The forlorn chair,
The beloved face,
No longer there.

I have to eat,
Yet have no taste,
To be alone,
Without your dear face.

Sitting in front of me,
Your whole being,
Smiled with impish glee,
Sharing ideas on Life's meaning.

Always for justice,
And the underdog
How can I have a fire
Without a log?

Your flame is out,
But my ember glows.
How much I loved you
No one knows!

Suzanna Wilson

A Wonderful Feeling

Just to say I love you
That I really care.
My life is made complete
Just knowing that you're there.

Always there beside me
With a love so true.
It's a wonderful feeling
Between me and you.

A feeling that will last forever
And as the years go,
Always remember my darling
That I'll always love you so.

Julie Brown

Tribute To My Wife

Ours was a holiday romance
They said it wouldn't last
But I would like to tell you
That 15 years have just passed.

We have many hobbies
Like walking in the park
We don't have any children
But we've little dogs that bark.

My wife's name is Janet
She's very good to me
But sometimes when I'm troubled
She'll make me a cup of tea.

We went away on our honeymoon
To put our love to the test
And we really enjoyed ourselves
Building our love nest.

So we are very happy
As all can plainly see
But all this would not come about
Without my Janet you see.

David Sheasby

Passing

Just like the moonbeams of the night,
The lady's eyes always held your sight;
They sparkled on and on and on,
In daylight flew, and now she's gone.

To go with that beguiling glance,
Did she not think once of romance?
What of this valley that opened wide,
And took my sense right o'er the side?

Had she no soul, was I just a mat,
To be cast off, and end all that?
Was love allowed, was it a crime?
Perhaps, perhaps . . . some other time.

Alistair McLean

Faded Love

The blossom of love is sterling delight
Awareness of everything not in full sight
Happiness encircles with dizziness throughout
The world and its problems a total blackout

Time however as it does to all men
Heals or tarnishes according to them
Living together and stresses and strains
Creates vulnerable lapses and timely attains

Poverty too plays an important role
Especially when sentenced to a spell on the dole
Out of the window flies many a notion
As desire is engulfed in a selfish motion

Familiarity breeds contempt they say
When abandonment without the right to play
Taking for granted is surely about
As indifference interferes towards haughty self-doubt

Faded love is thus a worn out flower
Neglected as such by nature's power
Starved of contentment, devoid of loving care
It withers towards a desolate despair.

Anthony Mc Geehan

Before The Morn

You were there, clearly in my mind
So deeply in the silent night
A thought just fleeting, yet so kind
To stop my heart from taking flight.

The still of night, waiting the dawn
Of a fresh day, to lighten care
Yet you were there, before the morn
Taking my mind so unaware.

Years have passed with joy and sorrow
Times when I've felt travel-worn
As I once more face my tomorrow
I feel you there, before the morn.

Molly Rodgers

My Love

You were the sunshine of my life,
You were all that I hold dear
My life is very empty now
Filled with darkness, sorrow, fear.

I long to hear you call my name
And hold me very tight,
Send all my troubles far away
And put my world to right.

I want you there beside me
To give comfort when I'm sad
I even miss your ravings
When I made you mad.

Our anniversary's here again,
So many heartfelt years,
No celebration flowers
Just me with all my tears.

One day we'll meet again my love,
I hope it won't be long,
Till then I'll do my best my love
And try to carry on.

Farina May Jenkins

A Love So Strong

I worship the ground you walk on,
Feel like a princess with you
You make me feel safe in your strong arms
Like the world can't touch me.

We've been through more than an old married couple.
Helped each other through pain.
We share so many special things forever.
The best day of my life was saying I do to you and you the same.

For all the things yet to come
I know I can face anything with you,
A love so strong,
I love you.

Gillian Elaine Brakewell

My True Love

First love is wonderful,
We couldn't bear to be apart.
All our dreams for the future,
Now where do we start?

Money was scarce but
We made our own fun.
Pure happiness prevailed,
Although luxuries we had none.

Contentment and sharing,
Supporting and caring,
Rising above the problems of life,
Which at times was quite wearing.

Forty years later,
Where has the time gone?
Our family are grown,
We are now both home alone.

The joy of grandchildren
And great grandchildren too,
The cycle of life never stands still,
Just as I will always love you.

Joan C Igesund

A Quiet Christmas With One's True Love

A yuletide log and a festive tree,
A sweet sherry and a warm mince pie.
No need of extravagance for a Christmas merry,
My one true love and I.

A silent night of soft white snow,
Festoons of decorative fun.
Tinsels and glitter and mistletoe,
The love of my true one.

'Morecambe and Wise' on the old TV
An archive of seasonal wealth.
A quiet Christmas on the cosy settee,
My one true love and myself.

Peter Terence Ridgway

Together

Stones are washed ashore
They've travelled here and there
If they could talk I'm sure
They'd have lots of things to share.

To and fro, upon the wave
In fine and stormy weather
The ups and downs remind me of
The times we spend together.

One love, one stone
That travels through life's sea
One love, one stone
To resemble you and me.

Through the ups and downs
The lows and highs
The laughs, the frowns
No more goodbyes.

The stone may settle ashore
The stone may go to sea
But wherever life may take it
Together will be you and me.

Jacqueline Madden

Femme Fatale

Now sometimes fate plays us a different hand
Than the one we imagined, the one we had planned
Our best intentions, hopes, wishes and dreams
Can turn into nightmares so easily it seems.

The pain of the body eases the pain of the mind
The suffering and torment that's so easy to find
Sometimes it's hard, when love withers and dies
In the cold light of day to understand why.

Better not to regret a love that you shared
Even if things went wrong than to never have cared
When I love someone my commitment is total
Until I fell for that femme fatale.

John Robert Smith

My Valentine

As Valentine's Day approaches
I think more and more of you
Because you are so special
So wonderful and true

Every day you're in my thoughts
The seeds of love you've sown
You really are so lovely
Like no one else I've known

Since we've known each other
You've totally changed my life
Now I'm wondering
Whether you'd be my wife

Before we came together
Life was incomplete
Now I'm on a pedestal
Up there with the elite

So as I send these wishes
My feelings in every line
I'd like you to know dear
That you are my valentine.

Martin Selwood

To A Lover

How I recall those heavenly nights, when moonbeams cast their spell
When you and I shared everything, with nothing left to tell,
I held you close within my arms and whispered soft your name,
And touched your hair with fingertips, life's never been the same!

I know we both had former loves, they'll never fade away,
But time has passed for you and I, it's now another day,
Time to look forward once again, and live life to the full,
A life that's love and happiness, a life that's never dull.

You know I love you, sweetheart dear, you'll never know how deep,
I think you love me too, my dear, but you've just let it sleep,
Time to wake up that love, my dear, and bring it the fore,
Let us always share that love, and 'twill last for evermore.

George Baker

Lost Love

She sits by the window on an upright chair,
Staring aimlessly into the sky.
She's all alone in this big, big world,
And can't for the life of her, understand why.

Her eyes are wet, as she inwardly sobs,
Remembering life as it used to be.
She recalls the time with the man that she loved,
And the time when their lives were free.

A tear rolls down her pallid cheek,
And moistly stains the blouse she wears.
Her face is sore, where she's dabbed her eyes,
And wiped away the tears.

Her hair is permed and immaculately styled,
Just the way her husband always admired,
So she dreams of the bygone days,
And the time that they shared for a while.

But now he's gone, and won't be back,
His illness was too much to bear.
So she sits at the window all day, and recalls.
The years that they once did share.

Jim Bell

Love Is No One's But Ours

A meeting place shrouded from onlookers.
The darkness an enveloping presence,
The stillness as poignant as the plight itself.
It's no one's secret but ours.

A thousand emotions in a single touch,
Impassioned in one perfect kiss.
An ever-intensifying maze of the mind,
It's no one's experience but ours.

Flawless in the essence of being,
Immaculate in the perception of love,
So natural in its concealed beauty,
It's no one's completeness but ours.

Gianna Pollero-Payne

Fifty Golden Years

How can I write in just a few lines
About our lives together,
The laughter and the tears,
All the treasured years.

Half a century gone,
We have grown old together,
We have walked upon the heather
In all kinds of weather.

Been blown across the seas,
Walked under trees
Looked up at the stars
People watched us from afar.

Our love has stretched to eternity
Like no other love on Earth,
Yes! we've had our ups and downs
We wear our love like a crown.

The doubters gave us just six months
They said it would not last,
But I wish they could see our triumph
For fifty golden years have passed.

Sheila Moore

Over Yonder

Over yonder my true love waits
Over yonder my true love lays
I can't see her, but she can see me
Over yonder my true love waits

Over yonder my true love waits
Over yonder my true love lays
I make her happy, she makes me happy
Over yonder my true love waits.

Over yonder my true love waits
Over yonder my true love lays
I know I can't see her, but
Over yonder my true love waits.

Jayden Gittens

Love, A True Story!

When I was only eight years old
My love story was about to unfold.
I didn't know that I was smitten
And the 'Love Bug' had already bitten.

We played together as children do
But there was a tenderness between we two.
And as the youthful years passed by
No other girl could catch my eye.

In the desert of my heart
A beautiful love was growing.
Just like the seedling of a rose
My love grew and my heart was overflowing.

We were married, quite young in fact
We wanted to be together,
So we started our 'Love Song'
And wished it to last forever.

It did for over fifty years
Through laughter and through tears
Until one day it came to an end,
Yet the 'Love Song' will never end.

William Clements

Michellé

My love for you Michellé
Burns in arc-white fusion
With everlasting flame.

I'd give my life
And passion rife
To have you feel the same.

My only aim
Is crystal-clear
For the one I worship
And revere;
To be with you in paradise
And always hold you near.

Kevin Setters

A Love Song

Will you be there at my waking
When sleep rolls away like a mist?
Will you be mine for the taking
Or pretend to be shy and resist?

Will you bring me floral tributes,
The splendour of rosebuds in bloom,
With sepals enfolding their beauty
And fragrance that graces my room?

Will you be mine through the winter
When noises are muffled by snow,
When our world seems locked in silence
And rhythms of life start to slow?

Will you stay with me till springtime
Wake slumbering plants from their rest?
Will you watch the summer heighten
At its blossoming, burgeoning best?

Grow mellow with me in autumn
As colours bedazzle the trees,
And when our green days are over
We will learn to love at our ease.

Celia G Thomas

Time To Run

Much too young to become a partner's wife,
I'll manage without daily housework strife.
Had to run from the love word, no can do,
But I'm sad, because he's left feeling blue.

From the beginning, the signs were there to see,
On the first date, he said he loved little me.
I tried to tell him not to fall too fast,
When my failed romance memories flashed passed.

Maybe I should have handled it better,
Perhaps met and not sent a goodbye letter.
Believed friendship was about having fun,
Didn't know he would go crying to Mum.

S Mullinger

Fire

Love is a shadow
That falls over thought.
Fills cold hearts with fire,
Where reason flounders,
Destroyed by her sparks.

Two furnace-fused minds,
Welded, locked in a
Synthesis. The fast
Flight of passion's pace,
Tempts oblivion.

I'm enslaved by pure
Liberating flames
Burning inside her;
Shot with silhouettes
Of drunken desire.

Keep me imprisoned
In her shadow's kiss.
A sunburst of dreams
Feeds my driven dawns:
Fires her soft shadow.

David Norris-Kay

True Love

I close my eyes and you are with me. Your smile is
Sincere and inviting, your lips hold the promise of joy.

Your eyes look deep into my soul, you court me with
Gentle persuasion, you are so tender and true, attentive,

And kind, your one wish is only to please me, as
Together our lives we combine, your smile is sincere and

Inviting, as every dream I employ, you tenderly stroke
Through my hair, every movement I feel with such intensity

And you move me with such a degree, and whisper the answer
That I yearn to hear you say, I love you dearly from my heart

And never part, having me to share our love together, linked
By mutual love forever, my fervent hope is you will treasure
Magic moments spent together and never part.

Imogene Lindo

The Captured Heart

The captured heart
Should beat freely
Within its gilded cage
Never knowing the searing pain of fear or rage.

The captured heart
Should beat contentedly
Within its barricade
Fulfilled by the sacrifices and promises made.

The captured heart
Should beat defiantly
Within its crimson walls
For memories will sustain it whatever may befall.

The captured heart
Grows not weary
Though freedom softly beckons.
The captured heart
Surrenders not to hours, minutes, seconds.
The captured heart
Continues . . . for love is liberty.
The captured heart continues for all eternity.

Fiona Jane Yerofeyev

Love Blooms Eternal

In spring a young man's fancy,
Turns to thoughts of love they say,
But my thoughts of you, my darling,
Are loving every day.

Not only in spring, but in autumn,
In winter and summer too,
Through all the changing seasons,
My heart is filled with love for you.

And though we both grow older,
Years come and then pass by,
I will love you still my dearest,
Till the very day I die.

William John Dovey

I Dreamt Last Night

I dreamt last night that your girlfriend had died
It made me feel all sad inside
I comforted you - your head laid on my chest
While Anne advised you for the best
Your eyes were melancholy but remained quite dry
Your grief was silent - you did not cry
All your lust for life had drained away
I could not keep your loneliness at bay

I woke - relieved it was just a dream
And scared of how real my dream had seemed
And ashamed too of my glee
At how I'd felt when you were with me

I dreamt last night that your girlfriend had died
I could not un-dream it - even though I tried
All day today I've been racked with guilt
At what I dreamt and what I felt

I failed you by thinking these unconscious thoughts
And for feeling pleasure when you were distraught
I failed you when you were grieving -
I do not blame you for leaving

Lauren Hesford

Taken

There! I felt it, a bolt of lightning,
New hope, fresh dreams
It crept into my very being, it sank
And settled in my gut.
Oh dear God, let life continue like this
Not food, nor drink sustains it
But a glimpse of him, a smile, a touch.

Does he realise or even care?
The flush of my cheeks at his glance.
My sickness would worsen if he were to speak
And screams within, surely heard.

I stand in evening's light and watch
My inner self reach out to him.
He walks towards me and I search for words,
I'm struck mute as his perfect form tantalises my senses.

'Quick, quick,' I say, 'speak.'
But he's past me and reaching out to 'her'.
The girl behind me, the one who can speak,
The one who takes him away with delight
And leaves me cold, but 'melted'.

Veronica Barnett

One Romantic Night

We graced the dance floor
Close in each other's arms
We swayed to the waltz
Your laughter and voice
A melodious symphony of sound
I clung to your body, replete in our embrace
Wishing mine would melt into yours
I love your hair. Your earlobe, and face
I am tempted to trace, but I settle
For the graceful curve of your neck
As I place on it a loving kiss
I breathe in your scent
Not of the aftershave but of you
You gaze into my eyes and I'm in heaven
I am not afraid to express my love
Because we have been made one
The soothing music and the candlelit room
Destabilise my senses
I can feel your body next to me
Virile and alive as we share a kiss
And continue to dance into the night.

Debra Valley

Emotion With Every Good Effect

The emotion we feel with every passing day,
Is to think of others in every way,
Be it in the relationship mode,
Or just a friend across the road.
It isn't easy to keep your mind,
On just one person all the time,
But when a special love becomes an obsession,
We try to forget the road of depression,
And let the love come from our hearts,
To speak of nothing and never to part.
It is just a case of perseverance,
As long as you try,
To love this person honestly,
Until the day you die.
Let's face it, that is not always easy,
To go through life and never make mistakes
But we have to make an effort,
To mean all we feel and say how we feel,
So that we get the response we are waiting for.
Thus, shall we love each other in a poetic way,
And then go on living another day.

Iris Crew

Dementia

Sitting by your bedside
Watching
As your life draws slowly to its end
Talking
Very softly of the happy times
That we have known
Humming
Bits of songs that meant so much
Melodies of long ago
Swearing
At the gods that let old age
Rob you of your memories
Wondering
If you can hear the words I say
Or if you understand
Hoping
That you can sense
The love that still remains
Wishing with all my heart
That I could make you well again
But alas, I can't.

G R Bell

The Day I Fell In Love With Vivien Leigh

When I was young
My father said to me
There is someone in the movies
That I want you to see,
Somebody you will remember
As the years go by,
Someone to make you laugh,
To make you cry.
But she has gone, gone with the wind,
Although I love her dearly,
I know it's true we never met
But somehow I can't forget
The day I fell in love with Vivien Leigh.
That was long ago, it seems a mystery,
For the words my father told
That were meant for me.
But she has gone, gone with the wind,
Although I think of her memory,
I know it's true we never met,
But somehow I can't forget
The day I fell in love with Vivien Leigh.

Rod Stalham

The Dancing Flower

A family gathered.
A celebration, a birthday.

I bring you.
My dancing flower.

A new love.
A family curious.

Questions fly as the drink it flows.
Your charm infectious.

A room full of strangers.
Enchanted by you.

Then the music begins.
They see what I once saw

A movement unlike any other.
Your dance bewitches like moth to flame.

I stand proud.
They have fallen for you as I once did.

A dancing flower.
That I alone saw bloom.

Lawrence Crawford

My Unrequited

Again, lost words, spoken freely
In a whirlwind haze of sound and beauty.
A broken heart torn to pieces
So small and tender they cannot be reborn.

The beating, the tension and adrenaline
Rushing faster as I frequently see your face.
It's so hard to resist this aching
This loving need to be held by you.

But it's a hopeless heartache
When your love has been taken by yet another.
To feel snowstorms and blizzards
Without you beside me is like stealing the sun.

This unrequited love is for you
Except you shall never return it truthfully.

Samantha King

When Lovers Fall Out

We are drifting far apart
There are bridges we must cross
To keep our love together
Before our love is lost.

It hurts not, to say sorry
When we know we have done wrong
And love will overcome this
If only we are strong.

We are not a river
That only flows one way
We can turn the tide around
And start afresh today.

The days we have lost
Could turn to weeks
And love then turns to hate.

We should not let this happen
For our love can be so sweet.

I will not live forever
But I will love you as long as I live.

B J Shire

The Reckoning

And now the moment has come
We are parted
Suddenly, only me
Left behind and lost
Now only desolation - despair
Unfamiliar silence

And the vacant chair facing the telly
Is breaking my heart

Yet would I change a thing
To leave you to suffer the same
No my lovely, never

Praises be
As usual
You fell asleep first.

Thomas Cobley

Come Walking Out With Me

Come put your hat and coat on
Come walking out with me
Let's walk along the riverbank
And watch it roll free
We can listen to it humming
Love song for today
Come put your hat and coat on
Come walking out with me

We can hold hands, laugh, kiss, make love
Under the old oak tree
We can sit among the daisies watching the buzzing bees
Listening to the leaves blowing gently in the breeze
So put your hat and coat on
Come walking out with me

We will walk through the meadows,
The corn, wheat and hay
Through the orchard
Where the perfume's blossom fills the air
So put your hat and coat on
Come walking out with me

Hazel McMullan

You Came To Me

You came to me where shadows weep.
That wintry day I do recall:
The sky was black, the air was thick,
With too much love, with too much light.

The birds nor sang nor witnessed want,
I saw you there - though you not I,
'Neath dappled sky brilliant fragment,
In darkness, bide, 'twas only time

I ever saw, a sight as yours
So fiercely searing haloed frame.
But I mind not if you do dare
Approach again outside my door,

For lost in you inside my heart,
Where angels sleep, you came to me.

Layla Hendow

The First Love That I Had

The first time that I saw her was in a superstore,
I knew, that from that very day, I'd never loved before.
She suddenly became the love I'd dreamed of all my life.
The gladness and the joy I felt was sharp as any knife.
If only I could have her, to stay with me forever,
I'd give anything at all and swear to leave her never.

I crossed the floor and stood by her, her beauty
Filled my heart.
I knew for sure that she was mine
And we would never part.
We left the store together, my heart was beating fast.
I knew my love would always grow, forever it would last.
I took her home and sitting down, she sat upon my knee.
My arms were wrapped around her, as she snuggled up to me.

I gazed into her wide brown eyes and stroked her thick dark hair.
The tenderness I felt for her and love that we could share.
I held her close and whispered, how much she meant to me.
And told her how the love we shared was really meant to be.
My heart and mind was full of her, I felt so young and glad
I'll never love like this again, the first dog that I had.

R Clark

Time

When love grows cold
And fever's over
All your dreams
Like scattered clover.

Long gone ahead of time
When love was young
And love was blind.

Sunlight no more to touch your lips
And all your footsteps
Love doth trip.

But love goes on
It did not die
Just hid beneath
The wings on high.

S Bannister

The Story Of Love

Love is a wonderful
Silken shawl -
Love will comfort
When you fall,
Love is all things
To a child,
Baby sweet and
O! so mild.

Where would we be
Without love -
Human and from
God above?
It's precious, dear
And worth preserving,
Whether or not
One is deserving.

Thank you for love
In all its glory,
What a wonderful gift,
What a wonderful story.

Maureen Oglesby

The Unspoken Word

My dear, if I could only tell thee,
those imprisoned words, I want to say.
But my throat alas, confines me.
Read the message in my eyes, I pray.

Thoughts of love frustrate me so,
of fondest feelings I have for thee,
I pray that always, my eyes will show.
Then my heart will soar, like a spirit free.

How can I speak of love, with no soft voice?
How can I tell you just how my heart yearns?
I must love from afar, I have no choice,
but with a passion's desire, that fiercely burns.

I cannot speak yet of my heart's desire,
just read my sad eyes, so full of fire.

Len A Hynds

Kissing The Border

The stormy waves rolling over coral caves
There is illusion
The coral cave crunching in life and death
Bubbles underwater.

Storm and calm
Living together.

Earth and sea
Change their boundaries.

Love and hate
Kissing the border.

Earth and sky
Joining in crimson.

Clouds and sand
Dreaming together.

Fire and ice
Harmony healing.

Guns and love
There is no meeting.

Rhod Singer

Red Wine

I drink wine:
Red as the lipstick and crimson velvet dress
I wore on our first date.
Red as the ruby
In my engagement ring.
Rich red as the rose in the bouquet
I carried on our wedding day.

I drink wine
Red as the blood that flowed
When I miscarried.
And, to take away the pain of our goodbye,
I paint my lips red and don a velvet dress,
Fill my house with rich, red roses.
Then, step out into the night
And become a scarlet woman.

Joyce Walker

Moving Onward

I miss you when the daylight hours are wakening
I need you when the evening shadows fall.
I need your arms to hold me when I'm frightened
In this big world I suddenly feel small.

Our love was taller than the highest mountain
Our love was deeper than the stormy seas
We rode the roller coaster rides together
Our love was meant to last eternally.

Since I must face this world alone without you
I'll wipe the teardrops falling from my eyes.
I'll journey onward till my heart is wearied
Until our Lord has called me to your side.

So until then I'll while away the hours
I'll learn to cope, when evening shadows fall.
I'll find the strength to face each day without you
With help from God, I'm ready to stand tall!

I lost my husband Gilmour, in September 2006.
As time goes by, the pain eases and I don't cry so often.
But I still miss him terribly.

Shirley Prosser

You Are

You are the song I sing;
You are the word I speak;
Such joy I have never known before.

You are the breath I breathe;
You are the very life I live;
Such happiness I have never known before.

You are the wind on my face;
You are the sun that warms my back;
Such freedom I have never known before.

You are the very heart of me;
You are the soothing balm to my soul;
Such peace I have never known before.

Yes, just simply Lord;
You are.

Helen Smith

A Ghostly Sacrifice

Oh Catronia I am a child in these matters.
If I had chosen not to quarrel with you,
We would be together now instead of, apart,
With me speeding through this dark dank, miserable night

Desperate to reach you, longing to hold you tightly once
more in my loving arms
But reach you I must ———— Explain
How she came to me
Assigned as my potentate.

Made me interconnect with the past
- - in another present
- - another time.

Now I've erased that betrayal
Her lasting memory has gone

She no longer has the same hold upon me
She's just a photograph
— A Shadow in the mind
- A timely metaphor
For A Ghost in Flame.

Alan Knott

Strange Love Sonnet

(Syllables amiss)

Come wither hither free me
From love's first kiss
Tender touch, when I felt thee
Melting moments I still miss
Torrential raindrops pour
Whilst my dampened hair
Awaits your tousling more.
I know you can no longer dare
To look at me with wanton eyes
My mellow skin is lonely
A meeting of bodily contact cries -
I know your movements will be phoney.
I rang your bell - you came;
Strange is love: I felt only fain.

Jackie Perry

What Am I Supposed To Do Now?

Is there a day I can forget
I love you
Is there a second, a minute, an hour?

Is there a week I can forget
I love you
Is there a flower?

Autumn, winter, spring, summer
I love you all seasons
It will never die
I would never lie
I love you!

Is there a day I can forget
I miss you
Is there a second, a minute, an hour?

When I think of what I had
And what I lost
What am I supposed to do now
How am I supposed
To live my life without you?

Marie Haswell

Born To Love You

Will you trust me if I say to you
Until now our lives have been in tune
I want to say, what is true, I was born,
Born to love you

Will you hold me as I tell you how
How you touched me without reaching out
You arrived right on cue, so it goes,
I was born to love you

I was lost, my mind was out of control
I was saved when your heart spoke to my soul

Many things they are left unsaid
As we trust all the thoughts in our heads
Letting go of all I once knew, it just shows
I was born to love you.

Adam Lipinski

For The Love Of Our Granddaughter

Shakespeare wrote 'I compare thee to a summer's day'
And you bring sunshine to us in every way
You were very special from the day you were born
And in the months to come we saw your character form
You were an Angel at the Nativity when you were about three
Not on the stage, unhappy, climbed up and smiled with glee
We have seen you in pantomimes in musicals and plays
Sadly these activities have had a parting of the ways
Education is a must and you have exceeded expectations
But not we noticed, without a few altercations

You are now eighteen and you have the world at your feet
You were once our Lucy Locket, cute and sweet
Soon you will be seeking a university of your choice
And we will miss your smile and the sound of your voice
As grandparents we are proud, as proud as can be
We could stand you on a pedestal for all to see
You are a lovely young lady, quite a unique brand
And always remember, we will always be at hand
To give you support, no matter how life seems
So live your life and fulfil your dreams.

Celia Law

The Unknown Flowers

The unknown flowers speak to my heart,
Of my Christ and his people, spiralling and arisen;
They are fragile, of infinite wisdom, the flowers,
Captured in their dancing, green leaves of the larks.

They are a dance of love;

Dance that embraces us through the ages, encircling us,
Dance that enthrals us, into health and divinity;
Dance, where our partner, embraces us into infinity
It is a dance of love, that gives a partner,
The divine dance of Christ, even unto death,
And beyond, in the everlasting garden, of husband's patterns.
The dance of the unknown fragile, fragrant, flowers,

Of light, form, and heavenly empowerment,
The enlightenment of man's erotic dance, and delight.

Elizabeth R French

Forget Your Role

You took the trouble
At least you'd thought
At least you'd felt
If that was you - if indeed
That was you
But, I'd love you
I'd love you - for being so brave
And smashing past it all
You'd be a marathon
Don't disbelieve it
If what I thought happened
Did happen then you'd be brave

But if you could have told me
If you could have stretched it
That little bit further
If we both could
Your *heart* respected me
Whatever you said
Because you knew *mine*
Felt the same for you

Pat Roffey

Valentine's Message

When I was on my computer one day.
I looked on a dating site to find a way
to find somebody to love care and hopefully stay.
There I saw the man of my dreams
I was so happy I nearly screamed.
Valentine's Day was getting near
for me it was usually a time for tears
for most people either love or hate but for everyone it's never too late
keep trying and always care
for that special someone is really out there
I've found my husband, I'm really blessed
for now I've found true happiness
and so can you for we have to say
that for all of you there is a way
single or married happy Valentine's Day.

Rosalind Ann Webb

Affection

(John 3:16)

Old-fashioned subject yet ever new.
An inborn trait not only in
Humanity, animals too.
'Tis fascinating to observe children and pets
Protection and loyalty are evident, with each
progressive step.

Love knows no boundary, when attraction is real
Emotions go *'click'* then it's a done deal,
Mysterious bonds are formed beneath this banner
Gestures and glances are typical manners.

Bunty, a Highland terrier, was a classic example
She loved to play, an adorable champion.
But if she suspected foul play towards her mistress
Bared her fangs in genuine distress.

A God-given gift bestowed by Him
Marvellous and wonderful, unending theme
Blissful experience, abused today,
But God is love, come what may.

Annie Harcus

Forever Chasing Superstar

My forever chasing superstar, is all that I can be
A wind, the rain, a gentle charm, a wish that I could be
So appealing - she waits for me in dawn and early light
My forever chasing superstar, I follow into the night
The slightest of hope she gives to me
Like the smallest ray of sun
My forever chasing superstar, my journey just begun
As I run to chase the traffic, I see her passing by
My forever chasing superstar, a glimpse in my mind's eye
I breathe the air in the summer sky and wait for her to come.
I calm my soul as it starts to take flight and know that she's the one.
My forever chasing superstar, I see upon the field
I pinch myself and rub my eyes, as I know it can't be real
My forever chasing superstar, a bolt of light so new
Is in my mind and in my heart, that much I know is true.

Lee Cassidy

Of No Significance

Time and distance
Are of no significance.

I'm asked if the scent of lilac and sea air
Takes me to places or journeys somewhere?
And this song, that singer
Mark anniversaries I must surely remember?

I need no reminder or memory exchange;
I need no saint's day, no weather change.

You and I lie within every season, year blending into year:
Talking, murmuring, singing, sighing, you close against me,
Close and beautifully clear.
Yes, you are always with me, we form a boundless, unwavering union.

I am told you have passed to the other side:
Death has broken our communion.

I must, voices are slow, uselessly clear, must pay heed
To the here and now, its arrivals and departures.

But time and distance
Are of no significance.

Tessa Paul

The Wonders Of Love

Love is a most beautiful thing
It makes you happy
You can feel your heart sing
In the morning you awake
With a spring in your step
This is a feeling you
Will never forget
The world seems a happier place
You smile and laugh
There is a glow on your face
Problems seem lighter
When there is someone who cares
And you know they are willing
Your troubles to share
For that is true love.

Irene Mellowship

Allan

Do I love him,
Sitting half asleep
In front of 'Neighbours'
Or biting chipped nails,
Slouched in his chair?

Do I love him
In that silly cap
With the same old chat?
No time for myself
When he's always there.

And at night I wake
When the snores vibrate
And shake our double bed.
His mouth open, I stare.
But do I care?

When dreams break sleep
And fears fill dark hours,
Love's warm hand
Makes life easier to bear.

Paula South

The Pool

I saw your shape
Drowned in a watery pool
Deep below my feet
And thought perhaps
That you had left this world for that

And then I saw below me
And beside you
My own shape
Wavering but linked
As our hands touched

And wondered if those shades
Lived on inseparable
In their watery world
While we above
Walked our separate ways.

Pat Mackenzie

Our Journey Has Ended

I'm still nursing the tears
From years gone by,
Still clutching at straws
After we said our goodbyes.

Now you've closed the door
I cannot just walk in.
Can't you feel the pain
That is buried deep within?

Ensconced in self pity
I call out your name,
Rosemary, Rosemary
Remove all my pain.

It's no use me crying,
I know you are dying
To get rid of me.
Our journey has ended,
We must part.
I will live forever
With a broken heart.

Mary O'Dwyer

Love Is

Love is
Longing to live with whom, forever,
You're willing to die in their endeavour,
Love is lost on those in vain,
Lost on those that live for pain,
Love is the terminals of the train,
That runs from the heart that disputes the brain,
Love is the promise you always maintain,
Even when your priorities may detain,
Love is tailoring yourselves to suit
One another without refute,
Love is sporadic and everlasting,
Love is fulfilling, when you're fasting,
As the tedium is lost when you're together,
Love makes life brief for more than ever.

Anthony John Ward

Untitled

I sat by my fireside
My eyes filled with tears
I had just lost my husband
After only nine years.

My love died with him
My heart was filled with pain
The sun did not shine
There was only rain.

Then one day I met someone special
My love came alive again
The rain stopped
There was sunshine
No more pain.

Now I sit by my fireside
My eyes filled with tears
This time tears of happiness
For my new love
And my happy memories
Of those precious nine years.

Patricia Stone

Heartbreak

Darling we are now apart
Incantations of my broken heart
Block out memories of love forlorn
Grieve not for grief every morn
Love hurts, but in its bloom
Laughter and joy fill the room.
Destiny be burned in Hades' flames!
Gone is my love, you have claimed.
Fate stands aside, be gone!
Anger and desolation, now my song!
Eternally, I will remember
Each word, each smile, each look
Auras entwined, your love was mine
My soul, my heart, my love divine
Yours, until the end of time.

Jessie Shields

To My Husband

Over forty years of sharing
Both the pleasure and the pain,
The long and desperate struggle,
The laughter and the rain.
We have clung to one another
On the raft that's been our life,
We have honoured our commitment
And our pledge as man and wife.
We have shared the joy of caring
For love's token of each child
And I've seen the pure contentment
Resting in your tired smile.
It was hard but we survived it,
No one cared, but we pulled through
To enjoy life's present richness
And it's mainly down to you;
For your patience and endurance
Kept us going in the main
And, despite tremendous hardship,
I would do it all again.

Sandra Holmes

The Sky Above The Sea

I was a leggy teenager with a tangle of gilt brown hair
Who read romantic poetry and wore blue jeans with flares.

I fell in love and out of love, as girls of my age do
Until one summer evening - like Juliet so long ago,
Before 'night's candles' shone on high - I met my Romeo.

We played duets on the piano, rubbed church brasses when it rained
Found primroses at Easter and wandered country lanes.

He said my eyes were just the colour of the sky above the sea
And we planned a happy future, hoped for children - one, two, three.

Can a love be too perfect - perhaps not meant to stay?
For he went to sleep and left me, on a golden autumn day.

Now, more than forty years have gone before me,
Gilt brown hair turned silver-grey,
But my eyes are still the colour of the sky above the sea.

Meryl Champion

Romance - Bah, Humbug

I've read romantic novels and many, many books
But it's not like that in reality, that's not how it looks
I can't remember anyone meeting just by chance
In a fancy ballroom, waiting to be asked to dance
Life is not like that now, the romance isn't there
Nowadays it's the cinema and a bag of chips to share
No more the man's eyes gleam as the candle flickers
All they want to do now is divest you of your knickers
Try before you buy now is getting to be the norm
Then when you end up pregnant your parents kick up a storm
A quick trip down the aisle and you end up wed
He can't wait to get you home into his warm bed
Then the children come along, you both feel you're tied
That's when the so-called romance has been and gone and died
So all of you authors writing books, just please take heed
It's not like it used to be, not like the books we read
Nowadays it's mortgages, bills and kids and fights
You go to bed weary, no longer sex all night
It's so easy now to grow apart, forget about romance
Nowadays young couples just don't stand a chance.

Dorothy Fuller

Success To Life

I love my food, I always have
But now I have to stop
With no more cakes with cherries on
In the corner baker's shop.
You see I have a nasty bug
That tells me what to eat
But once a year at Christmas time
I can have a special treat.
All my tasty cakes I see lined up
On shelves so high
The chocolate ones with icing on
But I must just pass by
Meat I can have plenty of
But sweet things not a munch
No more trifles, no more crumbles
After Sunday lunch.
A moral to this story
Now I'm slimmer there's no doubt
I can look for pretty things
To wear when I go out!

Josephine Blackford

He Waits

A man and a woman so deeply in love
But the man, he ignored his wife
With so much to do in writing and speaking
To his work he devoted his life
Some time later, well into their marriage
The wife became ill and she died
The man sat alone and browsed through her diary
In which she had kept by her side
Reading words she had written about him. She said,
'Yesterday he spent an hour with me
And it was Heaven and I love him so
This time so precious you see'
Then on another day she had written
'I have listened for his steps in the hall
But now it's late, I guess he won't come,
Perhaps tomorrow he'll call'
The man wept, realising his neglect of her
And her desire just to talk with him
It's like God who loves and waits for us
To fellowship and our hearts to win.

Catherine M Armstrong

60 Years On

I was young and carefree
A clothes-mad teenager,
My uncle's mother-in-law
Introduced me to a stranger.
He was of gypsy stock
In mix-matched clothes
Brylcreem-ed hair and a white muffler
His neck enclosed.
My face must have said it all,
When he came to call,
For the date fell flat,
We did not have a ball.
We went to the flicks,
I don't recall what we saw,
We were as mis-matched
As the clothes that he wore,
He left town soon after that,
So I'd no chance left for a chat
That was the beginning and the end
Of my affair, with my relative's friend.

Joan Wheatcroft

Beyond Words

They lie side by side
They talk and they touch
They love each other so much
His hand moves to her head
He strokes her hair
He caresses her face
Her heart starts to race
She puts her arms around his neck
She moves nearer to feel
His body next to her
They embrace and they kiss
They melt with warmth and love
Oh! To be loved like this . . .
To be held so tight . . .
To know that he is there . . .
Is a feeling so wonderful they share
In realising that the love which envelops them
Is beyond words, keeping them together
All through the night
Until the morning light.

Mary Jo Clayton

My Love

So fifteen years have passed, my love,
Since the day we met.
No matter what life's dealt, my love,
I still love you yet.
So life deals us problems, my sweetheart,
We manage to struggle through,
And when the trouble's over, my sweetheart,
I still always love you.
So work keeps us apart, my darling,
That is beyond our control,
But precious moments with you, my darling,
Are etched within my soul.
So time alone is rare, my baby,
Well all I can do
Is make each moment special, my baby,
For I always love you.
So age has changed us, my dear,
Time keeps marching on by,
I desire you ever so, my dear,
And will until I die . . .

Anita Marlene Stridgen

Facets Of Love

'Love is a many splendoured thing', so the melody tells us
Which, when you're in love, you find to be true
Everything around takes on a 'rosy hue'
You walk along with stars in your eyes
Alight with love that you can't disguise,
To be together all the time
Reliving this feeling is so sublime.

Love affects us in many ways,
Like the love we have for golden days
When the sun shines brightly in a sky of blue
And everything's right in the world for you.
The love we feel for our newborn child,
Lying in their cots so meek and mild.

The love for our parents is very strong,
When you are with them you feel you 'belong'
Their love makes you feel so safe and secure,
Throughout your life you love them more and more
For partners, parents, children and friends
We hope that our love will never end.

Jean M Wood

My Only Love

I've felt I've always known you
Since the day that I was born
A bond that is between us
That never can be torn
You've loved me and cherished me
Through all of the days
Nurturing me and protecting me
With your gentle, loving ways
You shared your life with me
And not one day do I regret
For the magic was always between us
From the very day we met
And even though I'm now alone
And your face I no longer see
I want you to know, that deep in my heart
You'll forever be there with me.

Caryn Smith

Love Forever

The wind blew gently through the trees,
The grey clouds blew away,
There he was down on his knees,
And then I heard him say,
'Please marry me, you lovely girl,
I need you in my life, I love you,
My head is a whirl
Please will you be my wife?'

My heart was beating fit to burst
I just had to say, 'Yes'
And so I promised him my love
I offered him the best
'I'll be a good wife,' I had said, 'and raise a family.'
He said he'd buy a bigger bed
Then happy we could be.

He made me laugh, and I must tell you
As the years roll by
He still makes me laugh every day
I'll love him till I die!

Eileen Southey

From Me To You

Step by step I fell in love with you,
Step by step, it wasn't hard to do.
Kiss by kiss and hand in hand,
That's how it all began.
But the path of love is not always smooth,
Though I try hard not to complain.
Win or lose, it's part of the game,
Even if I love in vain.
Why should I care if love turns me down?
Why should I care it's a very big town?
There may be others more willing to share
The thrill of romance, so why should I care?
Our secret walks I'll go on my own,
No whispered talks when I'm all alone.
We'd have no secrets to share if our love affair was through,
So why should I care and yet I know I do.

Ina Higginson

My One True Love

On that special day in '74
I thought I couldn't love you more
But 35 years have passed
And I love you more now
Our love has lasted and as each year passes
And another begins
My love for you grows.

Without you I am not whole
With you I am strong
Whatever happens in life
Or if things should go wrong
Because we have each other
We will keep the other strong
Thank you darling for all these happy years
The thought of ever losing you brings me to tears
So I cherish every moment
Am thankful for every day
For 35 years of happiness
On that special day in May.

Susan Stuart

Dream

This dream will be of a tender purpose
To have your countenance, to draw yours into mine
A glimpse, an etched smile, a lip designed to care.

A while to watch and grow, though hurt, then repair
Using the accustomed years to take for granted and draw tears -
Must comfort and be aware of the surety of new birth.

The subtle look and copy from father to son;
A seeing eye, so young, yet in its image
Brings 'you', 'I', a regeneration without words are one.

From inner strength small faltering steps look to a horizon
Filled with the promise of faith
In youth, this dream will know no fear
But with the fullness of life
Will walk
In the shadows of ancestral steps with love.

Eileen Stockwell

A Work Of Art

Staring before me
Innocent and timeless
Is a blank canvas
Free as a boat
Talks to my imagination
Memories of journeys taken
Memories of every photo

Time to copy
An uncopied song
The tradition is alive
Honest and romantic
What will the day bring?
Another prayer
Another paint stroke
In its atmosphere of golden light
Oh how beautiful
Holding onto love
My reason for being
A work of art.

Paul Kelly

Love

Love is eternal.
Love does not die.
Love has no ending.
Oh heart, do not cry
For your lost darling,
He is still around,
Because true love like ours
Forever is bound
In deepest devotion
In this life and the next
Through every emotion,
Love's power won't rest
Till one day united
We again shall be.
Love is eternal,
And so are we.

Helga Dharmpaul

My Love

My love is powerful and mighty,
He is tender in his regard for me.
He can journey to the distant stars
Or stride upon the sea.

He looks at me with sweet desire
And turns my blood to raging fire.
I glory in his majesty
And am very proud that he chose me.

I love his eyes, that turn to me with sweet surprise,
His brow is pure and undefiled
And his lips are chaste and infinitely kissable,
And so is his nose.

I curl my arms around his strong neck,
And am made delirious by his nearness,
And the sweet manly smell of him,
He smiles a smile of pure delight at me,
And I am lost in ecstasy of anticipation
I just love him - he is perfection!

Carole Plant

Aphasia

Could I but tell you of the love seething within my soul.
How lightened would my burden be; how hushed the night and still.
This worn insomniac might sleep: easing those deep etched lines
Upon a face revealing hours spent tossing with the pains
That unrequited feelings ever brought to those who yearned.
Never finding the words to speak that love with which they burned.
Though knowing of a worldliness enclosed within my head.
A bumbling fool must hold my tongue whene'er I feel the need
To call your name that blessed name I fondly dwell upon.
But only whispered garbled sounds are even faintly borne
Out on the air, to go unheard as swiftly you pass by.
Not seeing this aching one waiting to catch your eye.
Wild hopes cruelly stalking my time with promises of bliss.
Must cling to me throughout my span, since nought could fill their loss.
Logic cannot win the fight as heart and mind contend
To tell me of a cause long lost. For then this life would end.

James Feakes

Love

Faded old Valentine cards
Tied with a red ribbon bow
Love that you sent to me
Long, long ago.
As I re-read each one
The years just melt away
Once again I am in your arms
Where I always wanted to stay.
But time and tide wait for no man
Or a woman that's true
But I would have waited forever
Just to be with you.
Hearts, flowers and lace
Yet even now I can see your face
And I often wonder, could it be?
That sometime, in some way
You ever think of me?
Could happiness be what the future holds in store?
If you, old Valentine, came knocking on my door.

Lynn Scatcherd

Unconditional Love

Sitting, with the morning sun shining bright
The cold autumn air subsides and warming
Autumn dew rolling down the windowpane
Reflecting sunrays upon your bright red hair
Fate put us together, I wonder why
When friends gather in my humble home
They always fall in love with you
Your beauty radiates all around your bodily form
As you rise from a cushioned armchair
Walking across the soft carpets on the floor
Nothing can describe you more than being a princess
My happiness bubbles when you sit on my knee
When I stroke your flame-red hair, I almost feel the heat
I love you so, you ask for nought
But you do require my kindness and love
My darling little ginger Persian cat.

Dugald McIntosh Thompson

Every Man Knows

Every man knows love, but sage men cannot
This emotive, motive force explain.
At once it is a source of ecstasy and pain.
One that humans can never restrain.
To cope with it cannot, it is plain man cannot train.
None know where it is seated, but scientists
Insist it must be somewhere in the brain.
Electric, magnetic, betimes hectic,
Driving existence with infinite persistence,
Against it useless be resistance.
Inspiring music and works of art, from
Life can never be forced apart.
Romantics imagined it is firmly lodged in
The heart, a primeval force with man from the start.
So different from the beast which seasonally,
The sex drive is unleashed.
It may express itself in passion, but changes
The key emotion to softness of sweet devotion.
Thank God for love, truly a gift from Heaven above.

Graham Watkins

The Nature Of Love

Love is something that cannot be defined,
Its threads are like gossamer;
The golden strands settle as by chance.
Around its chosen subjects, caught unaware.
Thus came my own experience of the heart.
How strange to find after fruitless searches.
Someone who mirrored myself in many ways -
Who could appreciate my curious sense of humour,
For whom I was the perfect companion.
This time my experience became a steady, moving stream,
Betrothed, then married we became - I was so proud.
Though we knew heartache and pain before the end.
There's one thing I learnt on looking back
Love only lets you remember the happy times
There is no sadness that they are no longer here
My only regret would be if they had never been.

Ann Furley

My One True Love

There are many types of love I find
From families to friends, a different kind
It's taken me nigh on sixty years
Struggling with my hopes and fears
Would I find my true soulmate?
Perhaps for me it was too late
But then he walked into my life
Supported me through troubles and strife
The kindest, dearest man who let
Me into his life 13th June when we met
I will never ever forget that day
Who could have thought it would turn out this way
So happy together I'm glad he's mine
And I am his for the rest of time
This lovely man who I adore
Contented cherished I couldn't want more
I wish that everyone had this
True love, friendship, it's just bliss
(This is my heartfelt poem to you all).

Anita Barnes

My Valentine

Forgive me should I dream of you
My Valentine
For I have held your hand in mine
In misty valleys of my mind
I have watched you from afar
Afraid to tell you, afraid to speak
I hope this card gives you a clue
Of how much I love you
Forgive me should I dream of you
My Valentine
For you are but the morning mist
That melts away with the rising sun
My heart is beating faster, faster
As you approach and pass me by
The words I wish to speak are lost
In the beating of my heart

David M Walford

My Dear

My dear you are gone away
My dearest dear
The love will continue every day
Although I cannot see you
My dear I know you're there
Some day my dear I shall come
We shall be together my dear
My dearest dear think of me
As you go on your new journey
As you travel in Heaven
My dear I think of you
I often dream of you my dear
Wonder and think of you my dear
I know my dear I shall join you
In God's own time my dear
I must wait my dear until
The mists have cleared away
Then I shall hold you near my dear
And never let you go.

Christina Hutchison

Many Facets Of Love

Love comes in many different forms
And is expressed in so many different ways
But what is love in a world so annihilated from it
That you can think and ponder and maybe wonder
That self can be distracted of all ability to show it?
What greater thing do we all need today
In a world so full of strife
Is but to unite us all together in love and unity
For a better world and way of life.
Love has many facets and here are just a few
Love is kind, understanding, forgiving peaceful
Pardoning errors, no anger, calmness
Oh, what a world we would have
If some of these values took seed
By applying these few facets
What a better place for all to be.

Pauline Potts

Defences

I built a wall
No one could see
And it was there
Between men and me
For years it stood
Proud and strong
That was until
You came along
A look from your eye
It started to shake
A kiss from your lips
It started to quake
With a touch from your hand
Bricks and mortar
Turned to sand
I stand before you
Without my protection
Hoping for no
Pain or rejection.

Ann-Marie Price

Broken Heart

I enter with caution, I hold up my guard,
This heart's been broken, it's going to be hard.
Behind the eyes, I look to see,
If next time round could be different for me.
Remember your words, with the way it was said,
Gone from my heart, but engraved in my head.
Feelings that passed, moments have gone,
Forever in my memory you will carry on.
I've turned a new page, this is my life,
I continue on through struggle and strife.
People you meet, people you know,
Some they stay, some they go.
I feel so alone, don't know where to turn,
I'm a fool in love, I may never learn.
When I'm down, I must pull it together,
Through the tunnel, it's now or never.

Lindsey Nicole Hazle

To The Absent Lover

When orange sunsets light the dusk
And paint the west anew
When red is shot with green and gold
And turquoise runs to blue
When saffron skies are laced with rose
I dream, I dream of you.

When hollow winds assail the house
And howl the long night through
When ragged clouds obscure the stars
And mask the moon from view
When squally showers lash the panes
I long, I long for you.

When a bright full moon sails up the sky
And stars are faint and few
The land agleam with silver light
Reflected in the dew
It's then that, madly, most of all
I ache, I ache for you.

Editha Russell

Sempiternal Love

The Law is my sempiternal shepherd; I shall always love thee.

You teacheth me to lie down in green pastures:
You loveth me beside the still waters.

You resteth within my soul: you loveth me on the
Paths of right-use-ness for my heart's sake.

Yea, though I walk through the valley of the
Shadow of death, I will fear no evil: for thou
Art with me; thy rod and thy staff they
Comfort me.

You sempiternally preparest a table of love before me
In the presence of mine enemies: you anointest
My head with oil: and my cup of love runneth over.

Surely goodness love and mercy shall fill me
All the days of my life: and I will dwell
In the love of the Law sempiternally.

R. J. J. Atkin

Only Love

Only warm and tender love
Can mend your broken heart
Only warm and tender love
Can give you a brand new start
On this war-torn world of ours.

So you search the world
Both near and far
For the one and only love
Who can mend your broken heart
For only warm and tender love
Can give you a brand new start
On this war-torn world of ours.

Then when you find the one for you
And the one who makes all your dreams
Come true
Then your life once more
Will be well worth living
On this war-torn world of ours.

Donald John Tye

A Rose For Love

From a rosebud
or red rose grows,
its redness glows

In the garden it stands
out from the rest

A rose stands for the true
meaning of love
Love is so much like a rose

From a bud a rose grows

If you pick the rose
from where it grows
next year a bud will appear
like love it grows

If you pick it now
it will not fade.

Samantha Groves

Moonlight Dance

Dancing in the moonlight
By a campfire
With a song
You are my singer
And my lover
As we glide towards the dawn.

Snuggling by the fireside
With your kisses
Oh so sweet
You move Earth
To give me Heaven
As you make my life complete.

So dance with me my darling
By the firelight
Sing our song
As we celebrate
Each other
And glide towards the dawn.

Ruth Callender

Poem For Lisa

So there I was, quite taken aback -
Gobsmacked, sure, but glad to see you.
I thought I had gotten over you,
Till long black hair glistened in the sun
And girlish eyes sparkled with loveliness.

Clichés ran naked through my speech
As we spoke. I was tongue-tied,
I was gunnelled with desire for you.
Is this too much? Is confession taboo?
Oh, but then you showed me that smile,
That knowing smile. I was captive.

Yes, indeed and I remain
Your bonded prisoner. Old poets hunched
A proof of love should be offered,
Gifted, melodramatically - so here it is,
The poem that's chained to my heart.

Daniel Walsh

Happiness Is . . .

The many facets of love
glisten like diamonds
endearing, enhancing and embracing.
Life radiates,
love dances,
bliss.

The many facets of love.
Music speaks potently
extolling, echoing and exciting.
Life rejoices,
love answers,
bliss.

The many facets of love.
Kitten purrs happily,
expressing, exciting and engaging.
Life relishes,
love responds,
bliss.

Margaret Ann Wheatley

Hope

The sun shines, a warm glowing ball in the sky,
melting the frost on the lawn from way up on high,
Wish it were as easy to melt the ice in my heart,
the ice which has lodged there since we've been apart.
I've had fun and I've giggled and I've laughed 'til I cried,
but nothing and no one can help from outside.

They say it takes time and that time is the healer,
but how can they know for they know not the dealer
who dealt me the hand that wrenched the warmth from inside me
and replaced that perfect pink feeling with a finger so icy?
It took only seconds to change laughter to tears -
to destroy what had been growing inside for years.

Then - out of nowhere - he crept into my heart,
and that finger of ice he slowly shredded apart -
allowing the flame of hope to grow warmer and stronger
and melting all within - an iceberg no longer.

Pat Salisbury-Ridley

Holding Time

If I could make time stand still
Hold the moments with my will
Tectonic plates would fall asleep.
The clouds above no longer weep
Nor whisper to the winds that blow
The secret sorrows that they know
And I would give you peace, my friend
Long before your journey's end.

If I could make time stand still
Hold the moments with my will
Like a mountain I would stand
Cool above the desert sands
And in the light before the storm
In the night before the dawn
I would free you from your pain
And I would make you whole again.

If I could make time stand still
And hold the moments with my will.

Eleanor Broaders

Down Memory Lane

Walking down memory lane,
I saw your face again -
Clear and bright,
Through a haze of light,
The vision is always the same.
I heard our song again -
Reminiscent of times we shared,
The melody never seems to fade.

Your laughter and voice,
So real, comes to mind.
The joys we left behind
And the tears that forever bind.

How easy it is to return in thought
And capture a time when love wasn't fraught.
Years just fall away -
Walking down memory lane . . .

Agnes L W Berry

Honeymoon

Fading sunset, speckles our room,
Fragrant, and yet gentle perfume;
Musk-rose flower blooms, birds on a limb,
Dusk's close hour looms, colours are dim;
Silver half-moon, silhouette trees,
Still, the lagoon, untouched by breeze.

Modest moonlight, silence within,
Body's delight, deeper than skin;
Craves groom for bride, plover for dove,
Wave's spume, ebb tide, lovers make love;
Darkness descends, spirits combine,
Partners and friends, I'm yours you're mine.

Golden sunrise, herald of dawn,
Molten-plum skies, new day is born,
Morning stroll round, birds start to sing,
Awnings rolled down, take to the wing;
Nestling kind arms, surrounding me,
Wrestling mind calms, love sets us free.

Andrew Stephenson

A Memory Of My Love

I can recall a foggy night
When through the swirling city mist
Came love, it was upon that night
Two people kissed.
On such a night we found our love
That lasted faithfully through the years
Until you had to leave this world
And I was left to hide my tears.
'Twas if that fog had come again
Conceals you ever from my sight
In memory I can walk once more
And still recall that heavenly night.
I'll walk with you down Memory Lane
Until the time, when with God's grace
The fog will lift and once again
I'll look upon my dear love's face.

Margaret Baguley

The One I Love

Message on the blackboard
Do not rub off

Take good care of yourself
Look where you are going

Left behind paying my way
Penny a day interested party

Foghorn blows
I will be there

Look me up
Overland, over here

Country calls
Are you in love?

I am
In love with love!

In love
With you too!

S M Thompson

The Photograph

(Dedicated to the soldiers of World War II)

She called out to him, before the sea took him to distant places
'Hey Harry, take this photo of me and the boy
You'll be glad of looking at familiar faces.'
She thought to herself, *when he's all alone with no joy*
His friends and the noise, slowly dying
He'll look at the picture and truly believe
It is still, well worth trying.
Striving to keep normality, true love and all that
Alive in your head and your heart
Whilst chaos and meaningless slaughter prevailed
This was precious, a hope, set apart.
A hope that one day when wars finally cease
When rancour and hate give way to lasting peace
This family would be whole once again, quite complete
To live without fear and enjoy victory
So wonderful, so sweet.

Carol Stocks

Remember

Remember it takes two to hold hands
and walk and talk and share a view,
fingers interlaced in gentle contact.

Two to send and receive the shock
of that electric feeling when one love
touches the other - even the brushing
hem of a skirt, or arm round shoulders.

Remember it takes two to kiss,
to notice how short is a minute of happiness,
or how long an hour when you're waiting.

We would be complete with no more
than a bare hut,
as long as there are the two of us.

Remember it takes two to fall in love,
two hearts before they can be exchanged,
two rings, two promises, two lives
entwined for life, for now, forever.

J M Gardener

Kathleen

Gentle breezes of the summer,
making the flowers and grasses sway
Eyes so full of love and kindness
welcome the dawn of each passing day

A smile that makes your whole being
radiate with elegance and charm
Your personality oozing out enthusiasm
measured by the lifeline on your palm

Each day facing a new challenge
as we struggle through our daily life
Giving me the strength and courage
sharing my problems with you, my wife

Our lives we have spent together
like a wonderful, never-ending dream
I love you now and for evermore
Happy birthday . . . dear Kathleen

Raymond Thomas Edwards

Song For Barry

I have loved you since before forever
And will love you still long after time is gone
We have shared together joy and sorrow
And my love for you is brighter than the sun

Would that I could share time with you
Yet I know that is not to be
For we each have our own path to follow.
And to travel, both must be free.

Yet ever will you stay within me
For I carry you deep in my soul
And wherever life's journey leads me
In the light of your love I am whole.

So 'til once again we are together
In love's light and strength may you be
For I've loved you since before forever
And love you deeper than eternity.

Muffet.

Jennifer Densham

When I Feel The Need

Active, truly alive, that's how you make me feel
The way you walk, talk, you ooze sex appeal
If only you knew what happens inside me
Your smiling face all I need to see.

The feeling is good, the connection is right
It'll take you to the highest heights
Open your arms wide and welcome me in
A feeling to behold, what a way to begin.

You and only you know how it really feels
Keep it hidden away or to the world reveal
Feelings never leave you, feelings never subside
Look up to the stars, take it in your stride.

Don't hold anything back, just live for today
Seize the moment, no hesitation, no delay
It only happens once in a lifetime, if at all?
Tomorrow's another day, plough through, don't stall.

Leigh Smart

Chapel Girl

(For Patty, for saving me)

Was outside the village chapel
First we kissed, beside castle grounds
That she stole my eager heart
Which skipped between almighty pounds

A soldier boy and his first love
But asunder was to be their fate
For she was far too young
And he was too foolish to wait

Many years were set to pass
Before once more their lips would meet
Tossed and torn on twisting paths
Until again sweethearts did beat

I finally have my darling girl
Destiny played a cruel game
It almost took a lifetime
For true love to find its aim.

Martin Davies

Fare You Well

Dear heart farewell. We would delay
This parting, but you'll never stay
Because there's sunshine on the fell,
Gold light along the low sea-swell,
And blue hills calling, 'Come away!'
Beyond the green paths arched with may
Small, springy, bouncing white lambs play,
Birds sing their clear glad roundelay;
Fat bursting buds warm days foretell.
Sweet heart farewell.

Still as you wander we will pray
You find world-wonder on your way,
And peace, the calm enchanted spell
Be on the land where you will dwell
Beside a blue and emerald bay
Till star-shine at the end of day.
Dear heart farewell.

Diana Momber

For Brian With Love

(Written for our ruby wedding)

After forty years of marriage
With all its ups and downs
I've grown to accept your pigeons
Ditto, you my dogs.

There's been days of secret weeping
When I felt in despair
But in my darkest days of sorrow
You were always there.

We've shared many precious moments
Been so very richly blessed
With our three beloved children
Each one Heaven-sent.

The love of God has touched us
'Tis surely plain to see
For now we have grandchildren
To complete our family tree.

Olive Barber

Pretty Claire

When pretty Claire did kiss me
I thought my heart might swoon
Her nervous smile, flushing cheeks
Albeit, over too soon
Such joyous smile
A man might see
Until his dying day
When pretty Claire did kiss me
My years did melt away
I became the suitor
Her fair hand to win
To spend our years together
How joyous bells would ring.

To cup her fledgling beating heart
In hands callous with age
Alas, too soon to part them
And watch her fly away.

John Cates

But You Are Gone . . .

Today my friend, we say goodbye
I watch you leave the station
Your train seems distant
But yet, so near
I reach out but you are gone . . .

Thoughts pass me by, present and past
As slowly you get further away
Echoes of your voice surround me
I turn but you are gone . . .

Slowly I walk, through the streets
See people, we had known so well
They ask if I have seen you
I have, but you are gone . . .

Alone I sit by the fire
In its flames I can see your face
I feel that you are still with me
I have memories, but you are gone . . .

Denise Marie Evans

Nanny Kathy

How could she go
When I needed her most?
Yet living on in my heart
Nanny - a ghost.

Didn't know she was ill,
Could I not have said goodbye?
I could have loved her more,
Why did I not try?

How could she leave when
I loved her so?
With all my heart
And now I'm low.

How could her bright eyes turn so pale?
How could they close? How could they fail?

When her face drained of colour,
My nanny's dead, God bless her!

Amy Carter (11)

My Love

My love, my love
I think of thee
Morning noon and night
The image always constant
Before my inner sight

The energies that move us
Always should bring change
But our love for one another
Is constant and the same

Wherever you may wander
Whatever you may do
My love shall be forever
So very close to you

Our love shall last forever
Until the end of time
Now and for eternity
Shall you evermore be mine

Errol Kavan

Unconditional Love

Within this big and beautiful world
There is a love unique,
It is always there to comfort you
When life seems very bleak.

From the moment you are born on Earth
Your Mum is there to guide,
Nurturing you - loving you
Always by your side.

Through all the years of growing up
She carefully watches you,
Giving advice and constant love
No matter what you do.

When fully grown her love still stays
Constant - honest - true,
A Mother's unconditional love
Will stay her whole life through.

Dot Young

Always

For her, it was not one of those
heart-stopping moments
they sing about in love songs
where your eyes meet across a crowded room

It all happened gradually and comfortably
He brought out the best in her
Made her feel wanted, attractive, confident
All these things she had been lacking
before they met

At that first meeting, when he took her arm
It was as though they had known each other for years
And she knew then that at last
she had come home

Later he told her
that it had been the same for him
And they both realised that, whatever happened,
This feeling would last forever

C M Lewin

Anastasiya

My beautiful darling Anastasiya
You are more lovely than Malaysia
Each day, for you I get a little crazier
My beautiful darling Anastasiya.

I think of you with each new dawn
My heart and soul, to you are drawn
Apart from you I am forlorn
United we will never be torn.

I hang here on your every word
My love for you the Lord concurred
My heart flutters like a bird
Our plea for love the Lord has heard.

You are indeed my precious flower
For you I'll build an ivory tower
Before you let all others cower
Our love has such almighty power.

Philip Tucker

The Crush

When they shouted, 'Hey how's it going?'
I would say, 'Cool' or a surly, 'Fine'
Hoping they did not see my wanting eye
Watch her a few heads down the line.

Rejection and ridicule
Ever present fears and foes
And the loneliness in my room
Listening to songs that feed my woes.

Pretending to ignore her
Then desperate for a glance
Scared that she will come up to talk
And scared I will miss a chance.

Fantasy and daydreams are a light relief
When she smiled, I was beyond belief
It sent me all in a flush
That's the curse and the blessing of my first
Schoolboy crush.

Stephen Prout

Driven Insane

Your face is in my thoughts
Each and every day
Even when we aren't so close
It's like you're not that far away

I have to stop this madness
It's driving me insane
My feelings just get stronger
I shouldn't feel this way

Every time I'm lonely
Your image springs to mind
Giving me some comfort
You're gentle and so kind

I just wish to be with you
Together we'd be one
Without you it's just cloudy
With you there's the sun.

Paola Borella

Madly Falling

Oh so beautifully
You breezed into my life
Like a zephyr swirling through a field of corn
You caused my wobbly knees to sway and my poor old head to nod
I stood there speechless, mouth gaping like a fishmonger's cold slab cod
When I did speak I'll bet you thought I was a tree-dwelling anthropoid
But then you cleverly touched my arm and made these crazy feelings void
You smiled that lovely smile of yours
And took my hand with your velvet glove
And calmly said, 'It will be all right, it's just us falling madly in love.'
Your deep brown eyes revealed passion's gloss and instinctively I knew
That you could love me deeply, truly, almost as much as I love you
We will cling together at least forever, reliving the lucky day
That you breezed into my life
Oh so beautifully.

Morgan Keith

Love Lost

In every place that once we knew
    I look for you in vain;
I listen for your voice
    That I shall never hear again.

Our favourite meals, now dry as dust,
    I take without delight;
Our bed, so cold without you
    Brings no comfort in the night.

We still had so much love to give,
    So many songs to sing;
No laughter now to cheer my world,
    No joy in anything.

Oh, my dear love, my broken heart
    Must learn to bear this pain;
Until that longed-for day
    When I can take your hand again.

Patricia Fallace

You Can't Adopt Anyone Over 18 - June Did!

June - I was led to believe you loved me like a 'brother'
Before - you adopted me because I felt for another.
Later - but you were talking about reincarnation, and you had yet another.
I didn't know you had girlfriend feelings.
My shyness, it was so revealing.
Later with yoga I had healing.
Your laughing at me put me off you.
The blushing made me worse.
The blushing was a curse.
My first true love feelings were for you true.
Later you revealed your true feelings for me.
But I couldn't hear the third party comments, you see.
It's people laughing at me - that caused the blushing.
The blood to my face it was rushing.
June, I embarrassed you by what I said.
You laughed at me - insulted my head.
Now you're married - I have to give you up instead
And get you out of my head.

Peter Goodall

What Is Love?

What is love? I don't know.
If you catch it would you know?
Is it the welcome kiss when you've been away,
Or the sunshine on an autumn day?
An open fire, making toast,
Or enjoying the things I like the most?

The joy of a bride through a veil of lace,
Or the first ever smile on a baby's face?
Early snowdrops on a carpet of snow
Is this love? I don't know.

Maybe it's all around
Flying in the sky, growing in the ground,
In the simple songs that children sing
Or the shiny gold of my wedding ring.

Oh you can catch it, yes it's true
I caught love from all these things and you.

Jo Stimpson

Cover To Cover

My skin
A blank sheet
Your fingertips
Like a quill
Tracing your name
Gives my body
A thrill
Turning my pages
Slowly at first
Then speed-reading the chapter
As I recite quickly
A verse
From cover to cover
And over again
An open book
No longer
As you read me
Once again

Samantha Williams

Ivan - My First Love

I love to walk down by the sea
It's exciting by the shore,
I love to see the birds above
But darling - I love you more.

I love to drive my open car
To hear the engine roar,
And feel the wind go through my hair
But darling - I love you more.

I love to eat my favourite food
Chocolate I can't ignore
And ice cream and apple pie,
But darling - I love you more.

However old I get
However old and grey,
I will always say to you
'Darling, I love you more each day.'

Anne-Elise Carr

My Heart's Delight

She is my heart's delight
Whom I loved at first sight
All through the summer long
We went gaily along
To spend sunny hours
Amidst the fields picking flowers
The sun in its splendour
Shone down as I kissed her
So tenderly 'neath the trees
Their boughs swaying gently to the breeze . . .
Ere the winter had passed
I wedded my true lass
In the church on the hill
And her beauty my whole world profoundly filled
Now we live at ease
In heavenly peace
Far away from the city's cries
In a cottage small - our own pure paradise.

Gwyneth Scott

The Dark Rose

Joy is to muse on bewitching charged hours,
On England's most natural and loveliest flowers;
Whose love is the best, gentle worth I suppose,
The fairest of petals should match the dark rose.

Gold is the magnet, the award that we seek,
All glory unquestioned, the highest burnt peak.
But kindness seems often a third of fourth prize
Like captured exposures deep in the soul's eyes.

Dreamt legends Arthurian, past courtship sublime,
To ride for your lady, whirled memories and thyme:
Her favour, a bright scarf, entwined on your lance,
And gleams of true daring were seen in her glance.

So seeds of our ethos grow nurtured or wild,
A proud parent's daughter, an auspicious child;
A bloom through the ages in magic that glows,
Each artist envisions their English dark rose.

Christopher Rothery

My Beautiful Dream

My only dream is to be with you
To share your life in all you do
I love you more than words can say
I want to make you mine some day
Each time I look at your handsome face
The more I want to be dressed in lace
Money and wealth and all that they mean
Are nothing to me, you're my beautiful dream
You tie a band around my heart that's pure as shining gold
I never want to let you go even when we're old
And so my dream will never end
'Cause you're my lover as well as my friend
And I've said in the lines before
I never want to let you go
For you're my world, the love of my life
And I'd give the world to be your wife
Yes, money and wealth and all that they mean
Are nothing to me, you're my beautiful dream.

Josephine Quinn

Candour

Girls play with men's emotions, which is historic.
A smile from their eyes and men are euphoric.
Some men have variety, lots of notches on the post.
Others are more secretive, no desire to boast.

Never retreat, when a girl uses her charms.
Just move forward, pull her into your arms.
Always keep her curious, your enemy is lust.
Match loyalty with mystery, love is trust.

There has to be passion, for your lady fair.
To emphasise your ardour, prove that you care.
Men can be naïve and clumsy, this I must establish.
But love that is mutual is our fervent wish.

If you are unselfish, it's easier to stay detached.
Smiling like Cupid as each romance is hatched.
Deep in my heart, hides my definition of perfection.
Answering the Las Vegas band, we dance and we're human.

Michael Malam

Coincidence

I looked up unsuspectingly
The fates decreed our paths must cross
For there through the plate glass window
You appeared
Your bicycle made a glorious arc
As you spiralled effortlessly across six lanes of traffic
Your character was in that move
Artful, daring, vital, determined
Wasted time pulsed through your veins
The present was never enough to encompass your visions
Luck would have it: the sudden downpour
Forcing you to seek cover under the nearest overhang
An oddity to fellow diners I hid myself from view
What sadness this distance: to think you are the father of my children
Yet I have learned, in spite of my heart, to fear you
To no avail the screams, the tantrums, the recriminations
Life must be lived another way
Our past the pain and the happiness behind us.

Monica Gurney

Free Love

I never heard no violins.
No twanging harps on angels' wings.
All I felt for her was purely lust.
With the pleasure that it brings.

I believe she felt nothing for me.
To her I was survival.
That as soon as I left her red lit room.
There would be a new arrival.

But I can't erase her from my mind.
There was something there in her eyes!
A loving heart held prisoner.
Behind bars of drugs and lies.

Now she is gone! So young to die.
Nobody cares but me.
She held her own love prisoner.
Now she has set it free.

John Bilsland

Love's Fate

How was I to know
On that momentous day
That the two of us should meet
And love struck straight away.

Our days were not arranged
Our plans just went askew
But fate stepped in for us
And brought me love and you.

How golden were our days
How wonderful was our life
Till all my dreams came true
The day I was your wife.

And as the years roll by
We know fate was a friend
For our love matured like wine
And will last until the end.

June Mary Davies

Together At Last

Where is that young man I've come to know
That I give a kiss to each night?
He fills my heart with a radiant glow
Is it a dream that goes in the light?

This young man makes me feel so good
That I have come to love so much
I would give him a hug if I really could
I hold out my hand but no one to touch.

Oh! I truly wish it was for real
Not just a dream of this young man
That we could go for a lovely meal
And off we would go hand in hand.

That day will come when we will meet
And I will see him and have a talk
Perhaps in a doorway or in the street
And then we will go for a long, long walk.

Phyllis Nichols

Loneliness

Loneliness comes as night falls
 And the pressures of day
 Fade away.

In the deep sough of silence
 That comes with the night,
In the midst of the sorrow and pain,
 No hand reaches out to comfort and hold,
No voice softly murmurs my name.

Like a river of dark
 My silent tears flow,
And carry me on through life's stream.
 The mist from the river swirls round me and on
And shattered are all my dreams.

So loneliness comes in the shadow of night
 Till the pressures of life
 Fade away.

B McCoach

Only 16

Whilst touring in Scotland approaching night,
We found a guest house, which looked alright.
We asked if they had accommodation,
'Yes,' they said, 'we have had a cancellation.'

After dinner, we went into the lounge,
My parents and me, just we three.
A sofa and chair we managed to scrounge,
When I saw a boy with his parents, just like me.

We exchanged many a furtive glance
And then his mother said just by chance!
'Would you like to join us for a drink?'
And I felt myself turning pink!

Through the years he was a constant friend,
This young man and me had grown quite close.
But something happened, which I didn't comprehend,
And we parted, leaving me sad and morose.

Carole McKee

For My Special Husband

I was told the memories fade away
I'm not sure that I want them to
So many reminders, day by day
Shall I share some of them with you?

The things I miss most are the cuddles
The hugs and the jokes which we shared
His help when things seemed so muddled
The kisses to show that he cared!

Just knowing whatever I asked him
He would give it *all* of his best
The teasing because he thought I was prim -
Then holding me close to his chest.

Why would I want to forget this
And all other memories too?
Forty-seven years of his hugs and his kiss
I *will* keep them all - wouldn't you?

Kay Purkiss

Always

So long we've been together
I'm just so glad you are mine
I'd never want to lose you
You're just there all the time.

Always there for a gentle hug
There in times of tears
There when I go to sleep
It's been that way for years.

I'll love you forever
The bond is just so strong
I just know you'll stay with me
Throughout my whole life long.

Others have come and gone, it's true
But no others could compare
I'll always love you most of all
My own loveable, tatty old teddy bear.

Margaret King

Coming Home

As the shades of night grow darker,
And the evening shadows fall,
I think of the one who is not here,
The one I love most of all.

I listen for his footsteps,
The key within the lock,
But the only sound that fills the air,
Is the ticking of the clock.

Do you know I'm waiting?
Do you know I really care?
I told you, but you heard me not
Because you were not there.

But one day we'll be together
Where there is no further stress,
We'll walk together holding hands
And share our happiness.

Joan Hepper

Lost Love

Do you mind if I say I still love you?
You know it's not meant to offend
If our paths ever meet one day in the street
Would you mind having me for a friend?

I confess I feel nothing but sorrow
Why did our affair have to end?
I live for today there is no tomorrow
Is there hope for me now as your friend?

Can I tell you just once that I miss you
That my world is no longer the same?
Would it make any difference at all if you knew
I regret treating love as a game?

When will this nightmare I'm having all end?
Will I manage to piece things together?
If you won't be my love then just be my friend
Say maybe, perhaps, but please don't say never.

Margaret Grainger

In Praise Of Jewellery

When the men in my life have all gone,
The diamonds still sparkle and shine.
The tears, disappointments, hurts remain long,
But the gold and jewels remain mine.

When love, kisses and red roses fade,
The petals fall to be swept away.
The rubies stay fresh and glow,
Keeping memories alive and darkness at bay.

When the chocolates are all eaten,
And the husband returns home to his wife,
The mistress knows that she'll always be beaten,
For every hour of love has its price.

As the perfume begins to linger,
And his attention is beginning to wane,
It may only be that ring on your finger
That keeps mind and body sane.

Viv Fitzpatrick

Valentine

Don't send me roses
They never last
Forget about chocolates
They're in the past.

Sing me no love songs
Under the moon
Only Sinatra
Can make me swoon.

Don't buy me diamonds
They won't impress
Don't buy me perfume
Or even a dress.

Just give me some space
To be who I am
Then I'll be happy
To call you my man.

Elizabeth Thorpe

Ode To Love

Love is a feeling from deep in the heart
An artist's expression with the brush strokes in art
The smile of a mother and her tender grace
When she first sets eyes on her newborn's face.

Love is the bond of laughter and joy
Developed o'er time of girl meeting boy
A gentle reminder when sealed with a kiss
When a bride changes names to Mrs from Miss.

Love is the gentle whispers in trees
As they dance and sway to the soft summer breeze
The warmth of the sun on the soft wet sand
Smoothed by the onrushing tide's watery hand.

Love is a word with no creed or call
A special emotion to be shared by us all
Whatever religion or the colour of skin
If we open our hearts, love will walk in.

George Gutherless

Life And Love

Fast his life of mine was dying
Blind already and calm as death
Snowflakes on her bosom lying
Scarcely heaving with her breath

Love came by and having known her
In a dream of fabled lands
Gently stopped and laid upon her
Mystic chrism of Holy hands

Drew his smile across her folded eyelids
As the swallow dips
Breathed as finely as the cold did
Through the locking of her lips

So, when life looked upward being
Warmed and breathed on from above
What sight could she have for seeing
Evermore but only love.

Elizabeth Ann Parkin

Love's Lament

Don't take me to your manor house
For ornate trappings leave me cold
Don't spirit me to far-flung beaches
For the sun makes my stamina fold

Don't tease me with idle bon-mots
For want of sounding like a sage
Don't fan me with your flattery
For beauty quickly dims with age

Don't shower me with hasty promises
For experience foretells you won't deliver
Don't buy me expensive trinkets
For such indulgence makes me shiver

Don't claim you and I are kindred spirits
For the Lord decrees such fateful treats
Just take me to your heart
For only then, will I soundly sleep.

Joanne Garzella

A Grain Of Sand

As I lay naked on the sand
I am here, exposed for you to understand
That the beauty in life is far from bland
I have the secret of love in the palm of my hand.

Here for all the world to see
Enhanced with swift delivery
I would like you all to be completely free
If you have time to listen to me.

I will spread my message, for you I will make a stand
Speak to every nation in every land
My victory is not such an exclusive brand
For we are all, but a grain of sand.

Sea will no longer divide us
War will cease to exist
I am able to put a stop to the madness
For my dream world will become impossible to resist.

Katrina Graham

Memories Of Yesterday

A lovely little cottage,
With a view towards the sea,
Belonging to my partner,
Who died just recently.

I've got such happy memories,
Which I'll never leave behind,
But he's lying in a graveyard,
Life is sometimes so unkind.

With heavy heart I've pondered,
On thoughts so dear to me,
Of things I would no longer do,
Places I may never see.

He was there to lend a shoulder,
Always an ear to lend,
He'll be forever by my side,
A true and faithful friend.

Shirley Ann Stalker

To The Love Of My Life

Love is something you cannot see
But I love you and you love me
I can't explain how I feel for you
It makes me happy, occasionally blue
The way I feel makes me know that you care
The good times, the bad times
Special things that we share
You're part of me and I'm part of you
Being together, being true
Caring, sharing everyday things
Getting married, wearing of rings
Each day is special to wake up by your side
Being there for me whenever I've cried
I love you because you treat me good
I need you because you know that I should
I want you like never before
My love for you will not be a chore.

Julie Dawn Ellis

The Meeting

The Elery Queen of the obscure and unseen
Occupies the bell chimes of a steely night
Tainted by fantasies of desires
Merge to meet at midnight
With haunted lonely lovers of despair
Reflecting at what might have been
In the days of wanton consciousness
Below the clock tower of a wasted youth
As life ebbs away
In the velvet morning of the soul
And the sunsets of the mind
Meet at dawn
Like perfect strangers
The air is melancholy with neglect
In life's basement
And the bosom of our guardian angels
'Neath the serpent of souls.

Finnan Boyle

The Sound Of The Sea

Hands resting on knees.
In the background
The sound of the sea.
Wriggling your toes
In the sand,
Then the motion of you
Waving one hand.
You stand up unaware
Of the sun catching your hair.
You laugh and poke
Your tongue out at me,
Then turn around
And run down to the sea.
A never-ageing nymph,
A part of my life.
A born fighter
And a loving wife.

Alan Mason

Enchantment

Our hands touched fleetingly
Your eyes so blue, holding my gaze.
The smile that I loved
And softest voice
Just captured me.
From then I knew my life would change.
Would never be just me,
Never the same again.
We were to be so blessed
With a lifetime of such happiness.
And if I could go back, retrace my steps
I'd treasure every moment,
Relive every memory and still want more.
Just to hold you close to me
And tell you that I love you,
Hearing you say you love me,
For all eternity.

Christine Clark

Lost

You gave me time
That I shall not forget
And breathless am I,
One dozen kissed red roses
Nay
One thousand would be too few
And speechless am I,
A whisper, gentle
Blushing at my ear
And timeless am I,
Enchantress
Spells deep woven
Throughout my soul
And selfless am I,
Your hand upon my cheek
And I am lost within you
. . . and without you.

Jonathan Grout

Memories

We have been married 52 years,
My husband still says, 'I love you!'
When we met, he courted me with chocolates,
Which we shared in the cinema,
He put his arm around me, I thought my heart would stop,
And later we enjoyed fish and chips,
He smelled of soap and aftershave
Which I can remember today.
We brought up four children, now grown up and moved away,
As they grew, we shared laughter and tears
I remember when it rained he took his jacket off
For me to wear, and he got wet.
Now years later, we say, 'Have you got your mac?'
He holds my hands to steady me, so I won't fall
Such silent love between us,
No chocolates now, but flowers which won't make me fat.
Oh! where did I put my hat?

Joan Margaret Waller

Far Below Zero

Her icy heart
And stone-cold ways
Became a melted icicle
A droplet that glistened
In his palm
Delicately
Fragile, untouched by another
He became her surrounding
Her undiscovered
As the surface
No longer frozen
Faded with tender sensitivity
For no other place
No other moment
Had reached far beyond her true feeling
Revealing
Emotion bounded by unexplainable connection.

Debra Smith

Love Poem

Love is touch
Love is feeling
Love comes from the heart
Sharing and caring
Emotions one being of love
To hold a newborn baby in your arms is love
Love shared from one to another
To share love in action, with a kiss or a cuddle
But the memory stays in your heart forever
Your arms around one other person
Presents, token of love we share with one another
Speaking, taking shows love singing
Expressions we share in love
Blow kisses to say, 'I love you!'
See love in your eyes.
Feel love from body vibes.
Our always in love.

Pauline Morrow

A Simple Love

I will tell you a story of a love so true
One that tells of my love for you
Born of a glance when our eyes first met
With a single look, our future set.
Grey-blue eyes, intelligent and strong
Trusting and warm, I read their sweet song
I drank in their beauty, bathed in their depths
Touching my heart, like a tender caress
Your smile said it all as we stood side by side
As I said, 'I do,' when you made me your bride
When we kissed for the first time as husband and wife
We knew it to be for the rest of our lives.
We have travelled so far, these many long years
And have stayed strong and true, without any fears
When asked if our lives were blessed up above
I tell them, 'They're blessed, quite simply with love.'

Denise Edmonds

Love's Meaning

Love begins when we are born
And placed for the first time in our mother's arms
From then it grows as the years go by
Until another kind of love appears
Love for our friends begins to dawn
As we get older we start to wonder
How will I know when I fall in love?
Then all of a sudden, two opposites meet
The mystery's solved and life is complete
Steadily love for each other grows
It isn't all easy, as those in love know
But in difficult times it lends its support
And strengthens us in its special way
So we can face the world each day
Love gives us something to be thankful for
And thankful we'll be for evermore.

Jean Salmon

Love

You are the sun that shines through me,
The refreshing summer rain.
You are the one who I live for,
Who eases all hearts' pain.
You are the one whose face delights . . .
Whose smile is just for me.
You are the one who makes each day special . . .
Can't you see?
You are my whole life,
Each hour of every day,
The one who protects me,
What more can I say,
Except that what makes my world
Is the fact that you are there.
To say those words . . . I love you.
To mean them and really care.

Joyce Hudspith

Only You

When I was only sweet sixteen
I fell in love with you.
Our wedding day was perfect
The honeymoon was too.
Later when the children came
We shared a joy so new.
Through all the years we've laughed a lot
And cried a little too,
We've been so very happy
The time it simply flew.
It's hard to take it in,
The way our happiness just grew,
I only want to say now
That from the start I knew
No matter what may come and go,
For me there's only you.

Vera Seddon

My Best Friend Requested A Poem:

You asked me to write this, so this I write for you,
I just don't know how long it will be, as I think a lot of you.

It does not matter if these words are too stubborn to rhyme,
But these words are sketched from the heart,
The heart that I call mine.

You're genuine, you're crazy, you're unique and one of a kind,
There's more to you than most people know,
Like a hard puzzle to complete, with swings
And roundabouts in your mind.

You want the best for yourself and you want the best for me,
This is why I love you, as you're incredible and honest, you see.

From the day I first realised my feelings for you,
I knew it would be hard work, but something I wanted to do,
You've always been my number one, as I'm at one with you.

Love I believe is a friendship on fire,
Finding someone you can collide with from the soul,
Best friends that connect in mysterious ways
And shine for you when storms begin to roll.

When you hold me tight at night, all the negatives flow away
And I feel everything will be all right until the next day.

Your smile makes me smile, connecting in mysterious ways,
You bring out the best in me in every single way.

I'm scared of getting old, but I'm not scared with you,
As I know together we can see it through.

Our future will be special, because we believe in fate,
Wanting the best will guide us on our way.

Life is a journey and one you have to make,
So come and hold my hand, I'll be with you
Each and every step of the way.

The little man was a joke, but one I hope comes true,
In years to come though, I don't mean to scare you!

The look in your eyes, the 'Sudocrem' smoothed face,
Your smell, your touch, are all the things I crave.

Suggestive manner and that evil laugh,
You're still a kid, even after dark.

The bathroom door wide open with you chatting away,
It has me in giggles in a good, but odd way.

You're my favourite person in this world, well-known fact,
Please don't run away again, or do your famous disappearing act.

I just want to say thank you for you being you,
I'm lucky to know you and have you in my life,
I'm not me in my life without you.

So, you're talented - gifted, with a voice from God,
You have the ability to influence, keep aiming up top.

Keep being successful, you won't be anything else,
Keep in touch with your heart and you will be happy with yourself.

Be proud Mr Jazzman, like your family and I are of you,
Don't let things eat away, in fact . . . stop this now,
Things may get depressing and tied up in knots,
But just take a step back and shout out loud.

You'll find inspiration with life and fate to write your songs,
Don't let the lyrics write your life though, it could all go wrong.

Let your life and dreams write the lyrics
Let your destiny happen as nothing will be a surprise
Take the adventurous walk that will lead you,
Magic will soon open your eyes.

There's a lot to still learn, learning is a lifetime;
Have faith though, it's good to be frightened.
Hold back on those tears that rule your past,
If I can do it, so can you, the nightmares will not last.

You're here on this Earth for a reason, if only we knew too much,
Life will pass you by and you run this risk of getting stuck.

Friends around you have the answer, you just find that key,
Your name is already tattooed on my heart,
I feel it's there, deep within me.

You're one of a kind, that notices, a unique man that cares,
A knight in shining armour; always catching my distant stare.

From behind the shadows, or up on stage,
You seem to acknowledge my thoughts brewing in a rage.

This may be no masterpiece; it's nothing about who we are,
Just see this as a collection of words forming our shooting star.

We may have to be apart in life to make things work,
But understand us as individuals, sometimes it will hurt,
Though do not worry, reach out and you'll see,
There is one star that shines just for you and just for me.

In this universe we learn nothing is written in stone,
Please know though, don't ever feel lonely;
You won't have to walk this world alone.

We're the only two of a kind - all this and above is just from my mind.

Gemma Turner

The Ballad Of Sir Mark And Princess Stacy

(For my friends)

The sky was clear, the sun was bright,
Along the road, came the gallant knight.
His armour shone, how it gleamed,
His hair like flame, his eyes blue-green.
A man of honour down the path he came,
Sir Mark of Halstead was his name.
His quest was clear, his quest was true,
To save Princess Stacy with eyes so blue.

Far from the lands of the good and kind
Neatly kept cornfields and sukebind.
In a land full of darkness and of hate
Poor Princess Stacy was in a state.
'Oh me, oh my,' she would wail,
'Who will save me from this nightmare fairy tale?
Where, oh where is my strong knight?
Sir Mark please save me from this plight!'

Sir Mark was on the road many days,
Searching the dark forgotten ways,
To distant lands without the sun
To find his beloved fair-haired one.
For many sunny days and starry night skies
For as long as the wolf runs and the eagle flies.
Onward and onward went Mark the Brave
His one true love he would save.

Many adventures our hero came upon
Fighting trolls, ogres and a giant dragon!
His battles were many, his battles were fierce,
His magic armour could not be pierced.
His strength was great and his arm strong,
Fighting for right, conquering wrong.
On he went, he kept going forward,
Not realising that his lady was bored!

At the Tower waiting in the dark,
The lovely Princess waited for Sir Mark.
Having been trapped there many days before,
By an ugly witch who hated her to the core!
Twiddling her thumbs and biting her nails,
'Oh, when will my true love prevail?
This waiting about is starting to get to me.
Why doesn't Sir Mark come very quickly?'

Alone she would sit combing her hair,
The blue-eyed Princess of hair so fair.
'Is this what it is to be a Princess?
Sitting around being some Knight's quest!
I've had enough, I'm getting out!'
Whilst tying bedsheets she heard a shout.
'Hello my love, are you there?
Your Knight, Sir Mark, is now here!'

Relief washed over the Princess' face,
At last he had finally found the place.
Seeing him there from her high window
She sweetly called to him below.
'You bloody took your time!
Don't just stand there, start to climb!
I've been here what seems like an age,
All because of a witch's rage!'

The tall tower was smooth and grey,
Scaling the walls seemed the only way
After many attempts he slid to the floor
Finally Princess Stacy shouted, 'Try the door!'
'There's a door?' said Sir Mark. 'Why didn't you say?'
She replied, 'I thought it more romantic this way!
After so long in my confinement, it might be good entertainment!'

With his sword he bashed and banged,
The door opened with a big clang.
To the beautiful Princess, Sir Mark said,
'Come, let us away from this tower of dread.
Let's go now, too long we have tarried,
We'll find a church and finally be married,
You're the one for me, the love of my life
And I want you for my beloved wife!'

The Princess, her heart fluttered in her chest.
'Dear Sir Mark, you have a new quest,
You may be strong and brave and true,
But love, it seems, got the better of you!
Marriage is not an easy path,
Dragons and battles an easier task.'
Sir Mark looked into her eyes so blue,
'You're my new quest, I love you!'

Then they kissed and hand in hand,
Began to leave the witch's land.
But where they had stood their love so true,
It seeped into the ground and it grew!
It became trees, leaves and flowers,
This true love had strong powers.
The land began to take on life,
Gone now, the darkness and strife!

It shows you the Power of Love,
It can blossom a tree, make the sun shine above,
The Princess and her Knight true,
Their love made the land anew.
Together, forever, now
Knight and Princess made their vow.
A new adventure now began,
A new story started or love song.

Kaley McDonagh

Happiness To Sadness

I wake with a smile on my face.
My mind is filled with grace.
I feel my brain is at rest,
My promise to make this day the best.
I don't think about sadness;
My goal is for happiness.

I leave out for a new day,
My life I leave to lay.
I don't know what I will see.
My existence is meant to be.
I avoid the feeling of sadness;
My being is for happiness.

I meet my love at the bus stop.
My sight spots a cop.
I worry but I am content;
My intellect has no need to repent.
I am cautious of sadness.
My objective is to feel happiness.

I glide to embrace my love;
My heart at peace like a dove.
I caress their warmth towards my chest.
My belief: there is nothing to detest.
I am unaware of sadness;
My imagination is within happiness.

I lean over my love's shoulder.
My touch is feeling a boulder.
I sense awareness near the cop.
My hearing senses the command: stop!
I can feel grave sadness;
My being can't see much happiness.

I doubt I will experience the cheerful;
My love lies beneath the blissful.
I solidify into a terrible state,
My mind blanks as of late.
I can't believe this sadness;
My senses block happiness.

I spot the cop with the thing.
My intelligence starts to bring.
I collapse into a heap;
My speech is filled with beep.
I am overpowered by this sadness;
My actions are not filled with happiness.

I wake with the blues on my face.
My mind is going to deface.
I feel my brain is in a state of unrest;
My promise won't be met at best.
I always think of sadness;
My goal won't see happiness.

I leave out for my last day,
My life I won't leave to lay.
I believe I'll know what I see;
My existence is no longer meant to be.
I am unable to avoid sadness;
My being feels no happiness.

I met my love near the church;
My sight spots nearby the birch.
I don't worry as I am content;
My intellect will need to repent.
I am aware of sadness;
My objective fails for happiness.

I glide to embrace my tool,
My heart at peace; unlike a fool.
I caress its touch near my chest.
My belief: what is this thing I detest?
I am unaware of the actions of sadness;
My imagination sways towards happiness.

I look over, my love is near.
My touch is feeling nothing to fear.
I sense awareness above;
My hearing senses the command: stop! My love!
I start to feel a lot of sadness;
My being completely blocks happiness.

I doubt I will experience the cheerful;
Myself lies beneath the blissful.
I solidify into a horrific state,
My mind jolts as of late.
I now believe this sadness;
My conscience blocked happiness.

I spot the tool within several hands.
My intelligence is blinded by clouded bands.
I myself knows, below I fell;
My life is now in the pits of Hell.
I am overpowered by this sadness,
My love looks below; no longer in happiness.

Clare Abbott

Love Unsullied

That adorable girl, full of life, full of verve
Carefree, humorous, she really has the nerve
Pretty she and smooth skin no need to serve
Brown eyes, brown hair, attracting everyone's swerve
Full of love, expressed freely with no conserve
Not easy for any man to miss or not to observe

Parents good friends, and in our society we meet
For many years with no more than a greet
But then something happens, and a furtive look I treat
Blushes all over, her acceptance far from discreet
An unspoken message, and from heart to heart a beat
Understanding that from now on no retreat

We meet with excuses, with clandestine flutter
For our society careful girls avoid the gutter
Of even suspicions that a word did she utter to a boy with no word
To the parents even a mutter
Ours was excitement, clean and without clutter
Till first kiss in secret, and then I find me stutter

But honourable I am, for the girl, her heart is now mine
And my heart open to her like a love's goldmine
She wafts and she sways in movements with design
To show me her love in a demure girly line
Our eyes meet and as if our hearts to each other mime
Short moments of company and long ones of whine

We realise our dreams, and with parents' consent we marry
We go to far places, isolated, wild but happily we tarry
Life is full of joy, and she copes like a fairy
In the wilds of Africa, the jungles and the deserts we carry
Our hearts together in joy, love, our life so breezy and airy
As though the world is but a store of happiness to quarry

We lose one child and in a short time our life sullied
But love is so strong and faith is never buried
We go about our plans and to England we journeyed
To further our fortunes and our dreams so often hackneyed
Life is so difficult, and cold, and our money loss so hurried
But she rises to the challenge and with her effort our life carried

We toil and we struggle, with course and night study
In early mornings she joins up with her nursing school friend
And buddy
And to the Royal College I go with lectures and seminar flurry
And join up in the evenings exhausted but ever so happy

Weekends we explore London and it's Chinese and curry
Visiting friends and walking the parks till rain lets us scurry

My part one fellowship achieved with first attempt
Unusual, but my faith in God to fulfil what I first dreamt
The course only midway, so I have a refund
The college is honourable and I am financially better kempt
I start my first job, in Essex, my first training's attempt
People with Cockney accent, but colleagues and staff magnificent

She excels in nursing, but midwifery her aim
Loved by her colleagues and her work is supreme
Our accommodation's basic, and she copes with acclaim
In work and with friends, we are together a real flame
No children yet, and our life in a carefree frame
She breezes through hospital tests, the results never lame

Till suddenly and with a gasp, she with morn sickness and expectant
We realise, aghast that her training because of pregnancy
Not warrant
Torn between her future and our need to preserve her pregnant
Our love for our baby unsurpassed and our thoughts never stagnant
That is our priority and her acceptance is so graceful and vibrant
We recalculate our lifestyle, our income and every bank statement
But with never a doubt, that this is our new hope and our love
So ardent
Never off our dreams and our vision of the coming infant

The grace of God, and so generous is providence
A new job with higher earnings, and full residence
Up the training ladder, and hope so much in evidence
My work so arduous, her care of herself and baby ever in constance
Delivering the baby, a moment of ecstasy, love, never a
Parallel semblance
A beautiful girl, complete, filling the room with joy and fragrance

What bliss, what blessings, how can we thank Thee God
How can we have Your love, Your tranquillity that is never awed
Even with sleepless nights and rightful worries gnawed
Yet grateful we are, and the lovely May we called
Quickly growing and smiles to us never flawed
New hopes and fresh duties, but we never shirked this new life dawned

A pram and a pushchair, but with more joyful news these are
Not enough
For another pregnancy and soon another child, and will life be
More rough?

Love's Many Mysteries

Perish the thought, welcome to our newcomer with sweet songs
Never gruff
A boy or a girl, cannot tell, for tests then only a bluff
A boy would be good, but this is only God's will and His stuff
But then God's love to us, our prayers He does not rebuff
A boy it is, and our thoughts of the future lad full of tumble
And scruff

My final exams passed, and I am a fellow and a surgeon qualified
A sigh of relief for the good fortune to the family verified
Mother busy with babies, home, but all difficulties defied
A future now rosy for family and secure for every child
Let them grow stronger, healthier and full of dignity and pride
Growing up physically, educated but with spirituality in every stride
That was the bliss that was, but our wisdom failed us and our Lord
Did us chide

Divergence and sadness, with difficulties and quarrels
A wondering why, when life brings goodness in barrels
A sinking of spirit and wills in constant battles
Marriage not sacrosanct in companionship and feelings in crackles
That sacred bond and vows are so serious and never just dabbles
But my love is ever present and with time and humility it
Always doubles

Marriage is for everyone in the other subsumes
With love all encompassing and each the other assumes
That partnership and joint life is all the thought consumes
In good time and bad, in this world and t'other one always presumes
This union is permanent and any love buried each instantly exhumes
This is my promise for her, my love with fragrance and
Sweetest perfumes.

Nabil M Mustapha

Life's Rich Tapestry

(Dedicated to Michael Dyne, my dearest love)

Now the snow is gently falling
As the day is dawning.
The house is still and empty
Upon a winter's morning.

Jack Frost comes a-calling
On the windowpane.
No sound of laughter to fill up a room,
Ravaged by old Father Time.

Old age is creeping, like a vine
Fuelling hurt from my past.
Loved ones lost by the score.
I think back to the years of my youth.

Games I played and how friends stayed;
How I fought to make the grade.
Seasons have come and gone;
Years slipped by and I had cause to cry.
Yet somehow, you do get by.

The summer sun and scorching heat,
Winter rain with some sleet;
Yes, I have travelled many miles,
Seen a lot of old men smile.

I learned to love and to lose
Wearing out so many shoes.
But at the age of fifty-one
I stopped living life on the run.

For in the eyes of a certain man
I felt a future slowly planned.
Now we live our lives together,
Happy forever and ever.

He stole my heart and that was clever.
Sometimes you have to lose to gain.
Your heart beats faster, bearing the strain.
Wild devotion like the sound of an ocean,
Though I still need the pills and calamine lotion.

In the summer, we will visit the sea,
Watch the waves rolling, slowly unfolding.
Cascading gently to the shore.
Catch the sand beneath our feet,
See the sight of a sailing fleet.

Love's Many Mysteries

Yes, we did make plans, tied up so neat;
Passion beneath a silken sheet.
Smelt the roses in a garden so complete.
Walks by his side in a wood where you can hide.

A bride's dress flowing,
That face all glowing
Feelings showing.
Both of us seeing the same view.
We both have so much to give.
Day by day, we learn to live.
For he has had heartache too.
A searing loss, mortal pain.

Though a broken heart has to mend;
To this fact, I do tend.
Some secrets we keep, not meaning to show.
Battle scars seem to grow.

But we must let go, get on with the show.
Feeling the power of love so strong,
For it is with each other we truly belong.
Yes, he sat beside me on a one-way train;
Gave me hope, kept me sane.

Now, each time when I feel pain
He holds me near, whispering gently in my ear;
Wiping away every tear.
So I hold onto him so tight
As shadows yield into the night.

I know I will love him to the end of my days;
Find a way out of a maze.
His troubled mind I try to soothe.
So when the storm clouds gather up above
We give each other all our love.

For I know the warmth of him is met
I never will bear any regrets.

Time endures us not to part,
With wishes dear to any heart.
For I knew it from that early start

Two thorn birds flying in from the west
To build, at last, a feathered nest.
For all my life, I have borne a crest;
A careful need to invest.

So as I gaze out the window and see
A scene set for a queen
I look back on my times gone by
Then let out a gentle sigh.
Sometimes a solitary task.

So I look to all that is to come;
Know my life has really begun.
With him I see the setting sun.

No longer needing to run and hide
For very soon, I will be his bride.
Then down the aisle I hope to glide.

A set of vows, a wedding ring;
Soon we will have everything.
Our hopes and dreams and all such schemes.

In his hand is a light
Shining out for all that's right.
No sorrow or pain ever again.

Yes, a lantern showing, then a path,
Then I will know we are home at last.

Hazel Shepherd

Forward Press Information

We hope you have enjoyed reading this book - and that you will continue to enjoy it in the coming years. If you like reading and writing poetry drop us a line, or give us a call, and we'll send you a free information pack. Alternatively if you would like to order further copies of this book or any of our other titles, then please give us a call or log onto our website at **www.forwardpress.co.uk**

Forward Press Ltd. Information
Remus House
Coltsfoot Drive
Peterborough
PE2 9JX

(01733) 898101